The Africana Human Condition and Global Dimensions

Edited By
Seth N. Asumah
Ibipo Johnston-Anumonwo
John K. Marah

Global Publications, Binghamton University
Binghamton, New York
2002

Flip

Library of Congress Cataloging-in-Publication Data:

New York African Studies Association. Conference (2001 : State University of New York College at Brockport)
The Africana human condition and global dimensions / edited by Seth N. Asumah, Ibipo Johnston-Anumonwo, John K. Marah.
p. cm.
This book consists of selected papers presented at the April 27-28, 2001 New York African Studies Association (NYASA) Conference, that was hosted by the African and Afro-American Studies Department at the State University of New York, College at Brockport.
Includes bibliographical references and index.
ISBN 1-58684-220-X (pbk. : alk. paper)
1. Africa--Politics and government--21st century--Congresses. 2. Africa--Civilization--21st century--Congresses. 3. Africa--Social conditions--21st century--Congresses. 4. African Americans--Social conditions--21st century--Congresses. I. Asumah, Seth Nii, 1954- II. Johnston-Anumonwo, Ibipo. III. Marah, John Karefah. IV. Title.
DT30.5 .N495 2002
960.3'3--dc21

2002004656

Published by:
Global Publications, Binghamton University
State University of New York
Binghamton, New York, USA 13902-6000
Phone: (607) 777-4495; Fax: (607) 777-6132
E-mail: pmorewed@binghamton.edu
http://ssips.binghamton.edu
http://globalpublicationspress.comceabfdeabfdeabfdceabfed

The Africana Human Condition and Global Dimensions

The Africana Human Condition And Global Dimensions

Edited By
Seth N. Asumah
Ibipo Johnston-Anumonwo
John K. Marah

An Occasional Publication for the African American Studies Program at the State University of New York at Cortland, the African and Afro American Studies Department of SUNY Brockport, and the New York African Studies Association (NYASA).

Dedication

☙❧

To
Tosha Asumah, Valencia Perkins
and Katherine Asumah
SNA

To
Ballai Anumonwo, Obi Anumonwo
and Kachi Anumonwo
IJA

To
Kwame Ballah Marah
and Nzingah Jalloh Marah
JKM

To
All those who are struggling
to eradicate oppression, and those who are
engaged in struggle for sustainable
development and prosperity
for the Africana World
SNA, IJA, & JKM

CONTENTS

ACKNOWLEDGMENTS

The production of this book has been possible through the assistance of several colleagues, administrators, staff members and students who are dedicated to the cause of the development of Africana people. We were greatly assisted and supported by President Paul Yu, of the State University of New York, College at Brockport, who enthusiastically supported hosting the April 2001 Conference of the New York African Studies Association on the Brockport campus. This enthusiastic support vibrated into the offices of the Vice Presidents of Academic Affairs, Administrative Services, Enrollment Management, Student Affairs, Brockport Student Government, the Organization of Students of African Descent, and the Office of the Assistant Vice Chancellor, SUNY System Administration at Albany, New York.

We also wish to thank Ms. Edith Zsuzsics, Administrative Assistant to the April 2001 NYASA Annual Conference, who was instrumental in facilitating, documenting, and organizing abstracts of papers presented at the conference. Our special thanks also go to helpful students—Mary Ewert, Amy Source and Sarah C. Willoughby—for their assistance in typing much of the manuscript and other pertinent student tasks.

We are deeply indebted to Professor Mechthild Nagel, Assistant Professor of Philosophy and Director of the Multicultural and Gender Studies Council at SUNY Cortland, who read several drafts of each chapter, always challenging us to further sharpen the ideas and perceptions of this volume. She provided us with the assistance needed from the beginning to the end of the project. Our special thanks to Valencia C. Perkins, teacher, Randallstown Elementary School, Maryland for the layout, design, word processing and technical assistance in developing this volume. We extend our gratitude to Dr. Parviz Morewedge and Shalahudin Kafrawi of Global Publications for their support, assistance and patience. It would have been impossible to complete this book on time, but for the support of our families and colleagues at SUNY Brockport, SUNY Cortland and Binghamton University, Binghamton, New York.

PREFACE

This book consists of selected papers presented at the April 27-28, 2001 New York African Studies Association (NYASA) Conference, that was hosted by the African and Afro-American Studies department at the State University of New York, College at Brockport. Some of the papers presented at the NYASA conference have found scholarly outlets both in this volume and other publications. Out of the fifty-four research paper presentations (including workshops on teacher education, African dance, and panel discussions on the "Wonders of the African World"), a number of scholarly papers that focused on the impacts of globalization on Africana people, their education, literature, science and technology, lived spaces, access to jobs, women's issues, and Afrocentric theory and praxis were selected for this publication.

In keeping to the theme of the April 27-28, 2001 New York African Studies Association Annual Conference, "Human Condition: Global

African Dimensions," this book, *The Africana Human Condition and Global Dimensions*, eclectically grapples with a number of pertinent issues affecting African people globally. The concept of globalization and its impacts on Africans will continue to be of great significance to African people throughout the 21st Century and beyond. Science and technology in African development, the education of African people in a shrinking multicultural global village, the issues of the treatment of African women in fiction and non-fiction, the changing nature of work and connections between home and work in technological societies for African people, as well as the paradigms through which African people see reality and virtual reality will also continue to be important concerns to academicians and laypersons alike. These are some of the real concerns that the selected research and continuing research papers herein attempt to critically examine.

In chapter one, "The Effects of Globalization on African Nation-States and Culture," Professor Seth N. Asumah sees globalization as the complex interdependence of nation-states and cultures in the 21st century, which has given a new meaning to how prospects and problems of the world could be interpreted or tackled. Global forces are shaping the identities and policy preferences of subordinate cultures and black nation states in unprecedented proportions. The increasing global market economy and culture, in which capital investments and foreign cultures can relocate rapidly, have caused black nation states in Africa and the African Diaspora to continue to surrender their own efforts in development, social capital, and indigenous cultures to be embraced in the global village. In this chapter, he examines the effects of globalization on Black nation-states, social capital and indigenous cultures for the 21st century. He further assesses the intensity and scope of neo-cultural imperialism and the socio-political hegemony of the beneficiaries of the meretricious global village.

In chapter two, Kenneth Vincent, critically examines the relationship between J.J. Rawlings, former head of state of Ghana, Thomas

Sankara, former president of Burkina Faso, and their perceptions on African populism. In this chapter, Vincent details how this son of the land of Nkrumah began as populist revolutionary and was thrown off the course by these neo-colonial institutions. Rawlings' Ghana has been heralded by these institutions as a perfect example of economic deve-lopment through structural adjustment; but the fallacies of neo-liberal economics are highlighted along with an examination of the populist alternative that Rawlings strayed from (e.g., Thomas Sankara's Burkina Faso). Vincent analyzes the role that Jerry Rawlings and Thomas Sankara have played in the development of African populism.

In the next chapter, Professor Darryl Thomas examines the impact of globalization on African-American workers. After the final collapse of the Soviet Union in 1989, the United States became the only undisputed world power. But this undisputed world power has always held African-Americans at the periphery of economic and political activities. With the avalanche of third world immigrants into the United States, African Americans are increasingly going to compete with this reserve army of labor. These new immigrants are going to undermine African-Americans' ability to bargain with capitalist America for higher wages and even decent working conditions. African Americans, as third world persons in the United States, in no small measure, will continue to be negatively affected by the process of globalization, a process that is already attracting cheap laborers from third world countries, that have started to compete with the African-American labor reserve in the southern states of the United States. It appears that, one of the major steps African-Americans must take is to become technologically adept, a stage only a few are able to obtain; the African-American masses are increasingly going to be left to compete for low wages with the increasing numbers of third world immigrants.

In part two, "Science and Global Africa," Professors Paulin Hountondji, of the National University of Benin, Cotonou, and Judi W. Wakhungu of the Pennsylvania University, University Park, observe Africa's continued dependence on western science, technology, research instruments and paradigms, journals and textbooks. Hountondji, in chapter four, sees very little communication among African scientists, who are mostly communicating with northern scientists. As African economies are outer- directed, so also are African scientists, some of whom have become intellectual nomads, in search of jobs and environments that would utilize their skills. In chapter five, "The Baby on the Back: Science, Technology and Politics of Progress in Africa," Professor Wakhungu exhorts the new African Union leaders to support the institutionalization of science and technology in Africa; both Wakhungu and Hountondji believe that, for genuine African development to occur, African politicians must use their powers for the scientific and technological development of Africa, as opposed to the "development" of their own pocketbooks.

In chapter six, "Infusing Critical Thinking in College and University Courses in Kenya," Professor Thomas O. Mwanika looks at the educational system of Kenya to determine the country's professional and educational needs; he utilizes the focus group methodology to generate directly the information and data from the stakeholders themselves. This chapter reports the results from the focus group on infusing critical thinking into course work. It also outlines the stakeholders' perceptions of the nature, value, and challenges of infusing critical thinking.

In chapter seven, "African and African-centered Educational Models: Critical Linkages of Theory and Praxis," Ranahnah A. Afriye observes that for many generations, the definitions of schooling and education have not been synonymous in the global African community. This can certainly be linked to the advent of African political and cultural subjugation to Arab and European people. Thus, in many cases, African cultural transmission and social values were subjugated in the context of schooling to those of their colonizers. Based on an examination of indigenous African educational systems from ancient times to the present, Afriye endeavors to identify some of the pervasive attributes that constitute this educational tradition; she then applies these characteristics towards an analysis of the US independent black institutions that aimed to counter the residuum of European cultural hegemony among the African-American population.

In the "Traces of Multicentered Places in the Spaces of Plantation Society," Lori Lee sees houses as interstices between space and place and that ideology is embedded in the walls of houses, which are also material expressions of the past; insights into contemporary social ideals are realized by analyzing household architecture. In this chapter, Lee examines household spaces in plantation society; the architectural layout is analyzed using a cognitive-structural perspective. The architectural data are fleshed out with the lived experience of individuals who inhabited the built structures. These perspectives highlight the "real" that reciprocally complements, challenges, and transmogrifies the ideal. The lived experience decenters the built environment from hierarchically arranged spaces into multilocal, multicentered places.

In chapter nine, "Getting to Work in Spite of the Odds: Commuting Patterns of African Americans in Rochester and Buffalo, New York," Professor Johnston-Anumonwo observes that disagreement persists about whether or not African American workers in US metropolitan areas are more distant from centers of employment than European Americans. This chapter reports on an empirical inquiry about a question of spatial mismatch of African-American residents in segregated inner-city neighborhoods away from growing job opportunities in suburban locations. Using census Public Use Microdata Samples, the analysis examines workers residing in Monroe County (Rochester) and Erie County (Buffalo), New York. The results show that, as employment opportunities continue to expand in suburban locations and not in central-city locations, African Americans, especially women, suffer the inconvenience of significantly longer commutes to suburban workplaces than European Americans with similar job and income profiles. The evidence from Rochester and Buffalo about the employment experiences of African-American workers in spite of transportation and locational difficulties strongly counters prevailing stereotypes of welfare-dependent African Americans.

If African American women in Rochester and Buffalo, New York occupy more precarious economic spaces, as compared to their European American women counterparts, Professor Davidson Umeh describes the difficult position of Igbo women of Nigeria in his chapter, "Dehumanization of African Women: An Analysis of Widowhood Practices Among the Igbos of Nigeria." In chapter ten, Professor Umeh observes that widowhood practices in Igbo land are very significant aspects of the funeral rites that are expected of a woman to her deceased husband. The cultural expectation in widowhood practices is oppressive and humiliating to women. Igbo women's health and human rights have suffered severe setbacks in an effort to comply with widowhood practices. Yet, little effort is made to address the implications of widowhood practices on women and their children. Cultural mores and traditions have structured women to accept the oppressive practices meted out to them at the time of their husband's death. The sanctions of significant other persons in the family and society make it difficult for women to express their views about widowhood practices. Dr. Umeh concludes that the Igbo society has to re-examine its cultural practices on widowhood. The practices have far-reaching harmful effects on the health of widows and their children. Culture is dynamic and various harmful widowhood practices need to be changed to enhance the human rights of women in Igbo society. A re-education program for wi-dows, community, and religious leaders in Igbo land will enhance the effort toward cultural changes in widowhood practices.

In part four, chapter eleven, "Nneka, or Mother is Supreme: Powerful Female Imagery and Feminism in the New Millennium," Professor Cindy Ibechem gives a critical, anthropological, and novel feminist reading on the construction of images of women in Chinua Achebe's classic novel, *Things Fall Apart*, and re-evaluates Okonkwo's mother's role as an influential figure in Okonkwo's tragic life. In this chapter, Dr. Ibechem proposes an inclusive, feminist anthropological reading of *Things Fall Apart* that acknowledges gender as a social construct, as she highlights the importance of women and powerful female figures in this Pan-African novel.

In chapter twelve, "African Aesthetics and African Literature: Developing an African-Centered Literacy Theory From Existing Philosophical Concepts," Nzingha Gaffin suggests an African-centric approach to African 1iteracy criticism. She observes that criticisms of African literature continue to be unduly influenced by constructs from European literary models. These evaluative criteria denounce the structure of African literature, dialogues and themes as inadequate, unrealistic and obsessed with the past. They play down the significance of African literature because it does not enhance or promote European hegemony. As such, critical interpretation of the literature falls short of the intended message of the authors and oftentimes contradicts the worldview and ethos of the culture informing the work. Nzingha's chapter offers an alternative analytical tool derived from existing African philosophical concepts, centered in the language and cultural consciousness of African authors. This methodology will enable us to examine the conflict between the African and European *asili(s)*, study the development of the novel and its characters from a *kugusta mtima (ic)* perspective and then proceed to evaluate the entire work *kuntu (icly).*

In the last chapter, "The Rejection of Blackness in African-American Literature," Dr. John K. Marah appears to have anticipated Gaffin's position in the previous chapter that "An alternative analytical tool is needed, one derived from existing African philosophical concepts, centered in the language and cultural consciousness of African authors." Using the philosophical concept of Pan-Africanism, Dr. Marah eclectically surveys the works of a number of African-American writers whose protagonists have rejected African prognatheism and their black skin color, because of European hegemony, colonialization, western education, media, and western standards of beauty. African people, globally, in fiction and non-fiction, have tended to internalize negative images of themselves. To combat this onslaught on Africana people, Dr. Marah suggests a global, Africa-centric education that will sustain Africana people in determining their own aesthetic standards.

The intellectually inclusive readings offered in this volume suggest that Africana people must be multidisciplinary and vigilant, critical, mobile, and must be constantly willing to learn from various disciplines, anywhere, at anytime, so that they are always prepared to help Africana people develop.

Seth N. Asumah and Ibipo Johnston-Anumomwo
— Cortland, New York.
John K. Marah
— Brockport, New York.
April 4, 2002

PART ONE

ISSUES ON GLOBALIZATION

CHAPTER 1

THE EFFECTS OF GLOBALIZATION ON AFRICAN NATION-STATES AND CULTURES

Seth N. Asumah
Associate Professor, Political Science Department
Coordinator of African American Studies
State University of New York at Cortland

The recent protests against the uneven effects of globalization on developing nation-states at Genoa, Italy, where the G8 nation-states met to shape the political economy of the world, were not epiphenomenal, nor were they an aberration. While the G8 nation-states of the United Kingdom, the United States of America, Germany, Italy, France, Canada,

Japan, Russia and their cohorts, transnational corporations, are celebrating the apparent benefits of globalization, most African nation-states are experiencing a new form of colonialism and exploitation. The World Conference against Racism in Durban, South Africa in August 2001 gave new meaning to hegemonic/peripheral nation-states' interaction, as demands of Africans and the African Diaspora for reparations for slavery, colonialism and contemporary racism renewed the protests against the power holders of the global village and global apartheid.

In this chapter, I argue that the global village presents a meretricious burlesque of so called "prosperity" for African nation-states, while the world's hegemonic countries are hiding behind the façade of equal benefits of globalization to further their exploitation and marginalization of the more vulnerable African nation-states. The world's hegemonic nations' actions in globalization are tantamount to neo- colonialism, quasi colonialism and cultural imperialism. Furthermore, African nation-states have relinquished their sovereign authority to transnational corporations and the West in order to be accepted in the global village.

Yet, from Algeria to Angola, and from Zambia to Zimbabwe, people of the African world are adopting similar tastes in food, dress, art, popular music, and entertainment. These tastes are specifically Western ones. Paradoxically, there seem to be a trend toward "cultural sameness" in our multicultural world. The African world is experiencing a cultural disintegration in order to adopt Western forms of lifestyle and protocol, and the African nation-states have lost their raison d'etre as sovereign states. The African nation-states' susceptibility to global forces has facilitated the *"Coca-colarization" and "McCulturalization*" of the African world — making them even more vulnerable to globalization.

Similarly, the trends in today's political economy, coupled with the economic integration of the world, and trade policy liberalization have all combined to produce an unstoppable movement toward globalization. Globalization has become a buzzword for academicians, consultants, journalists and policy analysts. Globalization has gained currency with statesmen and stateswomen. The term globalization, which could not be found in a respectable English dictionary a few years ago, now has acquired both legitimacy and an added aura of sacred, emigmatic desirability, concomitant with Western media propaganda. Is globalization beneficial to the African economy? Is the process of globalization so inevitable and irreversible that African nation-states have declared it a *fait accompli*? Has globalization increased the gap between poor African nation-states and the rest of the world? In the balance of this article, the questions above will be tackled in addition to examining the different phases of Western intrusion into the African world and the emergence of global apartheid.

What then is Globalization?

Globalization is the international reordering of priorities, values, cultures, technology, trade, communication, and the interdependent nature of international interaction. Friedman (2001) characterizes globalization as "a dynamic ongoing process [which] involves the inexorable integration of markets, nation-states and technologies to a degree never witnessed before, — in a way that is enabling individuals, corporations, and nation-states to reach around the world farther, faster, deeper and cheaper then ever before, and in a way that is also producing a powerful backlash from those brutalized or left behind by this new system" (p. 302). The nation-states and cultures that are brutalized and marginalized in the process of globalization are, without question, those on the continent of Africa. Because of the complex interdependence of hegemonic and peripheral nation-states, global forces affect subordinate cultures and nation-states in unprecedented proportions owing to the weaker positions of the marginalized entities in the global bargaining process.

Globalization, according to Held, McGrew, Goldblatt, and Parraton

(2001), is about the interconnectedness of regions of the world – from the cultural to the criminal, the environmental to financial — and the way and manner regional and local dynamics change, increase or decrease over time (2001, p. 135). They correctly note that globalization is not a single process, but it involves four different types of change:

1) It stretches social, political and economic activities across political frontiers, regions, and continents.
2) It intensifies our dependence on each other, as flows of trade, investment, finance, migration, and culture increase.
3) It speeds up the world to a point where new systems of transport and communication provide the means for ideas, goods, information, capital, and people to move more quickly.
4) It means that distant events have a deeper impact on our lives. Even the most local developments may come to have enormous global consequences. The boundaries between domestic matters and global affairs become increasingly blurred (p. 134).

Globalization, therefore, places emphasis on the universal application of national policy for a proper sphere of political influence. With the universalization of domestic policy, a more comprehensive view of globalization steers the world toward a "global village." The world is expanding, but the expansion is geared toward a village community of inequality. The expansion of the world is concomitant with a convergence of the political economies of different nation-states in a global village community. Producers and consumers, cultural imperialists and imitators, pauper nations and rich nations all come face to face in a supposedly "free" but unequal market. Mazrui (2001) asserts, "Globalization is thus the villagization of the world.... What has been happening in the twentieth century is a more extensive globalization of Global Africa, making the African factor on earth more truly omnipresent and omni-directional" (p. 3). Although global Africa has become a reluctant participant in the global village, there are a few African predatory regimes that benefit from their association with other global actors. Predatory regimes are African governments that have facilitated the marginalization of the Africans people by colluding with external agencies in the process of exploitation. Yet, Africans have provided moral leadership in the global village, from the United Nations to the World Court, and over the world, Black *faces* are becoming more common. Nonetheless, the aggregate effect of global Africa on the global village is negligible.

Yet, the African concept of the village is not the same as what is envisioned in the global village. The African village is more sociocentric and less exploitative. The global village, on the other hand, is just the most recent development of global political economy designed by Western imperialism and mercantilism over the past five hundred years (Nester, 2001, p. 519). Furthermore, Immanuel Kant (1795), over two hundred years ago, in his *Essay on Perpetual Peace,* projected socio-economic development, interdependence, and the evolution of international law and organization into a system that binds all sovereign states (pp. 790-792). Although Kant's vision about globalization is fast becoming a reality, given his Eurocentric and racist ideas, he could not have imagined African nation-states as co-equals in the global village. Furthermore, these African nation-states have lost their raison d'être as sovereign states in the present global village because of systemic dynamics beyond their control.

In order to comprehend the impact of globalization on the nation-states of Africa, one has to analyze the historical context of global interaction in the past five hundred years. The present global village as Nester (2001) notes, is a continuation of a process that started five centuries ago. Today's globalization is actually part of the fourth phase of Western imperialism and penetration into Africa by superordinate forces that used Africa as a platform for exploitation.

The first phase of globalization's effect on Africa was during the period of slavery, when Africa's human and material resources were taken by global traders and slavers, whose work only benefited Arabs, Europeans, and North Americans (Henriot, 2001, p. 2). The second phase of globalization was the period of colonialism, when the Portuguese, Italians, Belgians, British, French and Germans divided and conquered the African continent for their self-interests in 1884 - 85 at the Berlin Conference. Just as the present form of globalization indicates, the benefits for the West always outweighed what the African people acquired through the other processes. The third phase of globalization was the period of neocolonialism, the post independent era, where Africa's fate was still controlled by alien transnational companies and foreign nation-states. Trade patterns, debt arrangements, investment policies, and the general political economies of African nation-states were primarily controlled by former colonial powers in the neocolonial era. The fourth, the present phase of globalization, is a global village where interdependence has made Africa even more dependent on foreign powers and resources than the period of colonialism. Financial flows, technology, information highways, byways, and thoroughfares, movement of people, and cultures have direct benefit to the Western countries and corporations that have very little in mind about Africa. Moreover, the global village would be dysfunctional if the dominant actors failed to carefully implement the tenets of the catalystic agent of globalization — liberalization.

The global village is considered a gigantic marketplace where profit maximization of private corporations and nation-states advocate laissez faire principles through liberalization. This "free" market has no deference for the nature and function of non-Western nation-states and cultures. The global village has all the qualities of global apartheid in the sense that its sustainability is predicated on race, geography, as well as markets (Booker and Minter, 2001). In a neo-liberal marketplace affirmed by the norms, ideas and precepts of Anglo-American cultures, Africana vision for prosperity is infinitesimally dilute. Liberalization, therefore, drives the free market of the global village to the desired destination of hegemonic, Euro-American, democratic, capitalist nation-states.

What then is Liberalization?

Liberalization is a paradigmatic shift by government in social and economic policies to a noninterventionist stance. Stewart (2000) writes that:

> "Liberalization" encompasses all these moves toward reduced state intervention. It has both a domestic and international component. The international component comprises reduced restrictions on trade, capital flows, and technology movements (but significantly, not labor). These changes, along with new communication technologies and reduced transport costs are responsible for the "globalization" phenomena (p. 2).

Although Stewart does not clearly outline the domestic component of liberalization in the quotation above, yet paradoxically the African nation-states have become victims of the forces of liberalization in the domestic arena equally so as in the international sphere. In the process of liberalization, African nation-states that are producers of raw materials with relatively low value and sources of cheap labor set themselves up for exploitation with little state intervention.

The policy changes of liberalization, to facilitate globalization in Africa, have pervasive effects on the general political economy and social capital of these nation-states. Despite liberalization, the markets for African products have not increased significantly as those nation-states with well developed manufactory sectors and technological base. The developed nation-states always have the comparative advantage. Liberalization has a strong effect on growth without much development in Africa. It has a direct impact on poverty and income distribution within African nation-states (Stewart, 2000, p. 2). Growth without development, poverty and an uneven distribution all contribute to sociopolitical instability in Africa.

Liberalization's impact on income distribution is one of the most important effects globalization has on Africa, since changes in poverty levels are concomitant with changes in income distribution and economic growth. While Western nation-states have increases in goods and services during the process of liberalization, because they could easily penetrate the poorer countries of Africa, the nation-states of Africa only have to succumb to the dynamics of interaction dictated through Western liberalization policies. Recent evidence in developed nation-states indicates that more equal income distribution tends to be associated with higher growth rates. Meanwhile, in African nation-states, it could be argued that the effects of poverty have a more lasting impact on the society than that of income distribution (Stewart, 2000, p. 2). Nonetheless, the changes in poverty levels during the process of liberalization are the combined outcomes of changes in economic growth and income distribution. Yet, for the poor countries in Africa, changes in income levels provide less in terms of meeting basic needs because of the differences in needs of richer nation-states in the same global entity.

In general, African nation-states that are primary-goods export producers (PEP) suffer the effects of liberalization more than Western nation-states that are manufacturing-goods export producers (MEP), because MEP nation-states have the ability to penetrate the global market without much trouble. In fact, MEP nation-states control the global market. During liberalization, African countries, such as Ghana and Uganda, that are primary-goods export producers (PEP) may experience a slight improvement in income distribution in the short run because the incomes of small peasant primary-goods exporters may increase. However, in the long run, income distribution among these peasants may worsen with liberalization in that transnational companies enter the market, displacing the small peasants. Since trade liberalization favors Western developed countries more than African countries because of comparative advantage, the nation-states of Africa would generally suffer the effects of liberalization and globalization. Birdsal (2001) notes:

> In short, the effect of trade liberalization on inequality depends on the extent to which a countries comparative advantage lies in labor-intensive agriculture or manufactured exports; on the extent to which education has been increasing and is already shared; and, ... on the extent to which the opening of markets is part of a much larger economic adjustment, implying widening income differences between those able to adapt and less able (p. 43).

The following sections will address how the African nation-state attempts to deal with the forces of the global villages in order to maintain its raison d'être.

The Nation-States of Africa and the Global Village

In the present global village, nation-states all over the world come together to form a global community. Defined succinctly, the nation-state is the largest, most sophisticated, self-reliant, political configuration in the modern world. Nation-states have four basic characteristics: *videlicet*, territorial area, general populace, a government, and recognition from other nation-states. Territorial area is one of the most fundamental components of economic development. Size, location, and natural resources are concomitant with territory or, in simple terms, land. Land is also one major element that serves as a platform upon which nation-states extend their boundaries at the expense of others, and it represents the frontier of an increasing conflict over legitimate right between nation-states and society rights vis-à-vis state authority.

The respective inhabitants of nation-states are another great asset that these entities could have. As human resources, the general populace of nation-states may differ greatly in their history, precepts, norms, culture and their socioeconomic and political acumen. People make decisions in the global village, not computers. Productivity in any nation-state is dependent upon the type of human resources available in that particular entity. Education and training can provide skilled or semi-skilled labor and leadership. Intangible variables, such as knowledge, skill and leadership can lead to the production of tangible needs such as general infrastructures. African governments would have little to worry about in the global village if the majority of the general populace could be productive and reach a level of optimal efficiency. Population explosion, unemployment, refugees, health issues, and the preservation of human dignity are some of the problems that come with people in the nation-states of Africa.

The third characteristic, good governance is essential to the survival and sustenance of any nation-state in the global village. Governance refers to the arrangements and management of regime relations, and the laws and rules that create the framework to conduct politics in the global village (Hyden and Brattan, 1992). Here, formal institutional structures, sociopolitical processes, and their interaction with the general populace within the global village are the areas of contention. Governance in Africa in the process of globalization has become the most elusive "art form." The frequency and scope of predatory regimes, praetorian governments, struggle with alien political philosophies, ideologies, and resource scarcity have all contributed to making governance in Africa within the global sphere a risky business. But the nation-states in Africa must survive the entrances and exits of governments and regimes in order to compete in the global village.

The fourth and final characteristic of the nation-state is recognition from other nation-states in the global village. Recognition relates to the "acknowledgment of the existence of a new state or of a new government in an exiting state, coupled with an expression of willingness on the part of the recognizing state to enter into relations with the recognized entity or government" (Von Glahn, 1981, p. 82). More recently, recognition has become a political act with legal ramification. Recognition involves diplomatic exchange, concluding of agreements respecting the existence of the nation-state in question, and perhaps, membership in the United Nations. Recent global forces have made some of the elements of recognition somewhat meaningless since liberalization makes the borders and territories of especially weaker nation-states more vulnerable for entrance and exit of parastatal agencies, transnational corporations and powerful nation-states.

As the modern nation-states evolve in Africa and it acquires all the aforementioned characteristics, it retires into a new type of entity in order to respond to the demands and needs of the society in the global village. Nonetheless, the authoritative actions of the nation-state to shape and constrain the expectations, demands, and pressure from the general populace, global actors, and institutions are modified according to paradigmatic reorientation of the nation-state itself. Two paradigms, the state-centered nation-state and the society-centered nation-state analysis could be utilized to describe how the nation-state responds to the forces of globalization within the global village.

State-centered and Society-centered Nation-States in the Global Village

In accordance with the state-centered nation-state model, the state acts as an independent entity — an independent variable that turns its preferences into authoritative actions. The nation-state's autonomous actions often result in policy decisions that have little reflective value to the immediate society because it is more concerned about global interaction. Culminating in autonomous actions and reactions, the state's ability to tap into resources outside its perimeters is diminished. From structural development within the state to global dynamics beyond the state's apparatus, the nation-state propounds and make policy choices that have little meaning to the general populace of its own. African private actors, businesses, political parties, affiliation and affinity groups cannot easily transform their demands via the nation-state into preferable socioeconomic and political agendas because of global forces over and above their means.

The society-centered nation-state approach postulates a condition in the global village where the private sector, transnational corporations, intergovernmental organizations (IGOs) and non-governmental organizations (NGOs) within and outside the polity have symbiotic relations with the nation-state and the global village. The nation-state in this paradigm serves as a viable platform upon which different sociopolitical and global actors come together to iron out their differences and galvanize their interests. These characterizations of the nation-state presume that the state has already reached a "takeoff stage" — a stage of prematurity, where the nation-state can interact with global forces without being marginalized or exploited. In fact, very few African nation-states, if any, fit this analysis or are able to maintain themselves in the global arena.

The nation-states in Africa have been unable to acquire the society-centered nation-state status because of structural heterogeneity, which is the transfer of advanced but inadequate technology and institutions from Western nation-states to undeveloped areas in Africa. Globalization enhances structural heterogeneity but stifles socioeconomic activities because of the inadequate capacity of African nation-states to deal with alien forces within the global village. Moreover, the lack of a sustainable private sector in Africa places limitations on the type of support the general populace could provide to the nation-state. Absent viable support from the external sphere of the state, it tends to rely on its own resources, which are insufficient to deal with forces within the global village.

For obvious reasons, most African nation-states would prefer the society-centered nation-state paradigm to deal with global issues. However, the society is not sufficiently equipped to provide the needed structures to facilitate the operation of such a paradigm. Indubitably, there is no entity that is exclusively nation-state-centered or society-centered. However, most Western nation-states are closer to the society-centered nation-state paradigm. The fundamental questions to be posed in attempting to determine the status of the African nation-state in the era of globalization are:

1) How does the nation-state maintain its raison d'être in the global village?
2) How are the state's authoritative actions and inactions understood in reference to internal and external constraints during the process of globalization?
3) To what extent do African nation-states still maintain their sovereignty in dealing with socioeconomic and political forces in the global village?

A brief discussion of the different typology of state structures below will enable us to provide some answers to the questions about the nature of Africa nation-states in the process of globalization.

Typology of Nation-State Structures and Globalization

Frequently, nation-states have been labeled "weak" or "strong." There are times when some states have been called "super" or "great" entities. Both military and socioeconomic elements or indicators are used to denote the weakness or strength of nation-states in the global village. Even though different regimes have ruled the nation-states of Africa, the states themselves have been frequently characterized as weak and self-centered because of their inability to generate their own preferences and maintain relative harmony between the nation-state's corpus and global forces. By examining two variables, state autonomy and societal support, we can discern four types of nation-state structures and assess their ability to maintain their sovereign authority or lack thereof in the global village. The four structures are: strong nation-states, weak nation-states, syncretic nation-states, and acceptive nation-states (Asumah, 2001, p. 30). In this essay, only two nation-state structures, weak and strong, are relevant to the discussion, so acceptive and syncretic nation-states will not be tackled.

Strong nation-states enjoy high autonomy and societal support. Autonomy, according to Nordlinger (1981), is the extent to which the nation-state can translate its own preferences into authoritative action (p. 361). Societal support includes but not limited to both human and material resources that the nation-state could translate into socioeconomic and political "energy-sources" for reconstruction and sustainability. Strong nation-states translate their own preferences into action in the global village by acquiring high support from their own populace and other global actors. Strong states are corpuscular, in that they tend to control the global agenda without threat from other actors. The nation-state in this model is insulated from rules and regulations resulting from the process of liberalization. Strong nation-states are able to meet potential and actual global challenges. Nonetheless, global actors work with the nation-state rather than against it, since the global actors and strong nation-states have similar interests.

Conversely, weak nation-states are extremely malleable in the global village. Such states are decidedly susceptible and receptive to various forces in the global market. Weak nation-states are less insulated and liberalization rules and regulations easily affect the states' corpus. Weak nation-states are "soft-centered" with fragmented social control exercise by few local hegemons with little global influence. Most African nations-states are detained in the quagmire of weakness, and this is the reason why they are vulnerable and are more likely to be losers in liberalization efforts in the global village.

African nation-states, sandwiched between global forces and local demands, must now reconsider their functions and roles in the global village. But to imply that the African nation-states have totally lost their authority and power could easily distort what is happening in the global village. The complexity of the picture cannot be over emphasized. African nation-states today are least as powerful, if not more so, than their predecessors during the era of colonization and independence. Yet, the demands on the African nation-state have rapidly grown in this era of liberalization and globalization. African nation-states' power and authority are shifting. These nation-states now deploy their sovereignty and autonomy as bargaining chips in the continuing negotiation with parastatal, transnational, and powerful nation-states. What therefore is the actual impact of globalization on African nation-states and cultures?

The Fate of African Nation-States and Cultures in the Era of Globalization

Earlier in the 20th Century, both Vladimir Lenin and many internationalists projected the gradual demise of the nation-state – the withering away of the state, and that the highest state of capitalism is imperialism. In the 1990s, observers started revisiting Lenin's position and management consultants, such as Naisbits (1994), have suggested that the contemporary advancement of globalization and the activities of transnational corporations are creating a world beyond nation-state, cultures, and nationalities (p. 14). The present effects of globalization on the African nation-state only beg for a revisitation of the Weberian conceptualization of the state in order to determine the fate of the nation-state in the global village. Max Weber's defining properties of the nation-state include:

1) Defined boundaries under the state's control and an unchallenged territorial area. This property has been almost meaningless in the process of globalization in Africa since globalization supports economic, social, and political activities across frontiers, regions and continents.
2) The nation-state's monopoly of legitimate use of force to control

its borders and general populace within its territory. Here, African nation-states, because of the forces of interdependence, have little monopoly of legitimate use of force and influence even within their own borders. Great powers and transnational corporations' irrepressible activities in Africa have diluted the nation-state's authority and the use of legitimate force in conducting its affairs.

3) The reliance upon rules and regulations in the governance of its citizens and nationals. Here again, in the global village, the rules and regulations propounded by transnational corporations and Western nation-states prevail in the global village. The boundaries between domestic matters and global affairs have become increasingly blurred to an extent that the movers and shakers of the global village carry the day.

In reviewing the Weberian properties of the nation-state and how globalization has made the function and authority of the African nation-state questionable, one cannot confide in the sustainability of these nation-states. Yet, it would be erroneous to perform a premature autopsy on the African nation-state, even though there is sufficient evidence that globalization has intensified the crippling effect and paralysis of the states in Africa. In general, globalization has uneven effects on African nation-states vis-à-vis Western industrial ones that are clearly the winners in the global village. The chart below demonstrates the reason why African nation-states are ultimate losers in the globalization movement.

Mutatis mutandis, African nation-states will continue to be victims in the globalization movement. Africa's primary drawing card in the global market is as a source of cheap labor and producer of raw materials, which are relatively low in value vis-à-vis finished goods from the West. Despite the liberalization effort in the past ten to fifteen years, the markets for African products have not increased significantly compared to those countries with a well developed manufacturing sector and technological base coupled with comparative advantage (Mwangi, 1996, p. 1). Even though fiscal trade liberalization has increased financial mobility in recent years, African markets are vulnerable to external changes, dollarization, and external shocks. The facts below will not dissipate; they are the realities of globalization that African nation-states have to come in terms with before blindly embracing the global village:

- Multinational corporations account for 20 percent of the world's production and 70 percent of world trade (Held et al, 2001, p. 143). But most of these corporations are concentrated in the West; African nation-states remain consumer countries instead of producer nation-states.
- The global market has over 53,000 multinational corporations and 450,000 foreign subsidiaries that sell $9.5 trillion goods and services a year and African corporations play a negligible part of this (Held et al, 2001, p. 142).
- With reference to global finance, every day approximately $1.5 trillion (World Bank Report, 1999) is traded in the foreign exchange market which is controlled by a few thousand Western traders that determine the economic fate of African nation-states – "free trade" has never been "fair trade" for many Africans.
- According to the 1999 Human Development Report of the United Nations, a fifth of the global village inhabitants lives in the world's richest nation-states. This fifth controls 82 percent of the world's export market, 68 percent of international direct investment and 75 percent of all the telephone lines in the global village. The bottom fifth in the global village are mostly African nation-states and has less than 1.5 percent shares in the three categories mentioned above.

Uneven Effects of Globalization on Africa and the West

African Nation-States: Non-Beneficiaries	Western Nation-States: Beneficiaries	Reasons Why
1. Primary-goods Export Producers (PEP)	Manufacturing-goods Export Producers (MEP)	MEP nation-states control prices and access in the global village.
2. Consumer culture	Productive Output	Nation-states with productive output make profit, while those with consumer culture lack savings and investment.
3. Unskilled workers	Skilled workers	Nation-states with skilled workers capitalize on information technology and technocratic establishment that make gains faster than nation-states with unskilled workers.
4. Debtors	Creditors	Most African nation-states are characterized as heavily indebted poor countries (HIPCs) that are at the mercy of the IMF, World Bank and creditor nations of the West.
5. Small companies	Large companies	The economies of scale favor large companies in the global market.
6. Local Markets	Global Markets	Western nation-states and transnational corporations have the ability to penetrate the global market.
7. Women and Children	Men	Men have more influential positions, assets, and power than women and children in the global village.
8. Indigenous culture	Global culture	Cultural imperialism prevails in the global village, where the dominant nation-states' cultures are synonymous with Western culture and remain as the norm.

The evidence above indicates that the global village is not what some observers paint it to be. Africans are receiving a raw deal; a deal that may be worse than all the deals in the three phases of Western interaction with Africa combined. How does the global village affect subordinate cultures? How does cultural imperialism affect the psyche of the African people in the global village? The next section of this essay will briefly examine the effects of global culture on Africans in the global village.

Global Culture, Indigenous Culture and the Global Village

The euphoric prognoses by statesmen, stateswomen and political economists about the benefits of globalization to all the members of the global village are beginning to subside because many developing nation-states and African nation-states in particular have realized the extent of exploitation, marginalization, and cultural imperialism associated with globalization.

People, transnational, and multinational corporations move from one place to another. When these movements occur, those engaged in them take their precepts, norms, and cultures with them. Globalization of cultures, therefore, has a long history. Before the creation of the nation-state in the 18th Century, very little stood between tribes and stateless entities in Africa. Now many people may identify with the nation-state. The emergence of the nation-state and nationalism facilitated the process of cultural globalization. Nation-states in Africa have attempted to control language, forms of communication and education. Colonialism has complicated the process because all African nation-states had to deal with alien institutions and cultures. Many Africans continue to suffer what W. E. B. DuBois called "double consciousness" – the struggle with the African self and the European other.

Culture is central to understanding human life in the global village. This is the reason why it is pertinent to define culture, a term that could mean different things to different people and different disciplines. Anthropologists, traditionally, make reference to Edward Tylor's (1871) definition of culture as, "that complex whole which includes knowledge, belief, art, morals, law, custom, and any other capabilities and habits acquired by man [sic] as a member of society" (p. 1). Yet, Sowell (1994) characterizes culture as a term "concerned with political and socioeconomic constructions, moral arrangements, precepts, norms, practices and shared meanings of a particular group of people in a society" (p. 3). Culture is then both a process and an institution. Culture is much a structure as the economy or politics. Its roots lie with families, learning institutions, music, art, and sociopolitical institutions of the society. Culture is therefore important to social domination or the emancipation of a group within the global village. The complex question here is what kind of culture – global or indigenous- could enhance the people's ability to deal with both domestic and global issues in the era of globalization?

European cultural globalization rose with technological advancement in transportation and communication systems, which helped the West expand into Africa and other areas with new ideas of liberalism, capitalism, socialism, and science. Now the Internet, satellite and digital technology have enhanced the process of global culture. Through radio, television, movies, and the Internet, exposure to different cultures and values has been more rapid than ever. In a similar vain, globalization has contributed to the dissipation of indigenous languages and cultures of Africa. "*McCulturalization*," *dollarization*, and "*Coca-Colarization*" all pose a threat to indigenous cultures. The recent globalization of culture is spearheaded both by corporations and Western nation-states. Cultural imperialism has been more rampant than ever, where the dominant corporations and superordinate cultures' practices, institutions and processes have become the norm for the rest of the global village. What does this mean to personal and national identities in the global village? Perhaps the recent rise of multiculturalism and the assertion of affinity politics (race, ethnicity, and gender) are challenges to the cultural imperialism of the West in the global village.

Conclusion

The process of globalization is unstoppable and yet inevitable. Globalization is transforming the world but the transformation is concomitant with prosperity and gains for a few Western nation-states (including Japan) while most African nation-states are entrapped in a pool of destitution and instability. Globalization has increased the gap between the wealthy nation-states and the poorest ones, who are predominantly African. As Held et al (2001) correctly note, "globalization has disrupted the neat correspondence between national territory, sovereignty, political space, and the democratic political community" (p. 146).

Today it is fashionable to speak of the global village — yet African nation-states are not *bona fide* members of the village because, as the United Nations Human Development Program indicates, out of the 174 nation-states ranked on its human development index, the twenty-two lowest nation-states are African. The United Nations Least Developed Countries Report (1997), also note that 33 of the 48 least developed countries (LDCs) are in Africa. Henriot (2001) sums up this bleak picture for Africa in the era of globalization as:

> "economic fundamentalism" that puts an absolute value on the operation of the market and subordinate people's lives, the function of society, the policies of government, and the role of the state to this unrestricted free market. Throughout Africa, this ideology governs not only economic structures but also political arrangements. It assumes almost a religious character, as greed becomes a virtue, competition a commandment, and profit a sign of salvation. Dissenters are dismissed as non-believers at best and heretics at worst (p. 4).

Also, when globalization culture becomes synonymous with Western culture, there is a need for subordinate cultures to go back to their source of the essence of being *(Sankofa)* to search for productive elements that will bring new meanings to their lives. Indubitably, this is not the time for pessimism. Nevertheless, the nostalgia and trauma of slavery, colonialism, neo-colonialism, and now globalization always remind Africans. In a similar vein, Booker and Minter (2001) document the inequalities in today's global village as "foundation of the old inequalities of slavery and colonialism....Like apartheid in South Africa, global apartheid entrenches great disparities in wealth, living conditions, life expectancy and access to government institutions with effective power" (p.15). Globalization is not a panacea to most of Africa's problems, as the winners of the global movement will make the world believe. Africans should be careful in participating in a movement that champions the style of globalization that is blind to the needs of the majority of the members of the global village. If this present process of globalization continues into the next twenty-five years, African nation-states are likely to permanently reinscribe in a position of subjugation, exploitation, marginalization and life-threatening status that is mystified by Western rationalization of a free market and equal benefits for all members of the global village. Africans must continue to reexamine the global forces today in addition to returning to the African essence of community sustenance, reliability, and African worldview.

References

Asumah, S. N. (2001). The nation-state and policy making in Africa: Reconsidering the effects of structural variables and systemic dynamics. In Asumah, S.N. & Johnston-Anumonwo, I. (Eds.). *Issues in Africa and the African Diaspora in the 21st Century,* Binghamton, N.Y.: Global Publications Inc.

Birdsal, N. (2001). Managing inequality in the developing world. In Griffiths, R. (Ed.). *Annual Editions: Developing world. 01,02.* Guilford, CT: McGraw Hill/Dushkin.

Booker, S. & Minter W. (2001, July 9). Global apartheid. *The Nation.*

Friedman, T. (2001). The world is ten years old: The new era of globalization. In Kegley, C. and Wittkoft, E. *The global agenda: Issues and perspectives.* New York: McGraw Hill.

Held, D., McGrew, A., Goldblatt, D. and Parraton, J. (2001). Managing the challenge of globalization and institutionalizing cooperation through global governance. In Kegley, C. and Wittkoft, E. (Eds.). *The global agenda: Issues and perspectives.* New York: McGraw Hill.

Henriot, P. (2001). Globalization: Implications for Africa.
http://www.sedos.org/english/global.html

Hyden, G. & Bratton, M. (Eds.). (1992). *Governance and politics in Africa.* Boulder, CO: Lynne Rienner Publishers.

Kant, I. (1795). Essay on perpetual peace. In Gay, P. (Ed.) (1974). *The enlightenment.* New York: Simon and Schuster.

Mazrui, A. (2001). Africans and African Americans in the changing world trends: Globalizing the Black experience. In Asumah, S. & Johnston-Anumonwo, I. (Eds.). *Issues in Africa and the African diaspora in the 21st century.* New York: Global Publications, Inc.

Mwangi, W. (1996, January). Who gains and who loses from globalization and liberalization. *EcoNews Africa,* 5 (1).

Naisbits, J. (1994). *Global paradox: The bigger the world economy, the more powerful its smallest players.* London: Brealey.

Nester, W. (2001). *International relations: Politics and economics in the 21st century*. Belmont, CA: Wordsworth.

Nordlinger, E. (1987). Taking the state seriously. In Weiner, C. & Huntington, P. (Eds.). *Understanding political development*. Boston, MA: Little Brown & Company.

Sowell, T. (1994). *Race and culture: A worldview*. New York: Basic Books.

Stewart, F. (2000, January). Globalization, liberalization, and inequality: Real causes, expectations, and experience.
http://www.findarticles.com/cf_0/m1093/1_43/59480145/print.jhtml

Tylor, E. (1871). *Primitive cultures*. London: John Murray.

United Nations Development Program (1999). Human Development Report Index. New York.

United Nations Least Developed Countries Report (1997).

Von Glahn, G. (1981). *Law among nations*. New York: MacMillan Publishers.

World Bank. (1999). *World Development Report*. Washington, DC.

CHAPTER 2

AFRICAN POPULISM:

Observations on Rawlings' Ghana and Sankara's Burkina Faso —Journeys through Authoritarian Neo-Liberalism And Democratization

Kenneth Vincent
Student
University of Virginia
Charlottesville

Introduction

Since gaining independence, leaders of the nation-states of sub-Saharan Africa have employed numerous strategies to develop economically. Throughout the 1960s various leaders attempted socialist development, while others saw more merit in neo-liberal free market development. Many states attempted various other forms of state-led development, such as import substitution industrialization during the 1970s; others attempted development through orthodox Marxist-Leninist policies. In the early 1980s structural adjustment packages from the International Financial Institutions (IFIs), loaded with conditionalities mandating that African nations disengage the state from the economy, veritably took over the African continent. Neo-liberalism, especially since the end of the Cold War, has been the dominant development ideology governing African economies. Although it was not implemented on a widespread level, an ideology that can be called African populism guided the development efforts in some African nations during the 1980s. This people-centered ideology drew many of its tenets from Marxist doctrines, but it should not be confused with pure Marxist development strategies.

The most successful attempt at populist development occurred in Burkina Faso under the leadership of Captain Thomas Sankara from 1983 to 1987. Sankara achieved significant material advancements for the Burkinabe people during his four years in power, but was unable to see his full vision of a just and self-sufficient Burkina Faso come to fruition due to his murder in a bloody coup d'etat in October 1987. The other most visible effort at populist development occurred in Ghana, during the very early stages of the rule of Flight Lieutenant Jerry John Rawlings. Rawlings' regime abandoned its revolutionary populist tenets after a short while and went on to implement some of the harshest neo-liberal economic reforms on the continent.

This chapter is divided into two main parts. The first section will discuss the theoretical tenets of African populism and the practices of the Sankara and Rawlings' regimes in Burkina Faso and Ghana respectively. The Sankara regime in Burkina Faso will be used as an example of populism in action. This will be followed by an in-depth look at the populism of J.J. Rawlings. The second section will focus on the transition the Rawlings government made from revolutionary populism to orthodox neo-liberalism. The ideological conflict that preceded the transition, the role that international capital played in the decision-making process and internal and external factors that allowed for such a strict implementation will be highlighted.

I. African Populism Defined and Rawlings' Populism Examined

An Overview of African Populism

Africa has seen numerous varieties of socialism since gaining independence. Populist socialism, in general, can be characterized by intense nationalism, anti-capitalism, the exaltation of the people, and Marxist tendencies (Young, 1982, pp. 101-102). Most of the populist socialist heads of state in Africa had been leaders in the independence struggles of their respective nations, such as Modibo Kéïta, Kwame Nkrumah, and Julius Nyerere (Young, 1982, pp. 97-100). The initial emergence of populist socialist ideology in Africa was tightly intertwined with the currents of Pan-Africanism and anti-imperialist nationalism that swept the continent in the 1960s. The cornerstone of populist development on the practical level was development for the sole benefit of the people. Theoretically, popular participation in the democratic process was supposed to be a facet of the original populist-socialist regimes as well. However, popular participation was actually quite limited in these regimes and most of the decision-making was centralized (Young, 1982, p. 103). Populism took on several different forms in this era and failed to produce significant tangible results in the area of economic development (Young, 1982, p. 99). The first wave of populist socialism in Africa was almost doomed from the beginning due to its incompatibility with Western Cold War interests and a lack of capital.

African populism, of the nature practiced by Rawlings and Sankara, differs from the original populist socialism seen in Africa. African populism can be best explained by identifying its six basic tenets.[1] First, to mobilize civil society on a broad scale, populism needs a charismatic leader for its implementation. Both of the leaders examined here displayed legendary charisma that went far in helping them attain the levels of success that they did. Secondly, African populism mandates moralism in the functioning of the government. Thirdly, civil society is to be politically mobilized on a grassroots level. This participatory democracy can be extremely problematic (as will be shown below), but its core goal is to provide a legitimate feedback from civil society to the government. The fourth and fifth tenets believe in the social equality of all people and the ultimate repugnance of colonialism and neo-colonialism. The sixth tenet of African populism is popular development. Development efforts are to be focused on the condition of the people and a collective popular effort is to be made to carry out this human-oriented development.

Based on its focus on the people's condition, African populism can be broadly grouped with all of the populist-socialist movements the continent has seen. The traits of populism in Burkina Faso and (briefly) in Ghana that differentiate it from other forms of socialism are its focus on moralism in the government and on the political mobilization of the people. Moralism in the government became more of an issue in Burkina Faso and Ghana after two decades of state-led development brought about the problems of an elite civil servant class and government corruption. The earlier socialist governments did not confront these problems because they focused on the initiation of self-governance, which was inherently morally superior to colonial rule. Populism mandated participatory democracy most likely because the post-independence attempts at Western electoral democracy did not give the African masses sufficient opportunity for feedback in the government. African populism took the same revolutionary ideals exhibited during the initial surge of populist socialism in Africa and applied them to old and new issues.

The nature of the participatory democracy that Rawlings and

Sankara attempted to institute in their respective nations falls in line with the most basic philosophical notions of democracy. Rousseau's social contract, at its core, involves the political mobilization of all people through education. Actual participation was a crucial part of this. Africa's attempts at democratization prior to the birth of African populism did not provide a sufficient political voice to the African masses because colonial rule had stifled their political consciousness. Populist participatory democracy attempted to give the masses this consciousness and a voice in government. Although in practice African populism's empowerment of the people was not completely successful (especially in Ghana), it does represent one of the better attempts at involving citizens in the operations of government that the continent has yet seen.

African Populism in Action: Thomas Sankara's Rule in Burkina Faso

Many of these populist notions in Africa could be equated to empty rhetoric, but a closer look at the case of Thomas Sankara in Burkina Faso would suggest that populism is a legitimate method of governance. First of all, in Burkina Faso moralism in the government was central to the policy and practice of the Sankara regime. The profitability of being in the civil service went against the moralist ideals Sankara governed by. Sankara (1988) passionately opposed excesses within the civil service:

> Out of a budget of 58 billion [CFA Francs], 30,000 functionaries monopolize 30 billion and that leaves nothing for everyone else. This is not normal. If we want greater justice, every one of us must recognize the real situation of the masses and see the sacrifices that must be made so that justice can be done (p. 154).

Even today, contrary to all that is often said in regard to privileges of the governing class in African governments, very rarely are the salaries of government employees pointed out and criticized by someone from within the government. Sankara cut down on the privileges of the civil service by mandating that they donate a portion of their salary to a "Popular Investment Effort" (EIP), cutting out a twelfth month's salary, ending housing subsidies to civil servants, and adopting the modest Renault 5 as the official car of the state over the government's fleet of Mercedes Benzes, which were raffled off (Martin, 1989, p.67). Sankara honestly wanted the government to be transparent and dedicate its resources to the masses. The masses were politically mobilized with the organization of Revolutionary Defense Committees (CDRs). These committees were an institutional manifestation of the people's central role in development in Burkina Faso and were designed to provide genuine feedback to the government. At times, however, they were used to control civil society by opportunistic leadership at the local level, which represented a serious shortcoming of populist participatory democracy (Martin, 1987, pp. 78-81).

Nonetheless, Sankara's focus on the social equality of all people referred not only to traditional Marxist class struggle issues, but also went further to take a look at other evils in Burkinabe society. He demonized traditional society's treatment of women and people's subservience to traditional chiefs. Payments and obligatory service to chiefs were outlawed in Burkina Faso in 1984, and in the following year a National Conference on Women's Emancipation was held to promote gender equality (Sankara, 1988, pp. 18-20). Sankara also tried to make Burkina Faso economically independent; his civil service reforms were his method of trying to stabilize the economy rather than calling on the IMF (Sankara, 1988, p.159). Human development in Burkina Faso was the primary goal of the Sankara regime. Through popular participation during the four years Sankara was in power, significant advances were made in the areas of literacy, health, and infrastructure. River blindness, long the most severe health scourge in the country, was eradicated. Thousands of Burkinabe children were educated in indigenous languages, and meaningful irrigation and tree planting projects took place (Sankara, 1988, pp. 9-10). It is clear that populist development did take place here, and that Sankara's regime was more mass oriented than most of Burkina Faso's military regimes.

One factor that makes judgement of the Sankara regime difficult is the fact that it was cut short on October 15, 1987 in a bloody military coup d'etat led by Blaise Compaoré. The tragic end of Sankara's life, ironically, gives validity to some of the populist traits of his rule. Populist development in Burkina Faso died with Sankara, which would indicate the importance of a charismatic leader. The moralist nature of the civil service reforms that took place must have truly curtailed excesses taken by Burkina's civil servants; their discontent was largely what led to the coup and shortly after taking office, Compaoré announced pay raises for government employees (Martin, 1989, p.75).

J.J. Rawlings' Early Days: Populist Ideology and Popular Mobilization

Before Sankara took power in Burkina Faso, Jerry Rawlings had already taken power in Ghana through a military coup, relinquished it, and taken it back through another military coup. Rawlings' first takeover occurred on June 4, 1979 with the Armed Forces Revolutionary Council (AFRC). This government was led by junior officers who were dissatisfied with their situation and with the excesses taken by superior officers in the ruling military government (Folson, 2000, pp.124-125). They intended only to clean up the government and hand it over to civilian rule when the job was done. On September 24, 1979, Rawlings gave power back to a democratically elected government, reminding the newly elected civilian government led by President Hilla Limann that the revolutionary cadres that had allowed for his takeover would be "watching [the civilian government] with eagle eyes" (Rawlings, 1993, p. 483). Obviously, those watching forces were unsatisfied with what they saw, because the same group of officers, led again by Rawlings, took over a second time on December 31, 1981. Jerry John Rawlings would go on to be Ghana's head of state for twenty years.

Rawlings' June 4th revolution definitely qualifies as populist, at least in part, because the central goal of the AFRC involved moralism in the government. The AFRC sought to eradicate corruption of all kinds, by any means necessary. The suffering of Ghanaian society, coupled with the obvious excesses of the ruling military elite, impassioned Rawlings and his followers. The coup's primary purposes were to "clean up" the government of Ghana and restore integrity to the civil service (Folson, 2000, pp.127-128). To the AFRC, punishing the wrongdoers was just as important as ceasing the wrongdoing. Several high-ranking military officers, including former heads of state I.K. Acheampong and F.W.K. Akuffo, were executed by firing squad in June of 1979 (*Ghanaian Times*, 1993, p. 465). This was to serve as an example to all Ghanaian leaders that the revolutionary cadres on the left meant business, and that corruption was intolerable. There is no evidence to suggest that the AFRC had any intention of restructuring Ghanaian society or addressing Ghana's position in the international system. The ruling classes were weakened by the AFRC's brief reign, due to the fact that almost all of the ruling classes were somehow scrutinized. This gave the working classes a better position from which to bargain (Ninsin, 1989, p. 29). Rawlings might not have had an extensive set of goals to accomplish, but it certainly appears that the goals he did have were populist in nature.

The early period of the December 31st revolution provides a better example of genuine populism. The initial ideology of the PNDC's (Provisional National Defense Council) regime had several features that could be identified as populist, and many measures similar to those taken by Sankara were enacted. The PNDC's set of goals was broadly based and focused on much more than just the issue of corruption within the civil servant class and the upper echelons of the military. Rawlings (1983) seemed poised to drastically change the face of Ghana:

> ...this is not a coup. I call for nothing less than a revolution. Something that would transform the social and economic order of this country. The military is not in to take over. We simply want to be a part of the decision-making process (p. 1).

Rawlings' proposed revolution began by championing a set of ideals similar to those that Sankara would champion two years later. The two men came to power in the same way, and Ghana supported the Sankara revolution more than any other West African state (Englebert, 1996, p. 153). Rawlings' populist ideology was unmistakable. Ghanaian society was to be turned upside down and made more just. Along with corruption (the primary target of the AFRC coup), the PNDC government lashed out against foreign and domestic capitalists' vested interests and "reactionary" leaders in Ghanaian society, such as traditional chiefs (Ninsin, 1993, p. 103). Its initial development agenda appeared to be extremely people-oriented; if focused on the deprived sections of Ghanaian society, human rights, an economy that ensured the maximum welfare of the people, and educational and health care reforms (Panford, 1994, pp. 76-77). The PNDC also routinely spoke against imperialism. A pamphlet printed in May of 1982 entitled *The Policy Guidelines of the Provisional National Defence Council* outlined an ideology that focused on external factors. This document, which provides excellent insight into the political atmosphere in the early days of the regime, identifies the roots of Ghana's economic problems in "more deep-seated neo-colonial economic and institutional structures" (p. 3).

The PNDC projected this leftist ideology to the rest of the world.

The regime's initial foreign policy pronouncements were radical. Rawlings' regime denounced American imperialism and other unjust Western policies that it felt had harmed Africa. It harshly criticized foreign investors for profiting from Ghanaian labor and Ghanaian resources, and threatened to nationalize foreign holdings (Boafo-Arthur, 1989, pp. 151-152). The PNDC unequivocally rejected Western capital, which would later play a central role in nearly everything that happened in the Ghanaian economy. The dominant populist ideology promoted withdrawing from the world capitalist system altogether (Boafo-Arthur, 1993, pp. 136-137). Forging a just society in Ghana would necessitate removing it from this system which was said to be the cause of all of Ghana's economic woes. Although the PNDC maintained a de jure policy of non-alignment, it had very amicable relations with the Eastern Bloc, Libya, and Cuba. The government initially looked to these nations for financial support. Cuba's success at human development made it a model to Ghana, and even provided it with some of technical assistance (Boafo-Arthur, 1993, pp. 144-146).

Within Ghana, the most significant populist measures adopted in the early stages of PNDC rule were in the area of political mobilization of the popular masses. Revolutionary cadres (including leftist student organizations, junior military officers, and labor organizations) made up the initial power base of the PNDC. Rawlings' government sought to mobilize the popular masses to ensure the success of the revolution (Folson, 2000, pp. 129-130). Rawlings' skepticism regarding the just nature of electoral democracy (through nation- wide elections) caused him to initiate populist participatory democracy in the form of grassroots People's Defence Committees (Ninsin, 1993, pp. 101-103). Rawlings (1983) viewed these committees as essential to the success of the revolution:

> Popular participation in the decision-making process must be a reality. The development of the Defence Committees as true organs of revolutionary power is the only way that this can be assured (p. 28).

Electoral democracy, which had proven entirely ineffective under Hilla Limann from 1979 to 1981, did not give the lower classes of society sufficient opportunity to give the government feedback. The People's Defense Committees were supposed to check anti-revolutionary practices, and they also were to serve as agents of popular development. The greatest impact that the Defence Committees had was in the area of labor; labor advocacy throughout Ghana's history had come in the form of traditional labor unions. The leadership of these unions did not always function in the best interest of workers, and the PNDC sought to improve this situation by establishing Worker's Defence Committees (WDCs) and dismissing corrupt union officials (Graham, 1989, pp. 49-51). This tied the power base of labor closely to the government, placing labor in the precarious position of relying on governmental dedication to its issues. Looking solely at the initial mobilization of civil society, the December 31st revolution can definitely be identified as populist. These grassroots mobilization structures, however, would prove to have a short life span.

Populist Policies of the PNDC in Practice

Some of the first populist policy measures taken by the new government were in line with those taken by the AFRC. Corruption within the civil service remained a problem within the government of the Third Republic. Rawlings called for a "Holy War" within Ghana to end the sufferings caused by bureaucratic excesses and accused the civil service of the Third Republic of trying to "institutionalize corruption and decadence" (Rawlings, 1983, p. 2 & p. 41) The PNDC set up punitive measures to penalize these excesses. It established investigatory committees to seek out corrupt members of Ghanaian society, questioning any Ghanaian who had over fifty thousand cedis in their bank account (Hansen, 1991, pp. 93-94). Government-owned enterprises, which perpetually incurred heavy losses, were also targeted. Management personnel found guilty of offenses, such as the hoarding of consumer goods and graft, were dismissed and subsequently subjected to "revolutionary discipline" (Ninsin, 1989, p. 31). Rawlings wanted more accountability in the civil service, to combat people "who reap where they have not sowed," and to instill revolutionary values in the civil service (Rawlings, 1983, p. 86). It should be pointed out that all these moralist measures, while populist in nature, differed from those of the Sankara regime in that they were solely focused on extralegal excesses. Rawlings and the PNDC did not go as far as curtailing the privileges enjoyed by the Ghanaian civil servants, and there was little evidence of changes in their perquisites or in their salary scale.

Domestic policy measures were also taken at the beginning to address the economic hardships faced by the Ghanaian people. The most visible populist policy measures in this area at the beginning of PNDC rule were government-imposed price controls. Rawlings' regime placed controls on the prices of basic consumer goods to alleviate the prevalent suffering of Ghanaian society (the dire nature of which will be discussed in detail below). The government implemented these price controls by administering corporal punishment to traders who ignored the controls and burning entire markets that it deemed "anti-revolutionary" (Gyimah-Boadi, 1993, p. 6). The PNDC also took measures to improve the lot of the Ghanaian urban worker, again, due to the crucial role that industrial unions played in its usurping of power. The regime's first (and only) concrete pro-labor act was the reinstatement of one thousand workers, who had been dismissed for protesting the Limann government, to the Ghana Industrial Holdings Corporation (Panford, 1994, pp. 76-77). The rural peasantry also received attention during the PNDC's populist phase. Agricultural cooperatives, designed to provide for the communal production of food, were set up in rural areas on both the administrative district level and at the village level (Anyimadu, 1993, p. 63). All of these measures were evidence of populist leanings, but they were only temporarily sustainable and did not address the fundamental economic problems that Ghana faced.

The PNDC did propose some more broadly sweeping policies that addressed Ghana's fundamental problems. The "Revised Budget Statement for 1981-1982" and the "PNDC's Program for Reconstruction and Development" represented the first policy pronouncements with populist orientations. They focused on the usual prescriptions for economic development, such as increased efficiency in management and the mobilization of indigenous resources to increase self-sufficiency, along with reworking the tax structure to be less regressive (Folson, 2000, pp. 132-137). These policies left the question of how to remedy Ghana's subordinate position in the global capitalist economy unanswered. These pronouncements mentioned nothing about the issues of monocrop export agriculture and extractive mineral exploitation that Ghana had endured since British colonization. Ironically, the PNDC displayed the populist rejection of all forms of imperialism by denouncing the IMF and The World Bank; it also decried the IFIs' mandate for currency devaluation as an imperialist program to foster the exploitation of African resources (Gyimah-Boadi & Essuman-Johnson, 1993, pp. 197-198). This provided a symbol of the regime's initial solidarity with the working classes. Rawlings announced more sweeping measures to foster food self-sufficiency, such as the reorganization of the State Farms Corporation and the Food Production Corporation, and a crack-down on smuggling and hoarding; however, little evidence points to the materialization of these goals (Rawlings, 1983, pp. 63-65). On the whole, the nature of economic reforms that were proposed in populist Ghana remained technocratic in nature.

Thomas Sankara's tenure in Burkina Faso provides an example of revolutionary populism by which J.J. Rawlings can be judged. This is ironic in view of the fact that Rawlings was already in the process of phasing out populist measures when Sankara took power. It is difficult to argue that Rawlings and the PNDC were not at all populist; however, their populism could be identified as extremely mild and definitely short-lived. This could most likely be attributed to a combination of factors, including the difference in size between the two countries, the more powerful right-wing in Ghana, and the ideological commitment of Rawlings. Sankara's idealism and personal commitment to the people he governed surpassed most world leaders. It should also be pointed out that this stubborn and vigorous idealism partially led to the bloody coup d'etat that ended Sankara's life. Before examining that change from populist rule to neo-liberalism in Ghana, the populist rule carried out by Rawlings and the PNDC should be further examined critically, focusing on the violent nature of its implementation, the stopgap nature of its policies, and the ideological commitment of Rawlings himself.

Populist Rule in Ghana: A Critical Assessment

Reason would not dictate that a revolution focusing on the people's condition should be brutal in practice. Sankara's revolution in Burkina Faso proved that a populist revolution does not have to be brutal. The AFRC went about accomplishing the same populist goals exhibited in the Burkina Faso revolution in a much more violent manner. The handling of revolutionary justice provides the most obvious contrast between the two countries. The executions of Akuffo, Acheampong, and other top military officers set a violent tone that was sustained throughout the AFRC's brief period in power. The People's revolutionary courts in Burkina Faso tried upper level officials and civil servants for the same offenses. However, their punishments were limited to fines, expropriation, repayment of the funds stolen, and light prison terms (Martin, 1987, p. 80). According to *Catholic Standard* (1979/1993), a Ghanaian newspaper, the executions were supposed to serve as a "warning note to future aspiring political leaders and politicians" (p. 467). Moralism in the government should ideally come from a genuine desire to serve the interests of the citizens governed, not from fear of the firing squad. Sankara, a true populist, perfectly exemplified this.

The violent nature of Rawlings' attempt at populist rule is also demonstrated in some of the methods used by the PNDC in its efforts to take care of the Ghanaians' basic needs. The enforcement of price controls mentioned above revealed the capacity for brute force and violence of the PNDC. Members of the PDCs routinely beat market women who refused to adhere to the price controls, and people's livelihoods were destroyed with the burning of markets (Ahiakpor, 1991, pp. 588-589). These measures are akin to terrorism and assault rather than popular mobilization. Popular mobilization involving a society galvanized by a charismatic leader to fight for the betterment of its own condition is the ideal of populism in practice; this actually occurred in Burkina Faso. The PNDC's brutality in these cases seriously calls the populist nature of their ideals into question.

All of the policies that could be characterized as populist did not have long-term sustainability of broadly sweeping implications. The Rawlings government never addressed Ghana's position in the world economic order or the social structure of the country, and the government could not have sustained these policies. It would be presumptuous to dismiss all of the measures enacted by the PNDC as a facade of populism. However, it should be pointed out that consolidating power was its primary goal after taking over. Leftist forces supporting the government and within the government itself had to be placated during this period. This could explain why most of the measures taken to help the Ghanaian people benefited people in politically important urban areas. Absent from the early period of PNDC revolutionary populism were programs focused on health and education issues, or a formal plan to spend less money on high ranking executives in the civil service and more money on the people. All of these policy shortcomings, measured by the standards set by the Sankara regime, could be attributed in large part to the transition the government made to neo-liberal economic governance after only a short period of populist attempts at economic recovery. The central role of Rawlings' charisma in the initial mobilization of Ghanaian civil society, the genuine leftist support base and its presence in the government, and the state structures set up to mobilize civil society all indicate populist leanings in the early stages of PNDC rule.

The final method to judge the populist nature of the early PNDC is by examining the ideological commitment of Rawlings himself. It is obvious from an examination of his training, that Rawlings could not have been the chief ideologue at the time that he took power. Jerry Rawlings was a pilot. All of the training he received above the secondary school level had been military prior to his initial takeover. Rawlings saw injustices within Ghanaian society and sought to redress them. In reference to the absence of intense ideological motivation in his governance, he said, "I don't know law, and I don't understand economics, but I know when my stomach is empty" (Sakyi-Addo, 2001, p. 21). Sankara (1988) had a similar shortage of academic training and has been quoted as saying the same sorts of things, although he called Lenin's *State and Revolution* "a book that I take refuge in, that I reread often" (p. 203). I would argue that African populism *is an ideology whose main goal is the betterment of the material condition of the people* and that Rawlings' lack of an academic focus would not disqualify him as a populist. A more valid critique of Rawlings' dedication to populist rule can be drawn from the fact that he did not heed the urging of his leftist contemporaries and form a revolutionary populist government during the AFRC takeover in 1979 (Ahiakpor, 1991, p. 587). Rawlings' true shortcoming as a populist, however, was his level of dedication. During his rule, Sankara faced a number of the same internal and external pressures as did Rawlings, but did not give in to them in four years. The only thing that could change Burkina Faso's populist trajectory was his murder. Perhaps Rawlings' willingness to give in to these pressures could be viewed as a rational decision; he had an incredibly long-lasting rule that received much international acclaim. It seems tragic that dedication to the human dignity of one's countrymen is so difficult to sustain, and that populist rule on the African continent was never really fully implemented.

II. From Populism to Neo-Liberalism: Ideological Conflict and the Consolidation of the PNDC's Authoritarian Capitalist State

Now that it has been established that Jerry Rawlings had populist leanings, we must examine why his populist rule was short-lived. The PNDC implemented a strict economic recovery package financed by the International Financial Institutions (IFIs) that went against every populist ideal with which the government started. Ghana's economy was in a disastrous state when the PNDC took over, and addressing this situation was its first goal. Intense internal debate on how to reverse the decline in Ghana's economy followed, with the traditional rift between state-led, people-oriented, and market-oriented development. International capital played an extremely significant role in this debate, giving a victory to the right coalition. The severity of Ghana's economic problems and the nature of the PNDC government explain the extreme form that structural adjustment took in Ghana. The PNDC quickly transformed populist, grassroots mobilization state structures into those of an authoritarian state repression and the powerful forces that had long stood against structural adjustment were co-opted by the PNDC machine.

The Early Days of the PNDC: Ideological Conflict in a Dire Situation

When the PNDC took power, the decline of the Ghanaian economy had reached alarming proportions. Ghana's economy never recovered from the dependent economic position it occupied under British rule.

The entire economy largely revolved around the export of cocoa, which kept Ghana at the mercy of the international cocoa market. Years of inefficient state-led development measures had taken their toll on the economy. Poor financial management, the maintenance of an overvalued exchange rate, and inefficient pricing policies all had extremely adverse effects on the economy.

The government of General I.K. Acheampong was largely responsible for the period of failed state-led development, after the initial surge of it under Kwame Nkrumah was undermined. Many criticized the Acheampong government for shunning international capital and the conditionalities of the IFIs (Jonah, 1989, pp. 102-104). Infrastructure had deteriorated and cocoa exports had declined, leading to a drastic shortage of foreign exchange; Ghana's food self-sufficiency was steadily dropping. Between 1979 and 1982 Ghana experienced a series of crises that greatly exacerbated its economic woes. Rises in oil prices caused an acute foreign exchange crisis, a drought and brush fires caused severe damage to the agricultural sector, and the expulsion of nearly one million Ghanaians from Nigeria put an unbearable burden on the already fragile economy (Anyemedu, 1993, pp. 13-18). This situation clearly necessitated drastic measures on the part of the government, measures far more drastic (no matter what their ideological basis), than those initially enacted by the PNDC. It has been argued that the severity of Ghana's deplorable economic situation enabled the government to implement a harsh reform package because the situation could hardly have gotten worse, and civil society was prepared to try anything (Ihonvbere, 2000, pp. 68-69). Intense debate on the policy direction of the PNDC government followed.

Ghana, to a large degree, has been one of the intellectual epicenters of Africa since independence. The legacy of Kwame Nkrumah makes Ghana open to vibrant intellectual debate even on a grassroots level, which made it a very open place for the debate over economic strategy (Ihonvbere, 2000, pp. 74-75). Ghana has been ideologically divided along the same lines since independence. The faction on the left, associated with Nkrumah, has always been at odds with the right-wing faction, associated with J.B. Danquah and K.A. Busia; this ideological divide has been at the root of most of the political conflicts in Ghana's post-independence history (Anebo, 2000, pp. 264-266). The leftist faction favors a more socialist approach to development and attributes Ghana's economic problems to international monopoly capital. The right, on the other hand, sees little wrong with the structural aspects of Ghana's position in the world economy and favors friendly relations with the West, as well as a market-oriented approach to development. This divide, along with the lack of political stability in Ghana, can account for the lack of a consistent policy towards the IFIs since independence (Jonah, 1989, pp. 94-95). This divide could be seen within the PNDC government. The left, which represented most of the support base of the PNDC, sought to radically address the situation by attempting to break free from the world capitalist system and revolutionizing Ghanaian society. Rawlings made pronouncements that placed him on the left, and the populist ideals of the regime initially seemed firmly in place. The right favored a gradual and technical approach to arresting the economy's decline and favored approaching the IMF for stabilization assistance. Currency devaluation, one of the most sensitive political issues in Ghana for decades, dominated these debates (Hansen, 1991, pp. 102-110). Because of this divide, neither far-reaching populist measures, as exhibited in Burkina Faso, nor market-oriented reforms were implemented during the first stages of PNDC rule. It would be easy to look at the Ghanaian transition to neo-liberalism as pure neo-colonial intervention on the part of the IFIs, but it must be noted that the decision arose from an internal conflict.

The right, whose main strength was its propensity to attract foreign capital, gained internal advantages early in this debate. The first body organized to debate these issues was the Economic Policy Review Committee (EPRC), headed up by Dr. Joe Abbey, an avowed neo-liberalist. The PNDC also appointed Dr. Kwesi Botchwey to add balance to the committee. Botchwey earned his academic reputation at the University of Ghana as a committed Marxist. It seemed odd that these two would be put together, but it was of little consequence because Botchwey moved to the right side of the debate once on the committee (Hansen, 1991, pp. 94-96). This gave the right coalition a spokesperson for its policies. Dissension was also rampant in the ranks of the left. A member of the PNDC murdered three judges and a former executive from the Ghana Industrial Holdings Corporation, and he was to be executed. The left became factionalized, and radical organizations that had supported Rawlings as a populist became antagonistic to PNDC rule (Toye, 1990, pp. 48-49). When the aforementioned lack of ideological commitment on the part of Rawlings is factored in, it already appears that the left coalition's situation was extremely precarious. The deciding factor proved to be international capital.

The Role of International Capital

Ghana, like so many African nations that have turned to the IFIs, was economically powerless in 1983. No government wants to have outside actors managing its economy. Approaching the IFIs is a last resort that many African nations have been forced to do. Whatever development strategy Ghana planned to pursue, it needed foreign capital. No situation as dire as the one it faced could have been remedied without considerable external assistance. Ghana did not possess the resources necessary for an independent development strategy. Consequently, the country had to turn to the rest of the world for help, and its options became limited to whatever programs for which it could obtain external finance (Boafo-Arthur, 1989, p. 154). Emmanuel Hansen (1991), who can be placed on the left side of this ideological conflict, wrote that the left's "contribution to the revolutionary process was measured in terms of its ability to attract financial assistance" (p. 111).

The left sought foreign capital wherever it could. Libya, a nation undergoing a similar populist revolution under the leadership of Muammar Gadaffi, provided Ghana with some forms of piecemeal assistance, such as shipments of crude oil, but they proved unhelpful as far as significant capital loans. The same was true of the European socialist bloc (Boafo-Arthur, 1993, pp. 139-145). All of these nations could claim ideological solidarity with the Ghanaian left, but they simply did not have the resources to spread around. Ghana called on the socialist bloc when the latter's involvement in Africa was already beginning to decline from the peak of its involvement during the 1970s.

The West became the only remaining source of capital. Stabilization and structural adjustment funds from the IMF and The World Bank could become available, but not without conditionalities. Ghana also had to prove itself suitable for assistance. To accomplish this end, the PNDC had to renege on everything it championed during its populist days. Ghana, under the PNDC, had long maintained a policy of nonalignment. However, all of the anti-imperialist rhetoric had placed Ghana closer to the East, which undermined American support, a crucial factor in getting capital flows from the IFIs (Boafo-Arthur, 1989, pp. 157-158). Threats of nationalizing multinational corporations obviously made Ghana quite unattractive for direct foreign investment. The dire need for capital forced the PNDC to tame down its radicalism. Rawlings even went so far as to censure the Ghanaian press, which was controlled by the left, for creating a misleading ideological image of the PNDC (Boafo-Arthur, 1993, p. 149). To appease Western monetary organizations, the PNDC reconstituted the Economic Review Committee to be comprised of neo-liberal economists, while downplaying the role of more radical organizations (Ninsin, 1993, p. 105). For obvious reasons, the leftist coalition could not bring the same amount of money and power to the table as the right coalition could. This forced the PNDC to abandon all of the people-oriented measures it had originally championed in favor of neo-liberal economic policies. It seems that although the ideological conflict surrounding economic reform was internal, not to mention the doubts about the populist commitment of Rawlings' regime, there is strong evidence that international capital influenced the PNDC's abandonment of populism far more than any other single factor.

The PNDC and the Implementation of the Economic Recovery Program (ERP)

Before Jerry Rawlings, no other Ghanaian head of state had been able to hold on to the presidency for more than a decade. The struggle for power in Ghana had gone back and forth between the left and right coalitions outlined above, resulting in a lack of a long-term direction of development in Ghana prior to the PNDC takeover. Rawlings and the PNDC were unique because they took over with a support base from the far left and slowly drifted right, crushing or co-opting forces that opposed their new economic direction. The political environment that the PNDC provided was absolutely essential in the implementation of the ERP (Jonah, 1989, p. 114). The PNDC provided stability by relying on the charisma of Rawlings and on propaganda to keep a substantial part of civil society on the side of the regime. At the same time, it moved away from, and effectively destroyed, the left coalition; and it reorganized state structures (originally intended for political mobilization) to suppress dissent and consolidate authoritarian power.

Since the AFRC uprising in 1979, Jerry Rawlings maintained substantial popularity in Ghana. His fiery speeches and identification with the working class made him a hero to the people of Ghana, who gave him the name "Junior Jesus," in hopes that he would lead them to better lives (Sakyi-Addo, 2001, pp. 21-23). Rawlings had to convince the people of Ghana that the people's revolutionary duty mandated they endured the hardships ahead. He seemed prepared to be straightforward with the citizens he governed. In a speech marking the anniversary of the December 31st revolution, Rawlings (1984) outlined the rationale behind the ERP and did not hesitate to admit that there would be hardships ahead:

> I could, of course, be telling you very soothing and pleasant stories and attempt to make promises of easy time ahead. There is only one thing which prevents me from doing so, and that is the truth (p. 72).

Rawlings appealed to the Ghanaians to be dedicated to the revolution. He explained the long-term effects in a positive light and focused on the rural peasantry, who had long been ignored by the government, although they represented the backbone of the Ghanaian economy. The ERP did benefit more people in rural than in urban areas. Some have argued that this focus on the rural peasants appealed to Rawlings during the debate on economic reform because so many of the benefits of socialism accrued to the urban bureaucratic bourgeoisie (Clapham, 1996, p. 179). Aside from Rawlings' appeals, much of the crucial spin control regarding the ERP involved the issue of devaluation. For decades, devaluing the Cedi had been one of the most volatile issues in Ghanaian politics, and the ERP approached this topic extremely cautiously (Sowa, 1994, p. 13). This seemed logical due to the many negative social effects of currency devaluation on ordinary citizens. The ERP (1983) itself presents the devaluation (which initially came in the form of a split exchange rate) in a roundabout way, never actually using the "d" word (pp. 16-17). It is debatable whether these publicity measures had any impact at all on the staying power of Rawlings and the PNDC, although Rawlings' charisma must have played some role. Measures taken to consolidate power and crush opposition proved far more important.

After winning the debate on economic planning, the rightist coalition and the Rawlings faction had to neutralize the left. They had already toned down much of their revolutionary rhetoric to appease the IFIs; internal pressures became the next problem. The popular press, controlled by the left, was initially silenced. Rawlings told the editorial committee of *The Worker's Banner* to tone down its subversive editorials that harshly criticized The World Bank and the IMF (Hansen, 1991, p. 122). To fill positions formerly occupied by populist revolutionaries, the PNDC appointed old guard, rightist military officers and politicians to give the government a more conservative face (Panford, 1994, p. 86). The PNDC harassed members of the left coalition, but the left's attempted counter-coups in October and November of 1983 were unsuccessful. The National Defence Committee, which had been at the forefront of revolutionary populist activities, was disbanded in December of 1983 (Hansen, 1991, pp. 124-125). Populism within the PNDC had been totally eliminated. Rejection of the Western capital monopoly and emphasis on the structure of Ghanaian society would become a thing of the past. It should be noted that the reason the PNDC consolidated rightist rule more efficiently than any other previous government was that it came to power on a leftist program. When Rawlings and other PNDC officers allied themselves with the right side of the debate, they disarmed one of the most powerful factions of the left. Pressure from Rawlings' cadres had prevented Hilla Limann's government from calling on the IFIs for fear of another coup (Gyimah-Boadi, 1993, pp. 2-4). Ironically, in a 1987 interview, Limann praised himself for defying the IFIs and criticized the decision of the PNDC to turn to the IMF (Okunor, 1987/1993, p. 483). The ideological turnaround of the Rawlings faction was clearly one of the most important factors in the suppression of the left because it had formerly represented one of the strongest leftist factions.

The IFIs did not approve of the populist institutions set up to politically empower the Ghanaian people. Rawlings abandoned organs designed to channel the feedback from the popular masses for those that were designed to silence the dissent of those very masses. Rawlings' regime slowly became more authoritarian and autocratic throughout the 1980s. Although by many standards the PNDC was not particularly brutal, evidence definitely points towards the violation of civil liberties and human rights during its time in power (Gyimah-Boadi, 1993, pp. 8-9). To put forth a façade of democracy, the PNDC divided Ghana into 110 small districts, which were to hold grassroots elections. Although district assemblies did provide a forum for civil dissent, whenever they appeared to pose any sort of viable opposition, the PNDC quickly silenced them (Ninsin, 1993, pp. 107-111). Rawlings' December 31st takeover replaced an electoral democracy with populist participatory democracy. When the IMF and The World Bank criticized the organs of popular political mobilization established by the PNDC, these organs were stripped of their political power. Civil society no longer had an outlet to officially voice its discontent. This insulation of the decision-making process from popular pressure allowed for an economic program that was extremely hard on the citizens of Ghana (Callaghy, 2000, p. 58).

The most glaring example of how the PNDC transformed the organs of a populist revolution into a means of strictly implementing a structural adjustment package came in the area of labor. At the beginning, the PNDC sought to radicalize the labor movement. The PNDC criticized the leadership of the Trade Union Congress (TUC) for corrupt and undemocratic practices. Much of its support came from organized urban labor, and it wanted power to lie with the workers themselves (Ninsin, 1989, p. 32). Ghanaian workers, empowered by the revolutionary government, forcibly overthrew the TUC leadership in April of 1982. The demands of labor were then supposed to be voiced through the Worker's Defense Committees (Graham, 1989, p. 49). Mobilization of the people, in this case, was supposed to eliminate the corrupt middleman in this situation, giving labor more of a voice in government. Rawlings declared that, if labor union executives "had been true leaders, they would automatically emerge in these new democratic expressions" (Rawlings, 1983, p. 27). The populist period of

PNDC rule gave labor more power and more influence on the government. This power was based on the populist nature of the PNDC government. When the PNDC began to make its ideological transition to the right, labor was left behind. Largely to appease the IFIs, the PNDC eliminated the WDCs shortly after establishing them (Gyimah-Boadi & Essuman-Johnson, 1993, pp. 198-199). Keeping in mind that the Committees had replaced the traditional unions, it becomes easy to see that this measure essentially robbed labor of any voice it might have had. This is a clear example of why the PNDC was able to implement the ERP so strictly. Quieting the Ghanaian left represented the main obstacle in ERP implementation. The PNDC's transformation from the political expression of the left's power to the enforcer of the right's neo-liberal policies eliminated this obstacle entirely.

Conclusion

Flight Lieutenant Jerry John Rawlings took Ghana on an incredibly long journey. Many Ghanaians would say that this journey was far too long. This journey represented almost half of Ghana's post-colonial history. At the beginning, Rawlings and the PNDC seemed poised to attack the contemporary and historical forces that compromised the welfare of the Ghanaian people. International capital quickly quelled this revolutionary fervor, and Ghana became the vanguard of IFI-financed, free market development. The hardships imposed on Ghanaians under the ERP matched (and in some cases surpassed) those endured under state-led development plans of Dr. Kwame Nkrumah. The ERP looked better on paper, so the IFIs deemed it a success. The fact that the IFIs did not use the material condition of Ghanaian citizens as a measuring stick for the success of their programs provides considerable insight into the framework and methodology of the development plans they impose all over Africa.

When contrasted with African populism, the neo-liberalism of the IFIs looks less convincing on a theoretical level. The two ideologies cannot properly be compared using the case of Ghana alone because the PNDC governed in a populist manner for such a short period of time. Populism can be usefully examined using the case of Thomas Sankara in Burkina Faso and the ideological framework outlined by scholars. When populism is compared to neo-liberalism, glaring contrasts manifest themselves. Populism puts the condition of the people at the top of its agenda; under neo-liberalism it is an afterthought that is only partially addressed (as is evidenced by PAMSCAD). Populism seeks to practice democracy in a manner that goes to the core meaning of government by the people; neo-liberalism calls for electoral democracy, but the externalization of financial management takes away much of the element of choice in democracy. Populism approaches the national budget with the attitude of trying to cut corners to provide more for the people; neo-liberalism approaches the budget with only austerity in mind, with little regard for the social ramifications. These two ideologies could not be more at odds with each other. So how could they be found in the same nation under the same ruler?

Both populism and neo-liberalism are concerned with curbing the excesses of the government, and both of them have a focus on the rural peasantry. Rawlings, who did not possess much formal academic training, was possibly attracted to these similarities. Most importantly, however, the PNDC abandoned populism because it had to. In a hostile international environment during the Cold War, no nation with needs as dire as Ghana's could have successfully developed using populist policies. Thomas Sankara's success in Burkina Faso, which might have provided an example of a legitimate alternative development course, had he lived past the end of the Cold War, could be attributed to differences between the crises in the two countries, and above all, Sankara's undying ideological and moral commitment to the Burkinabe people. Ghana had no choice but to turn to the IFIs for assistance. Although international capital represented the biggest factor in this change, it did arise from an internal conflict. The right side of the internal conflict was simply given an overwhelming advantage through the IFIs.

This ideological shift from revolutionary populism to neo-liberalism within the PNDC hierarchy was most likely the chief factor in putting Ghana at the forefront of neo-liberal development. The PNDC gained power with the support of the left. It created a populist state that was to become the sole protector of the people. When it decided to purge the left from its organization and take away the channels of advocacy it had provided for Ghanaians, it was in a perfect position to do whatever it wanted. International capital co-opted the PNDC government, and in doing so took much of the power the left had enjoyed in Ghana. The PNDC became an authoritarian government, which did particularly well in implementing the structural adjustment package. It is interesting to note that IFIs success story happened in a country where all political dissent was effectively silenced, and the government did not have to be democratically accountable.

The preceding text is not intended to demonize the IFIs; their concept of development was a reaction to the failure of state-led development, and this essay is a reaction to the failure of market-led development. Admittedly, no one who works for the IMF or The World Bank gets up in the morning with the intention of deliberately harming people in Africa. In fact, I think the opposite could be true. The fact of the matter is that centuries of history have led to Africa's current economic situation and no development plan will fix all of the problems in Africa in just a short time. No matter what ideology one sees as the answer for Africa, it is difficult to imagine that Africa will be able to develop economically in the face of tightly closed American and European markets. Thomas Sankara's populist rule in Burkina Faso is not necessarily a perfect example of how to govern an African state. It simply reminds us that the point of development is not improving macroeconomic indicators by themselves, but it is the betterment of people's lives.

Notes:

1 This synopsis of African populism was outlined in a series of lectures by Professor Guy Martin at The University of Virginia. His work is drawn upon heavily for this part of the paper as he is one of the very few people that has written on Thomas Sankara's political thought and revolutionary practices in English.

2 This paper is an abridged version of a longer work entitled: "From 'Mis-Education' to Education: Applying the Precepts of African Indigenous Educational Models." Copies of the unabridged paper are available from the author by request.

3 This information is based on an interview with a former NCDC student. He referred to the school network as "a family." For him, this was one of the most significant facets of his education at the school. He, his family, and his classmates often remained at NCDC during after-school hours, participating in organized community programs or informal socialization.

4 For example, the school reminds students to do "black things" each day. Refuting the prevailing cultural precept, "black things" are defined as good things, e.g., respecting your classmates, sharing, working hard, etc. (Information obtained from NCDC interviewee).

References

Asamoa A. (1996). *Socioeconomic development strategies of independent African countries: The Ghanaian experience*. Accra: Ghana Universities Press.

Ahiakpor, J. (1991). Rawlings, economic reform, and the poor: Consistency or Betrayal? *The Journal of Modern African Studies 29*, 583-600.

Anebo, F. (2000). Voting patterns and electoral alliances in Ghana's 1996 election. In Nnoli, O. (Ed.). *Government and Politics in Africa* (pp. 264-266). Harare: African Association of Political Science.

Anyemedu, K. (1993). The Economic Policies of the PNDC. In E. Gyimah-Boadi (Ed). *Ghana Under PNDC Rule* (pp. 13-42). Oxford: Codesria.

Anyimadu, A. (1993). Some Institutional Aspects of Agricultural Development Policy Under the PNDC. In E. Gyimah-Boadi (Ed), *Ghana Under PNDC Rule* (pp. 63, 68). Oxford: Codesria.

Boafo-Arthur (1989). Trends in Ghana's Foreign Policy After Nkrumah. In E. Hansen & K. Ninsin (Eds.). *The State, Development and Politics in Ghana* (pp.137-162). London: Codresia.

Boafu-Arthur, K. (1993). Ghana's External Relations Since 31 December 1981. In E. Gyimah-Boadi (Ed). *Ghana Under PNDC Rule* (pp. 136-149). Oxford: Codesria.

Callaghy, T. (2000). Africa and the world political economy: Caught between a rock and a hard place. In J. W. Harbeson & D. Rothchild (Eds.). *Africa in world politics: The African state system in flux* (3rd ed.) (pp.57-58). Boulder, CO: Westview Press.

Catholic Standard, The (1993). In E. Ziorklui, *Ghana: From Nkrumah to Rawlings* (p.467.Accra: Em-Zed Books Center Publishing. (reprinted from the newspaper issue published on June 24, 1979)

Clapham, C. (1996). *Africa and the international system: The poli-*

tics of state survival. New York: Cambridge University Press.

Englebert, P. (1996). *Burkina Faso: Unsteady statehood in West Africa*. Boulder: Westview Press.

Folson, K. G. (2000). Ideology, revolution and development- The years of Jerry John Rawlings in Ghana. In Okwudiba Nnoli (Ed.).*Government and politics in Africa* (Pp. 124 -137). Harare: African Association of Political Science.

Ghanaian Times (1993). In E. Ziorklui, *Ghana: From Nkrumah to Rawlings* (p. 465.Accra: Em-Zed Books Center Publishing. (reprinted from the newspaper issue published on June 16, 1979)

Graham Y. (1989). From GTP to Assene: Aspects of industrial working class struggles in Ghana 1982-1986. In E. Hansen & K. Ninsin (Eds.). *The state, development and politics in Ghana* (pp. 43-72). London: Codresia.

Gyimah-Boadi E. (1989). Policies and politics of export agriculture. In E. Hansen & K. Ninsin (Eds.). *The state, development and politics in Ghana* (pp. 222-241). London: Codresia.

Gyimah-Boadi, E. (1993). The search for economic development and democracy in Ghana: From Limann to Rawlings. In E.Gyimah-Boadi (Ed). *Ghana under PNDC Rule* (pp. 2-4, 6, 8-9). Oxford: Codesria.

Gyimah-Boadi, E. & Essuman-Johnson, A. (1993). The PNDC and organized labor: The anatomy of political control. In E. Gyimah-Boadi (Ed). *Ghana under PNDC rule* (pp. 197-199). Oxford: Codesria.

Hansen, E. (1991). *Ghana under Rawlings: The early years*. Lagos: Malthouse Press.

Ihonvbere, J. (2000). *Africa and the New World Order*. New York: Peter Lang Publishing.

Jonah, K. (1989). Changing relations between the IMF and the government of Ghana,1960-1987. In Hansen, E. &. Ninsin,K. (Eds.). *The state, development and politics in Ghana* (pp. 94-115). London: Codresia.

Martin G. (1987). Ideology and praxis in Thomas Sankara's populist revolution of 4 August 1983 in Burkina Faso. *Issue: A Journal of Opinion, 15*, 77-90.

Martin, G. (1989). Revolutionary democracy, socio-political conflict and militarization in Burkina Faso, 1983-1988. In P. Meyns & D. W. Nabudere (Eds.). *Democracyand the one-party state in Africa* (pp. 67- 75). Hamburg: Institut für Afrika Kunde.

Ninsin, K. (1989). State, capital and labour relations, 1961-1987. In Hansen, E. & Ninsin, K. (Eds.). *The state, development and politics in Ghana* (pp. 15-42). London: Codresia.

Ninsin, K (1989). The land question since the 1950's. In Hansen, E. & Ninsin, K. (Eds.).*The state, development and politics in Ghana* (pp. 165-183) London: Codresia.

Ninsin, K. (1993). Strategies of mobilisation under the PNDC government. In E. Gyimah-Boadi (Ed). *Ghana under PNDC rule* (pp. 101-111). Oxford: Codesria.

Okunor, A. (1993). Limann is happy unemployed. In E. Ziorklui,(Ed). *Ghana: From Nkrumah to Rawlings* (p. 483). Accra: Em-Zed Books Center Publishing. (reprinted from *Africa Concord,* published on February 19, 1987)

Panford, K (1994). Structural adjustment, the state and workers in Ghana. *Africa Development 19.*

Rawlings, J. J. (1993). Address by his excellency FLT.-LT. J.J. Rawlings on the occasion of the inauguration of the Third Republic at Parliament House on 24th, September, 1979. In E. Ziorklui (Ed.). *Ghana: From Nkrumah to Rawlings* (p. 483). Accra: Em-Zed Books Center Publishing. (Reprinted from the speech transcript published in 1979).

Rawlings, J. J. (1983). *A revolutionary journey: Selected speeches of Flight Lt. Jerry Rawlings*. Tema: Ghana Publishing Corporation.

Rawlings, J. J. (1984). *Forging ahead: Selected speeches of Flight Lt. Jerry Rawlings*. Tema: Ghana Publishing Corporation.

Republic of Ghana, economic recovery program: 1984-1986 (1983). Accra: Government of the Republic of Ghana.

Sakyi-Addo, K. (2001, January-March). End of an era. In *BBC focus on Africa*. London: BBC World Service.

Sankara, T. (1988). *Thomas Sankara speaks* (S. Anderson, Trans). New York: Pathfinder Press. (original speeches given between 1983 and 1987)

Sowa, N. K. (1994). *Governance and economic performance in Ghana*. Legon: Department of Economics.

Toye, J. (1990). Ghana's economic reforms, 1983-7: Origins, achievements and limitations. In J. Pickett & H. Singer (Eds.). *Towards economic recovery in sub-Saharan Africa* (pp. 42-62). London: Routledge.

Young, C. (1982). *Ideology and development in Africa*. New Haven: Yale University Press.

CHAPTER 3

AFRICAN AMERICANS AND THE CHALLENGE OF GLOBALIZATION:

Between Technological Imperatives and Third World Immigration in the 21st Century

Darryl C. Thomas
Associate Professor and
Chair, Africana Studies Department
Binghamton University

The rise of the United States to a hegemonic position in 1989 when the former USSR finally collapsed created contradictions in its domestic race relations. Those who are located at the periphery within hegemonies are also the least integrated within their domestic political system. American policymakers had to come to terms with their domestic Third World population, i.e., African Americans, Native Americans, Latinos, and Asian Americans, in order to modernize their racial dominance. Traditional race relations became increasingly inappropriate for under the new order that emerged at the end of the Second World War. The African Americans' struggle against American Apartheid, that is, Jim Crowism, provided a framework for the struggle against America's racial regime by the dispossessed — the nonwhite population.

The Civil Rights struggle had its origins in the post-Reconstruction era as African Americans began to devise new strategies to challenge their subordination. Black nationalism, bourgeois reformism, Black feminism and Afro-Marxism of various stripes emerged as alternative approaches to this struggle. Booker T. Washington, W.E.B. DuBois, Mary Church Terrell, Ida B. Wells-Barnet, Marcus Garvey, and Paul Robeson emerged as champions of these divergent strategies. In the postwar era, Dr. Martin Luther King, Jr., Ella Baker, and Malcolm X challenged America's racial order through bourgeois reformism, Black Nationalism and revolutionary Black Nationalism and ushered in a new racial dispensation.

African Americans' conceptualization of democracy and freedom has historically been at odds with the practice of white America, especially with reference to their experience of disenfranchisement and systematic segregation, and as economic outcasts. Still, African Americans have held fast to their vision of a democratic social order. African Americans visualize a society with unfettered access to political, economic, and social rights, regardless of race, class, or gender. African Americans have referred to this vision as freedom. This vision of freedom has become a nightmare for African Americans dwelling in capitalist America. As a result, African Americans have had to search within and without for solace as they face the realities of capitalist America (Marable, 1991, p. 229).

African Americans have also had to struggle over the question of their identity since the slavery period, when they were referred to by their oppressors primarily on the basis of their skin color. To be "black" or a "nigger" in a social order based on exploitation was to be a prisoner of one's skin color and the victim of the idea of immutable inferiority conveyed by an entire nation. From the arrival of the first Africans during the colonial period to the new era of Global Apartheid and Globalization, white Americans continue to identify their national collective interests with those of European geopolitics, culture, philosophy, and values, and have perceived "blackness" through the destructive and false social construction of "race" – implying permanent inferiority and dominance for African Americans. From the First Reconstruction Era (1865-1877) to the Second Reconstruction period (1954-1980), new eras of Global Restructuring (1980s) and Globalization (1990 to the present), African American and their descendants in the United States have never accepted their oppressors' definition of their identity. The slaves always looked backward, recalling their African roots, which became articulated through language, syntax, verb tenses, and idiomatic expressions. They forged within this system of oppression a deep sense of cultural and national identity as Americans of African decent.

This chapter examines the relationship between globalization, technological imperative that has accompanied globalization and the quality of life issues that confront African Americans. Increasingly, quality of life issues for African Americans are tied to the forces of globalization. The increase immigration flows from divergent sectors of the world system also has ramifications for African Americans. Likewise, investment flows into the United States from Germany and Japan also impinge on African Americans. Hence, the traditional role of African Americans as a labor reserve, playing the role of the 'last hired' and the 'first fired,' is no longer operative in the new era of Global Apartheid and Globalization. African American laborers have come to increasingly compete with a new global army of labor reserve. The question as to whether the forces of globalization have made African American laborers obsolete with the arrival of the new global army of labor reserve emerges.

Between Global Restructuring and a New Era of Globalization

Starting in the 1990s, the discourse that once centered on the specificity of the New World Order lost ground to the forces of globalization. Scholars and practitioners alike considered the processes of globalization as natural, inevitable, and beneficial to every sector of the world system, including African American workers located on the fringes of capitalist America. Some observers even declared that we had reached the "end of history" through the triumph of planetary capitalism and a third wave of democratization. The concept of globalization normally includes the spatial reorganization of production, the transfer of industries across borders, the dispersion of financial markets, the diffusion of identical consumer goods to distant countries, massive transfer of populations and the inevitable conflicts between immigrant groups and established native communities in formerly tight-knit neighborhoods, and a worldwide preference for democracy. This conceptualization of globalization involves framing a multilevel analysis: economic, political, cultural and ideological (Mittelman, 1996, p. 3). We have certainly entered the age of globalization as when the world system has truly become a global village (Marah, 1998). The current global predominance of transnational corporations has incorporated a diversity of nations, peoples, and cultures. The world system is being shaped and defined by the digital-information era. As a worldwide phenomenon, globalization is a coalescence of varied transnational processes and domestic structures, allowing the economy, politics, culture, and ideology of the dominant nations to mandate the less developed regions of the world. The globalization processes ranges from the spatial organization of production to international trade, and the integration of financial markets. Driven by changing modes of competition, globalization compresses the time and space aspects of social relations. In a word, globalization is a market-induced and not a policy-induced process (Mittelman, 1996, p. 3). Rapid innovations in microelectronics, material science, and biotechnology have led to what some have labeled a new "technological revolution" or the "creative destruction" phase of capitalism. Research and development in science and technology involve complex and expensive laboratory facilities, and in some cases, increased use of proprietary research; Nano technology has made possible the transition from mass production to flexible specialization, producing smaller batches of differentiated goods faster and more efficiently (Stallings, 1995, p. 114). Lester Thurow has observed that, "for the first time in human history, anything can be made anywhere and sold everywhere" (Thurow, 1996, p. 114).

Elsewhere (Thomas, 2001, pp. 153-175), I have compared and contrasted conflicting Third World zones with reference to their ability to carve out a niche for themselves in the new international division of labor. The result of this analysis suggested that East and Southeast Asian Nations performed much better than their counterparts in Africa and the rest of the Third World. Several states in Latin America (Brazil and Mexico) and their counterparts in Europe (Portugal and Turkey) were exceptions to this trend. The comparison revolved around what Gary Geriffi (1996) refers to as "producer-driven networks" and "buyer-driven networks." Producer-driven networks are centralized, vertically integrated producer chains, found in capital intensive sectors such as autos, computers, and aircraft. Subcontracting involves manufacturing of parts in various countries around the world for later assembly in appropriate locations. Buyer-driven networks are decentralized design-intensive industries such as clothing and footwear. Subcontractors produce finished goods according to specification for retail outlets in advanced market countries. Stallings (1996) draws attention to the fact that the new premium placed on technological expansion has made it difficult for African and other Third World nations to break into higher value-added production, at the same time that the cost of not doing so has also risen (p. 9). This new international context of development reinforces our notion of global apartheid. While there are certain niches for specialization in low value-added goods, countries that rely exclusively on these products run the risk of falling further behind. These same actors face the traditional problems of low-income elasticity's demand for basic food items, textiles, and low-grade steel as well as the spill over in terms of training and technology are lost. Those countries that continue to concentrate their exports on commodities and raw materials are at even greater disadvantages because the new technology minimizes the use of such commodities.

In this age of globalization (capitalism—postindustrial, post-Cold War, transitional, informational, and high-technology-driven), global capitalism has the capacity to produce and distribute any commodity on a worldwide global scale. This new capacity of global capital has transformed the existing fragile bargaining power between the North and South. This new phase of capitalism is undermining the ability of Third World states, both individually and collectively, to negotiate their interests, in terms of earning, better prices for the products their products, improved working conditions, sustainable environmental industrial policies, and increased employment opportunities for their citizens.

Increasingly, the market exercises the accountability function normally associated with the state. These markets now perform the contractual functions normally associated with citizenship, they can vote for or veto government economic policies; they can also force governments to adopt particular policy preferences and not others. In addition, private investors vote with their feet, moving quickly in and out of countries, often with massive amounts of money. The global capital market makes it possible for money to flow anywhere, regardless of national origins or boundaries, although some countries, such as Iraq and Libya, are often excluded. The financial market has created innovative new methods that allow foreign investors to reap huge profits. These instruments now include derivatives, i.e., futures, swaps, and options. Global capital has incorporated the neoliberal regimes as critical elements of its arsenal in order to influence the fiscal policies and outcomes of states. International financial institutions have emerged as key sites for the formulation and implementation of neoliberal regime during this era of globalization. Operating under a variety of names ranging from neoliberalism, neoconservatism to neoorthodoxy, the new international consensus on international finance features three main elements: macroeconomic stability (especially smaller fiscal deficits), a reduced government role in the economy (deregulation and privatization), and greater openness to the outside world (reduced barriers to trade and a more receptive approach toward capital (Stallings, 1995, p.12). Starting in the early 1990s, most advocates of the free market ideology were very optimistic that the benefits of unfettered financial markets outweigh the potential problems. The proponents asserted that freeing up trade is good; why not also let capital move freely across borders? These same proponents assumed that free capital mobility among all nations was exactly like free trade in goods and services, a mutual-gain phenomenon. Hence, restricted capital movement, just like protectionism, was seen as harmful to economic performance in each country, whether rich or poor (Bhagwati, 1998, pp. 7-12). Capital mobility has not lived up to its high expectations, particular with repeated crisis that have wreaked havoc on emerging markets. Example abounds with the Mexican peso crisis in the mid-1990s, the Asian and Russian financial market conflagration of the late 1990s and the financial and economic meltdown in Argentina in the early part of 2002. The latter financial fiasco is accompanied by the bankruptcy of Enron, the American energy giant, the failure of financial transparency present questions about corporate governance, as well as the free market approach to global financial markets.

Fernand Braudel observed that capitalism is not just a means to organize the economy. Capitalism, in each of its divergent historical formations, has also been a particular system of values, patterns of consumption, social structure, and form of state. Each configuration or form has also projected a conception of world order. The new capitalism, with its global vocation, incorporates all of these things. At the same time, the divergent models of capital accumulation found in the Anglo-American, German, and Japanese formations, as well as alternative models of economic organization in the Peoples Republic of China and East Asia, are being exported as paradigms to the Developing World (Cox, 1996, p. 557).

The end of the Cold War conflict in 1989 transformed the way scholars look at the world system. The concept "Third World" no longer has significance in the post-Cold War era. At the same time, the New World order does not quite capture the continuities and discontinuities that are operating. Instead of Third World zones or regions that have fixed geographical representations, we are witnessing the evolution of a Third World or peripheral capitalist sector within the Northeast and the Northwest. Hence, our developing theme: "the world is a ghetto," means that a large segment of the world's population is excluded from the benefits of globalization or more accurately, market democracy. There are islands of wealth located throughout the globe, surrounded by a vast sea of poverty. Increasingly, large number of people from the developed regions of the world are joining this sea of poverty. However, some are combating their impoverishment by drawing attention to citizenship rights based on blood ties, and increasingly, skin color. The state has established an array of immigration laws and welfare reform packages that limit economic and financial benefits to a restricted number of people, particularly people of color and their European counterparts who are not from the core sectors of the Northwest. These welfare reforms are very similar to the structural adjustment programs instituted in African and Third World states under the supervision of the International Monetary Fund and the World Bank. Affirmative action and equal rights policies are in retreat throughout the globe as neoconservatism and the politics of indifference prevail in the political arena.

This new situation has propelled many African, African Diaspora and Third World people to exit via immigration to the Northwest, pursuing both political and economic asylum, from the South to the North. The growth of immigration flows from the Third World has influenced the pace of economic and financial growth among African Americans. African American economic progress has also been influenced by the pace and scope of foreign investment in the United States during the new era of global restructuring and globalization.

Convergence of Race and Restructuring of the U.S. Economy

At the end of the 1960s the postwar economic boom came to an end with a decline in the general living standards and occupational mobility that had distinguished the twenty-five years since the Second World War. By the end of the 1970s the U.S. economy had endured three recessions, and price escalations had resulted in stagflation. American multinational corporations began loosing their competitive advantage at home and abroad as they failed to increase productivity and extend their profit margins. This structural crisis led to the wholesale exportation of industrial jobs, automation strategies, and created instabilities in financial markets. Starting in 1973, the real income of U.S. working and lower-middle-class families began to decline. The increase in female labor market participation kept it from sliding further. U.S. corporations responded to this crisis in profits and job sites' control by cutting labor costs. The postwar social contract between labor and management lost legitimacy as production sites were constructed overseas, forcing domestic wages down and outsourced products to nonunion suppliers. Traditional leaders of heavy manufacturing sectors underwent dramatic restructuring and dropped a considerable portion of their industrial capacity in the process (Noel Jacob Kent, 1993, p. 63).

Starting in the 1980s, Black economic progress reached its zenith and began to shrink as economic stagnation and decline became the dominant feature in the U.S. economy. The end of the economic boom was a calamity for African Americans' economic aspirations. African Americans became increasingly insecure, given their location in the unstable and semiskilled jobs in the secondary sector. African American primary sector workers were clustered in declining goods-producing industries such as steel, automobiles, and rubber. The stable African American working class lost ground to plant closings, automation, and the export of jobs. Manning Marable (1991) has estimated that approximately 550,000 African American workers who lost their jobs were victims of a structurally racist system (Marable, p. 7)

After the crisis of the late 1960s and the early 1970s, capitalist business enterprises moved with all deliberate speed to reorganize their productive systems to reduce the cost of labor and to rollback the power of unions. The deindustrialization that followed had a negative impact on black workers, who worked in a large number of factories in such cities as Detroit, St. Louis, Chicago, Pittsburgh, and other industrial cities. These corporations were driven by a desire for higher profits, close proximity to natural resources, access to local markets, and most critically, cheap labor. The increase proletarianization of select Third World zones accelerated the departure of large and medium-sized corporations from the U.S. and Europe. In the 1950s one-third of all U.S. jobs were manufacturing. By the mid-1980s, only 20 percent of all U.S. jobs were in manufacturing, and by 1990 that had declined to between 10 to 14 percent; and it is projected that by 2005, the number could drop to between 2.5 and 5 percent (Lusane, 1997, p. 10).

The increase hypermobility of capital, particularly that involved in textiles, apparel, electronics, footwear, etc., caused these manufacturers to refashion significant proportions of their operations into a global division of labor. Many of these firms moved the labor-intensive aspects to areas where wages are low and unions were nonexistent or under repressive government control. These corporations continued their research, development, design, engineering, testing, and coordinating aspects of their operations in the United States. In recent years, some firms have exported some of these arenas as new ways to cut costs and increase profits (Wilson, 1995, pp. 208-209). Labor costs in the Third World are a small fraction of the labor cost in the United States. For example, in 1982 the average hourly wage for a production worker was $11.79 in the United States, $1.97 in Mexico, $1.77 in Singapore, $1.57 in Taiwan, and $1.22 in South Korea. At this juncture, South Korea and Taiwan became the Third World production sites for U.S. multinational corporations (Bluestone and Harrison, 1998).

Increasingly, African American youth found themselves caught in a structural and demographic vise. They entered urban labor markets at a time when these markets were undergoing dramatic restructuring from goods' production and distributive function into sophisticated information processing, financial, governmental and business services. Industrial restructuring precluded the hiring of an entire cohort of the 1970s African American young people. A large sector of African American youth no longer participated in the labor market and became fodder for the developing lumpenproletariat, which later was labeled the "underclass." The grouping of African Americans constituting this category is a result of structural displacement and cumulative racism. They are essentially unemployed workers beset by automation, export of historically urban blue collar jobs, inadequate transportation, and job information networks, poor education facilities, and the lack of marketable interpersonal skills (Wilson, 1996).

As capitalist business enterprises engaged in their ceaseless quest for cheap and tractable labor, they abandoned the traditional bipolar racial segmentation of labor and no longer confined their quest within national boundaries. Jacqueline Jones (1998) observes that employers with mobile forms of capital sought local supplies of immobile workers; thus a particular region of the United States might offer surplus supplies of illegal aliens, or destitute sons and daughters of isolated rural folk, or inner-city blacks or Latinos, all potential employees willing to work for cheap wages. African American workers, who historically were located in the lower tier of the work force found themselves in the midst of a new competitive arena, as multiethnic and multiracial distressed communities proliferated throughout country. As a direct result of their resistance to various forms of labor exploitation, black people as a group continued to bear the stigma of "troublemakers," in contrast to allegedly quiescent "Fourth Wave" immigrants from Latin America, East Asia, Africa and the Caribbean. Jones (1998) notes that, in every sector of the economy, employers responded warily to blacks at all levels of the work force, because blacks were declaring, in the words of Thomas Rush, an airline sky cap, "I look at everybody at eye level. I neither looked down or up. The day of the shuffle is gone" (Jones, 1998, p. 370).

The African American middle classes experienced decline in their growth rates around the middle of the 1970s. College-educated African American cohorts were finding it more difficult to translate their training into middle-class incomes. American corporations continued to practice racial and promotional discriminations while the public sectors that had been more open to minority labor participation stagnated as the fiscal crisis of the country reduced employment opportunities at the local, state, and federal levels. The convergence between white and black middle classes came to a halt as lower middle class black families found two incomes more fundamental to self-maintenance than their white counterparts. African Americans also experienced difficulty in maintaining their lower middle class status in an increasingly fluctuating and competitive economic and political milieu.

Towards a Global Army of Labor Reserve

The new fourth wave of immigration has created a global army of labor reserve, which has undermined the bifurcated labor segmentation and African Americans' role as a domestic army of labor reserve. To date, African Americans have been culturally, economically, and socially affected by the recent surge in immigration flows. African Americans have experienced increasing differentiation in socioeconomic characteristics at the individual level and bifurcation between the middle class and the poor (Oliver and Shapiro, 1995). These patterns of differentiation and bifurcation are primarily the results of the global restructuring processes underway in urban labor markets and the rapid growths in immigration. Uneducated and poor African Americans have been trapped in the inner city, where ladders of social mobility have disappeared and where entry to low-skilled jobs is barred by employer discrimination and immigrant employment networks (Wilson, 1996). Middle-class African Americans have experienced unprecedented social mobility; nevertheless, many still confront racial discrimination in the housing market, which constrains residential mobility (Massey and Denton, 1987).

Min Zhou (2001) has observed that the appearance of large number of non-white immigrants transformed the racial composition of the urban population, rendering the bipolar racial paradigm null and void (p. 222). African Americans as a group have not yet moved up the racial hierarchy. The caste status of African Americans has moved further down the ladder as a result of the incorporation of new coloreds or Third World immigrants into what Myrdal (1944) referred to as the "moral problem in the hearts and minds of Americans" (p. 16)

In their struggle for liberation and equality, African Americans are confronted with a daunting dilemma — how to deal with being a U.S.-born minority competing with foreign-born minorities, whose members have come from different backgrounds, many exhibiting a majority mentality, and heading in different directions (Min, 2001, p. 222).

African Americans also confront fierce economic competition from these new immigrants. The availability of a large pool of laborers from the expanding immigrant communities may contribute, at least indirectly, to exacerbating the economic situation for African Americans in urban areas. The oversupply of labor allows employers to lower wages for qualified workers and discriminates against African Americans, who insist on livable wages. In addition, immigrant-employee-networks, developed initially to help coethnic members find jobs, erect entry barriers against African Americans who are outside these networks. What is more threatening is that African Americans, especially the educated class, suddenly find their hard-won occupational niche suddenly shared by immigrant minorities (Waldinger, 1996).

Direct Foreign Investment, Race and Growth

This rest of this chapter will examine the relationship between direct foreign investment in the United States and the extent that African Americans in urban areas could benefit through job creation. I will explore the relationship with special reference to German investment and the extent to which African Americans are partners via the job market. Furthermore, are German manufacturers are seeking to evade African Americans as a result of their propensity to be concentrated in areas of high unionization? This question reveals the other side of the globalization and global restructuring processes.

In recent years the United States has emerged as an important site for foreign investment by other advanced capitalist states. In the past, the United States was the leading foreign investor in both the Northern and the Southern Hemisphere. Since the 1980s, however, the United States has emerged as the leading debtor nation. Initially, the growth and proliferation of direct foreign investment has consisted of acquisition of pre-existing American firms rather than establishing new firms. Starting in the 1980s, foreign direct investment has been targeted at manufacturing and goods production sector of the U.S. economy. During the 1960s direct foreign investment came primarily from European and Canadian investments, with the English-speaking countries alone accounting for 60 percent. Most of the corporations involved in such investments have had long histories of participation in the U.S. economy, i.e., Canadian railroads, Royal-Dutch-Shell petroleum interests, and Swiss chemicals and pharmaceuticals firms (Lipsey, 1993, p. 137).

The European pattern underwent dramatic changes in the 1970s as the United Kingdom's share declined slightly while the Canadian one decreased at a faster rate. Both France and Germany became more important source of direct foreign investment in the United States. The changes in foreign direct investment also reflected the comparative advantage of these European investors. Over seventy percent of the Netherlands-owned affiliates remained in the petroleum industry in 1959, and their share decline but was still around half in 1987 and far above the other countries. Affiliates from West Germany (Germany was still divided along Cold War lines at this time) and the Netherlands had exceptionally large outlays of their sales in chemicals. The Japanese have carved out a separate niche in manufacturing, Japanese affiliates were, to a large extent, involved in distribution of products produced in Japan, reflecting their competitive advantage in producing motor vehicles. Later, they would locate some production facilities close to the U.S market; the United Kingdom had concentrated its efforts in food production (Lipsey, 1993, p. 138).

German firms have made their niche in chemicals since 1974 and as a result, 34 percent of their affiliates' employment was in this industry; while other countries averaged around 11 percent employment in this sector. By the 1980s, Germany's affiliates in the U.S. were still more heavily concentrated in chemicals than any other country. At this juncture, they began diversifying and were making entrance in the non-electrical machinery. Germans also made their presence felt in the automobile industry. They are also following the lead of American and Japanese firms by locating their new productive facilities in the South to court cheaper labor and to be away from areas where unions have a strong presence.

Over the last two and one-half decade, the Sunbelt has emerged as the preferred location for manufacturing. The South can no longer considered as this nation's most underdeveloped region. It is home at least five states that created the most jobs during the 1980s and the 1990s and the region has been the preferred location for the expansion of new manufacturing plants since 1991. The population growth in this region is twice the national average with more than 20 million new residents in 1990 alone. Recent census data reaffirm this regional trend and the South is the preferred new location for migration flows as the new century unwinds. The economic output grew by 4.5 percent in the middle 1990s, in comparison with 3 percent for the nation. Charlotte, N.C. and Atlanta, Ga. led the nation in job creation in the 1990s (*New York Times, National Sunday,* July 31, 1994, p. 20).

The automobile industry, both foreign transplants and domestic have made their pilgrimage to the South, bringing their multimillion-dollar auto plants with them. Some of the new arrival plants include a $1.3 billion Nissan plant, located in Smyrna, Tennessee creating approximately 6,000 jobs; 5,000 jobs in Spring Hill, Tennessee; and the $2 billion, 4,000 jobs Toyota plant in Georgetown, Kentucky. These corporations have moved South to take advantage of the warm weather, low cost of living, hospitality toward business and non-unionized labor environment (*New York Times, National Sunday*, July 31, 1994, p. 20).

Germany's automobile giants, Mercedes Benz, and BMW of North America have located their new plants in the South. BMW invested over $450 million in Greer, South Carolina and created approximately 2,000 jobs. Mercedes Benz of North America has invested over $300 million in the early 1990s creating 1,500 jobs in Vance, Alabama. The recent merger between Mercedes Benz and Chyrsler has intensified the global reach of this German auto giant. Since 1990, the top five metropolitan area destinations for African Americans were in the South. They are 1. Atlanta, Georgia, 2. Norfolk, Virginia, 3. Washington, DC, 4. Raleigh-Durham, North Carolina; and 5. Dallas and Fort Worth, Texas. Alabama's Black belt and the Mississippi Delta lag behind in economic opportunity for African Americans *(New York Times, National Sunday*, July 31, 1994, p. 20).

German auto giants are shifting their transplants to the southern region of the U.S., attracting large numbers of African Americans to this new zone of opportunity. These auto giants are participating in the reindustrialization that is sweeping the region. The South has all the trappings of a Third World zone, seeking foreign investment from domestic and foreign firms. The German firms have also located in nonmetropolitan areas in the South. Transnational corporation location decisions impact African Americans with reference to the forces of globalization. Once again, we may not find African Americans competing with an anxious labor pool from the Third World nations from the Southern Hemisphere that will continue to challenge the efforts of globalization. Yet, the global village might keep African Americans at the losing end in this process of globalization.

References

Bhagwati, J. (1998, May/June). The capital myth: The difference between free trade in widges and dollars, *Foreign Affairs* 77, (3), 7-12.

Bluestone, B. and Harrison, B. (1998). (Ed.). *The great u-turn: Corporate restructuring and polarizing America.* New York: Basic Books.

Cox, R. W. (1996). Globalization, multilateralism, and democracy. In Cox, R. and Sinclair, R. (Ed.). *Approaches to world order* ed. Cambridge: Cambridge University Press.

Geriffi, G. (1996). Global production system and Third World development. In Mittelman, J. *Globalization: A critical reflection.* Boulder, CO: Lynne Rienner.

Jones, J *(1998). The dispossessed: America's underclass from the Civil War to the present.* New York: Basic Books.

Kent, N. J. (1993). To polarize a nation: Racism, labor market and the state in the U.S. political economy. In Young, C. (Ed.). *Rising tide of cultural pluralism: The nation-state at bay.* 55-72, Madison, WI: University of Wisconsin Press.

Lipsey, R. (1993). Direct foreign investment in the U.S.: Changes over three decades. In Froot, T. *Foreign direct investment.* Chicago: University of Chicago Press.

Lusane, C. (1997). *Race in the global era: African Americans at the millennium.* Boston, MA: South End Press.

Marable, M. *(1991). Race, reform and rebellion: The second reconstruction in Black America.* Jackson, Mississippi: The University of Mississippi Press.

Marah, J. (1998). *African People in the Global Village: An introduction to Pan-African studies.* Lanham, Maryland: University Press of America, Inc.

Massey, D. & Denton, N. (1987). Trends in residential segregation: Blacks, Hispanics, and Asians, 1970-1980. *American Sociological Review* 52:805-825.

Min, Zhou. (2001). Contemporary immigration and the dynamics of race and ethnicity. In Smelser, N.J., Wilson, W.J.& Mitchell, F. (Eds.). *America becoming: racial trends and their consequences* Vol. I (pp. 200-242) Washington, DC: National Academy Press.

Mittelman, J. H. (1996). *Globalization: A Critical Reflection*. Boulder, CO: Lynne Rienner.

New York Times, National Sunday, July 31, 1994

Oliver, M. & Shapiro, M. (1995). *Black wealth/White wealth: A new perspective in racial inequality.* New York: Routledge.

Stallings, B. *(1995).Global change, regional response: The new international context of development*. Cambridge: Cambridge University Press.

Thomas, D. C. (2001). *The theory and practice of Third World solidarity*. Westport, CT: Praeger Publishers.

Thurow, L *(1996). The future of capitalism: How today's economic forces shape tomorrow's world.* New York: William Morow and Company.

Waldinger, R. (1996). *Still the promised city: African Americans and new immigrants in postindustrial New York City*. Cambridge: Harvard University Press.

Wilson, C.A. (1995). *Racism: From slavery to advanced capitalism*. Thousand Oak, CA: Sage Publications.

Wilson, W. J. Jr. (1996). *When work disappears: The world of the new urban poor.* New York: Alfred A. Knopf.

PART TWO

SCIENCE AND GLOBAL AFRICA

CHAPTER 4

SCIENTIFIC DEPENDENCE IN AFRICA TODAY

Paulin Hountondji
Professor of Philosophy
National University of Benin, Cotonou
Benin, West Africa

A View From the Outside

To define what I mean by scientific dependence, I would like to quote extensively from Jacques de Certaines, a French biologist who was partly educated at the University of Dakar in Senegal:

> In the African universities where I was trained, there was a scientific teaching quite valid in the subject matters I had to learn, but it taught

> dependence rather than real science. I mean that, for three years I was told how biology had developed through experiments that necessitated the use of facilities unavailable on the spot. Therefore in order to do biology, students had to go abroad. Such and such scientific results were published in such and such journals, but these journals were European or American, and one had to read them abroad. In short, during three years, thanks to teachers who were good ones and of whom up to sixty percent were African, I received good teaching and learned, at the same time – but for me, this was, of course, not as serious as it was for my fellow students who did not return to France – I learned that, in the end, all I could do as a biologist in the future would have to be done under the control of American centers, American periodicals, with European facilities, and that all I could ever do at the University of Dakar was to duplicate European experiments, or to conduct minor experiments that would have to be submitted, for publication, to European journals. All this apparently good teaching only led to a feeling of dependency toward those places where science was really being done. I was told, in a sense: here you are working on the margins of science; if you really want to reach the heart of the matter, you will have to leave. All my fellow students from that time have continued doing biology; some of them have become secondary school teachers, but those who wanted to do research actually left. How could such a dependent teaching lead to real development? (De Certaines, 1978, p.41)

I like this testimony by De Certaines because it shows how different scientific training and scientific activity are, as a whole, in developing countries as opposed to industrialized ones. It expresses with great accuracy a feeling shared by most students of African universities (even if they unfortunately do not take it seriously enough) – the feeling that, whatever their special fields might be, everything that matters for them is located or taking place elsewhere. Elsewhere, outside Africa, are located the most fully equipped laboratories, the best universities, the most powerful research centers, the editorial teams and offices of the most prestigious scientific journals, the most complete reference libraries and publishing houses, and last but not least, the world's major concentration of practicing scientists. Elsewhere, therefore, most of the events considered to be important scientific occurrences take place, especially the scholarly debates and discussions that, at any given time, shape the real configuration of each discipline – in other words, the methodological and theoretical paradigm of what is known as valid science.

Now, how do African scientists react to this situation? They hardly question it. They tend to take it for granted. And that is why, once again, De Certaines's testimony is particularly revealing. If the French biologist could avoid falling into the same trap, if he could afford such a critical perception of his own situation as a student, it was because he had previously been educated in a different manner and in a different context, while remaining conscious all along that his new African experience was merely temporary. In most cases, this critical distance does not exist. African scholars assume that, having been born and educated at home, they will be starting their scholarly training and, their scholarly careers "on the margins of science," far from the heart of the world's scientific and technological activity. They believe that only a stroke of good fortune may someday enable them to step up from the periphery to the center. They usually accept without question the necessity of stepping up, of progressing from the abstract to the concrete, from the margins to the heart of knowledge. Moreover, they assume that this "stepping up" should be reserved, in Africa and the Third World as a whole, to the happy few who can afford to... "go." They do not seem to notice that the relationship to science is quite different in industrialized countries where people do not have to... "go," to travel thousands of miles from home, in order to practice real science.

Having made this point, we should seek to go beyond the subjective reactions to this situation, to analyze the objective facts that account for it and make it intelligible. In other words, we need to identify the specific, inevitable, and structural shortcomings of scientific activity in Africa and, perhaps, in the Third World as a whole. To such analysis, I wish to contribute the following hypothesis: scientific and technological activity, as practiced in Africa today, is just as "extroverted," as externally oriented, as is economic activity; its shortcomings are, therefore, of the same nature. That is, they are not cognate or consubstantial with our systems of knowledge as such. On the contrary, they derive from the historical integration and subordination of these systems to the world system of knowledge and "know-how," just as underdevelopment as a whole results, primarily, not from any original backwardness, but from the integration of our subsistence economies into the world capitalist market. We have to think about the analogy between these two kinds of subordinating integration, about the similarity between these two kinds of underdevelopment. I would like to elaborate on this point.

Southern Science in Retrospect

Historically, science and technology, in their present form on the African continent, can be traced back to the colonial period. When I make this statement, I do not in any way mean to diminish the importance of pre-colonial knowledge and "know-how." On the contrary, I believe that the whole matter is really about the fate of this pre-colonial heritage, its real place and status in the context of so-called modern science. It is about the way that pre-colonial knowledge has been set aside, marginalized, deprived of its internal dynamism and power of self-regeneration and self-criticism, prevented from absorbing, assimilating and freely developing contributions from outside for its own benefit. It is about the way that pre-colonial knowledge has been reduced to silent, dumb juxtaposition with imported forms of knowledge which in the long term assures its decline and death. The real issue today is how this so-called traditional knowledge can be actively, critically reappropriated by African societies in a way that does not entail traditionalism, passéism, or collective narcissism, but rather enables these societies to address the new challenges that face them.

In the process of scientific investigation, as understood in our times, the decisive stage is neither the collection of data which, in a way, initiated the whole process, nor the application of theoretical findings to practical issues, which is the final stage. The decisive stage is what comes between them — the interpretation of raw information, the theoretical processing, often through experimental machinery and methods, of the data collected, and the production of those particular kinds of utterances that we call scientific statements.

Under these conditions, it becomes evident that the one essential shortcoming of scientific activity in the colonies was the lack of this intermediate stage, of this central operation of theorizing. We only used to have the first and third stages: 1) The data collection, the feverish gathering of all supposedly useful information, was carried out, so that it could be immediately exported to the so-called "mother country" for theoretical/experimental processing and interpretation, and 2) a partial, occasional, and limited application of the results obtained from metropolitan research was made to some local issues. The middle term, the intermediate stage in the whole process, took place on the territory of the ruling country, outside the colony.

The colony itself lacked laboratories and other facilities necessary for basic research; it even lacked universities, or when it had them, they were so poorly developed that they could promote, at best, the proto-theoretical procedures necessary to enlighten the data-collection process, and the post-theoretical procedures necessary for applied research in its final stages, the only ones that took place in the colony, if they took place at all.

Thus, science in the colonies was characterized by a theoretical vacuum, the lack of those intellectual and experimental procedures which, being at the heart of the entire enterprise, depended on infrastructural facilities that existed only in the ruling country. This theoretical vacuum was substantially the same as the industrial vacuum that used to characterize economic activity in the colonies. In the process of imperialist production, colonial dependencies served primarily as sources of raw materials and, later, as new markets for the finished products of metropolitan industry. The raw materials collected, through mining or agriculture, were not used locally but exported to the ruling country, which processed them in its factories, partly for its own consumption and partly for re-export as finished products. Colonial economy was, in this sense, extraverted (i.e., externally oriented); It was organized in such a way that it responded to the demand of industries located elsewhere, and more generally, to the consumption needs of people in the ruling country.

In its minimal formulation, my hypothesis is that scientific research in colonial dependencies went hand in hand with economic activity and developed along the same lines. Laboratories were missing just as industrial plans were missing in the colonies. The theoretical vacuum was just as specific to colonial scientific activity as the industrial vacuum was to economic activity. In the overall process of the production of knowledge, colonies functioned as immense data banks, as storehouses of bare facts and information that were exported to the ruling country, just as they used to serve as storehouses of raw materials that were exported to the same ruling country. There is, therefore, a global parallelism between the two processes.

We can follow this line of argument even further. My maximal hypothesis would be that the theoretical vacuum as well as the industrial vacuum are but two forms of one and the same phenomenon; more precisely put, scientific activity may well be a specific mode of economic activity in the widest sense of the word, in the sense that economy is understood as the overall process of the human transformation of nature, not just monetary exchanges involving agriculture, industry, and commerce. In this complex and many-sided process, economy in the narrower sense (i.e., production and circulation of material goods) remains basic and plays a paradigmatic role vis-à-vis all other aspects. This understanding of the term means that the various aspects or levels of human productive activity (human economy in the wider sense) retain an irreducible specificity, while being conceptualized, at least externally, on the model of economy in the narrower sense.

Within this context, the colonizer's introduction of so-called modern science in the overseas territories was really the introduction of an impoverished science, an ersatz science, deprived of the inner, constituent element, the intellectual theory-building activity that makes science science; however, this in itself was merely a side-effect of the same colonizer's launching of so-called modern and market economies in these territories. The capitalist mode of production was basically new with respect to the traditional one, but it was deprived of the industrial activity, the sense of initiative, the propensity to incur risk, that make this form of economic organization productive in the colonizer's own country. The theoretical emptiness of colonial science is but a side-effect of economic domination, of forced integration into the world capitalist market, but within a subordinate sphere: a consequence of what Samir Amin has called the peripherization of Third World economies. To what extent has this situation been changed by decolonization?

View from Inside (New Forms of Scientific Dependence)

In the former colonies political independence has brought about an increase in the number of research facilities and, sometimes, an improvement in their quality. We now have more and more universities, research institutes, libraries, scientific journals, and publishing houses. We have more and more scientists and academics, better and better-equipped laboratories, enhanced scientific potentialities that no longer allow us to denounce the "theoretical vacuum" in Africa. Yet, the question remains: what has emerged from these new potentialities? How profoundly have they changed the relationship between North and South, between former colonial dependencies and ruling countries, in the field of science and technology?

One thing has certainly changed: in a number of sectors the periphery (the South) is no longer exporting raw, untreated data because the preliminary process of transformation is increasingly taking place there. In some cases, all the necessary processing can even be done on the spot in well-equipped laboratories and research institutes. Nevertheless, in our countries, scientific activity remains basically extraverted, alienated, dependent on an international division of labor that tends to make scientific invention a monopoly of the North, while confining Southern countries to the importing and application of these inventions.

This phenomenon can be observed in a variety of ways. First, as far as equipment is concerned, not only the most sophisticated, but even the simplest technical apparatuses in our laboratories are made in the North. We have never produced a microscope. We do not master even the first step in the chain — the making of research instruments, the production of the means of production.

Second, despite the growth of libraries and publishing houses in our countries, these facilities continue to lag far behind those in industrial countries in both quantity and in quality. African scholars still remain largely dependent on foreign libraries and documentation centers for their scientific information and updating. More generally put, they rely on an international scientific information system that includes computer-based devices and is largely controlled by the North.

Third, as a consequence of these first two limitations, African scholars are bound to remain permanent scientific tourists. In the present state of affairs, no scholar from the Third World can claim to be doing top-level research in any field without traveling, without betaking himself physically to the universities, research centers, libraries, and laboratories of industrial countries. This amounts to institutional nomadism, a restless going to and fro, at least as long as one wishes to continue living at home, among one's family and the people of one's own country, without renouncing the possibility of doing research.

Nomadism is by no means the monopoly of the African or Third World scholar. It is also the usual condition of scholars from France, Britain, Germany, and many other countries insofar as these scholars too are increasingly attracted to countries like the United States and, more rarely, Japan. However, this flow of scholars and scientists from North to North does not have the same meaning as the flow from South to North because it does not testify to any internal inconsistency or imbalance of the research process in second-tier capitalist countries. Each of these countries has developed autonomous, independent, self-reliant research activities, even though the level of achievement is perhaps not the same. In this field as in other fields, the difference is a difference of degree, not nature, whereas there is a difference in nature, an essential, functional, structural difference between industrialized and so-called developing countries.

Fourth, the notorious issue of brain-drain must really be viewed and re-interpreted from this point of view. Brain-drain is not a problem in and for itself. It is merely an extreme form of institutional nomadism and, therefore, a side effect of the global extraversion that characterizes contemporary societies. The desire to do better research is not the only reason why scholars from Africa and the Third World choose to expatriate. Yet beyond the many subjective motivations of individual scholars, beyond the economic, political, and other objective factors that may account for the expatriation of scholars, the process is also, from a macro-sociological standpoint, an inevitable consequence of the international relations of production in the field of science and technology. For this reason, it makes no sense to condemn an individual African scholar for not staying at home. The problem must not be posed in terms of individual responsibility, but in terms of global structure, if we expect to understand the underlying problem and to find a solution for it.

Fifth, if the political independence has fostered the acquisition of technical equipment for research, the only effect of this development has been that theoretical data processing is now partly performed in the South rather than solely in the North. However, this geographical transfer of responsibility for one stage in practice of science does not put an end to the North's monopoly of theory. It merely means that scientists from the South become more involved and enjoy greater responsibilities to participate in the process without having to leave their countries. But there is still no organic link between these laboratories or research institutes and the society that hosts them. The objectives they attempt to attain generally have little to do with artificial islands floating on the surface of the sea without any roots in the soil on the bottom. The insularity is one of the main features of scientific dependence.

Sixth, the research facilities that became established since independence tend to be used largely for applied research. There is still a collective prejudice against basic research, which is thought to be too costly, quite useless for developing countries and, therefore, appropriate only to the North. It even happens that, although adequate facilities sometimes exist, we still refrain from doing basic research out of conviction. The prevailing ideology in our countries is utilitarianism or pragmatism. Obviously inherited from the colonial period, this ideology illustrates the degree to which we have internalized the norms of the colonizer.

Seventh, being aware that their publications will be read more in the North than in the South, African or Third-World scholars are tempted to address issues that are primarily of interest to a Western public and, in one way or another, relevant to the state of knowledge in the West. If they do not do so, they may have no scientific audience at all. This is one of the most pernicious forms of extraversion: theoretical, or socio-theoretical extraversion, the fact that we allow the content of our scientific production, the questions we pose, and the way we deal with them to be preoriented, predetermined by the expectations of our potential readers. Resisting this temptation is, of course, possible. But it is difficult, and the fact that we, and only we, as scientists of the Third World, have to resist such temptation testifies once again to the specific difficulty of doing research in our countries.

Eighth, as a consequence of this socio-theoretical extraversion, research at the periphery is often predisposed, especially in the social sciences, to study exclusively the immediate environment and to remain bound to the local context, confined to the particular, unable, and, what is more serious, unwilling to raise one's speculations to the level of universal. One might regard this centripetal orientation of research as a sign of theoretical liberation vis-à-vis the dominant topics of Northern research, a sign that the scholar from the South is willing to deal, first and foremost, with issues concerning his own society. But the fact is that, throughout the history of the sciences and especially that of the social sciences, territorial specializations were produced by the West. Originally, they were aimed at satisfying theoretical and practical needs of the West. Africanism itself, as a practice and as an ideology, is an invention of the West. Insofar as African scholars lock themselves into this ideology, they are agreeing to play subordinate roles as informants, learned informants, for Western science. It is of course legitimate for Southern scholars to be interested in their own milieu, but as long as this interest remains exclusive and ill-mastered, it will continue to generate dangerous traps for them.

Ninth, scientific research is often conducted directly in the service of economic extraversion. Such is the case of the agronomic research. Until recently, agronomic research was, in most African countries, almost exclusively devoted to searching for ways to improve export crops such as palm-oil, coconut, cotton, cocoa, and coffee. This is obviously the crudest form of scientific and technological extraversion. Only recently were new research programs initiated to deal with food crops that are cultivated primarily for mass consumption. But even today, these new programs can hardly be considered successful.

Tenth, the present situation of so-called traditional knowledge and "know-how" is obviously one of the most serious indices of the ongoing process of underdevelopment. In this connection, the development within Western scholarship of what has come to be known as ethnoscience (i.e., the systematic survey of the precolonial corpus of knowledge as transmitted through oral tradition down to the present generation) must be understood in all its ambiguity. Ethnoscience, and all its various branches (ethnobotany, ethnozoology, ethnomedicine, ethnopsychiatry, ethnophilosophy, and many other disciplines) imply the acknowledgement of endogenous systems of knowledge and "know-how." These systems used to be coherent and efficient, and within their own context, they still are. However, the attempt to objectify these systems, to dominate and master them, inevitably reduces them to a dead corpus once their inner, positive constituents have been endorsed by and integrated into the living, dynamic, progressive corpus of so-called modern science.

Eleventh, the dependency on foreign languages as a prerequisite for access to any research activity in most African countries is also an index of scientific dependence. One might argue that the learning of foreign languages is an enrichment rather than an impoverishment and should therefore be viewed as a means of facilitating access to the universal that I advocated in my eighth point. Yet how does the dependence machine work? In the present state of affairs, we scientists of the Third World are expected to inquire exclusively into the peculiarities of our immediate environment (a seemingly centripetal movement) and then to give an account of our research results in a foreign language for the benefit of a foreign public. Under these conditions, the inward orientation of research is but the first step in a process that continues to be directed outward. The alternative is to invent a new scientific practice that our peculiarities would occasionally be enlightened and appear as peculiarities. Furthermore, an account of this universal knowledge should be given in languages that would make it possible for the majority of our own people to share, appropriate, develop, and if need be, make practical use of it. Such a proposal implies a sort of Copernical revolution and invites the formulation of a radically new language policy, at least in some of our countries.

The twelfth index of scientific dependence is the lack of communication among scholars from Africa or the Third World. The fact is that these scientists are much more involved in a vertical exchange and dialogue with scientists from the North than in any horizontal exchange with their fellow scholars from the South. The internal space of scientific discussion and debate is non-existent or very poorly developed in and between our countries. Inter-African governmental and non-governmental institutions have been established in an attempt to correct the situation. But much remains to be done, and such efforts must be evaluated in light of the dependency relationship I have outlined in this discussion.

Thirteenth, a number of universities and research institutions in the South are actively cultivating what I would term a system for the reproduction of mediocrity. To take just one example, if the responsibility for training young scholars and scientists, to people who have never proved themselves to be good scholars or scientists, to people who have never written a scholarly article but who are good members of the Party or clever, noisy empty barrels, then you might well be nipping in the bud the talents of dozens or hundreds of potentially good African scholars. Universities in the West share some responsibility in this situation insofar as they are sometimes less rigorous in testing African and Third World candidates than in testing candidates from the country itself. Knowing that the degrees granted to such students will not generally entitle them to look for employment in the host country, their examiners often treat them with condescendence and permissiveness.

I am not suggesting that this is always the case. Some examiners in Western countries still evaluate the work of African and Third World students more severely than that of other students. Conversely, tolerance towards foreign students may, in some cases and to some extent, be traced to the awareness that they have had to overcome greater obstacles and difficulties than European or American students. Yet despite these obstacles, a large number of African scholars do achieve excellence in their fields, and these cases of real excellence should be proposed to African students as models and norms, not as dubious successes or as examples of sheer mediocrity. We should constantly seek to raise levels of achievement or at least to maintain them, rather than lowering them. From this point of view, the best policy is certainly not the hasty production of second-rate doctors designed to fulfill the special needs, as perceived by the West, of African or Third World countries. It is just the opposite. We should aim at fostering and encouraging excellence in all fields, so as to engender collective advancement and, in the long run, a methodical, critical appropriation (or reappropriation) of all knowledge and know-how that are available to us through our heritage. And we should use this knowledge and know-how to promote a free, autonomous, self-reliant development of what are now peripheral societies.

Conclusion

The thirteen indices of scientific dependence listed above are merely tentative and should be regarded as suggestive rather than definitive. In one of my previous papers, I enumerated nine features of scientific dependence in contemporary Third World countries. In others, I mentioned only five, or even less. Thirteen is an arbitrary number. It could easily be reduced to a lesser figure or increased to a larger one. Nevertheless, the list illustrates and makes clear the nature of scientific extraversion. By the same token, these thirteen features underscore the urgent necessity for a more systematic enquiry and analysis.

The study of the relationship between science and society is the specific object of a fairly new discipline, the sociology of science. Not more than fifty or sixty years old, this discipline has, until now, focused on the relationship between science and society within industrial societies, leaving aside the crucial issue of scientific and technological relations of production on a world scale and ignoring the conditions of the production of knowledge in so-called developing countries. What I have attempted to demonstrate is that a new chapter in the sociology of science remains to be written about this specific range of issues.

The critique of ethnophilosophy, as formulated by a number of African scholars, including myself, needs to be deepened, enlarged, and placed into the wider critique of ethnoscience or, better still, into a critique of the entire process of marginalization. The question of ethnophilosophy has too often been misunderstood as a dogmatic denial of African traditional wisdom, as an extension of the colonialist disparagement of African cultures. A counter-critique of the critique of ethnophilosophy has therefore emerged; it aims to reformulate the coherence and intrinsic value of our traditional systems of thought in the face of what is often regarded as a Westernized, elitist (i.e., artistocratic and bourgeois), idealistic, positivist, scientistic view of philosophy. From another standpoint, this movement is a reaction against what has been seen as an underestimation of the value of oral speech and a concomitant fetishization of the written word. I once asserted that the critique of ethnophilosophy has never sought to denigrate precolonial system of thought and that this counter-critique was itself based on a populist concept about the nature and role of philosophy. This debate could continue on its own right, but at the present time, it seems to me useful and instructive to place the discourse of African philosophy side-by-side with that of African zoology, botany, medicine, and other specifications of Africanist discourse as a whole. We could then take a sociological look at all of them. In each case, we could examine how they function and the extent to which they favor or oppose the dependency machine. Throughout this reevaluation, we should keep in mind: how can we, today, make Africa free and self-reliant in the field of knowledge and know-how (as in the fields of economy and politics)?

As I understand it, the issue of scientific dependence is ultimately a political one. It will never be solved or accurately perceived as long as the ruling cliques and powers-that-be lack a clear vision of the challenges that face our countries, as long as their major and often only concern is the maintenance of their power—a power that they desire for the sake of sheer power, power erected into an end in itself, an absolute goal, disconnected from the real problems of society. By drawing attention to these problems, and by analyzing their impact upon society, African intellectuals can raise the level of awareness among the people and thereby contribute to changing the present state of affairs. And that in itself is more than sufficient reason for intellectual effort in Africa today.

Note:

This chapter was reprinted in this volume with permission from Indiana University Press.

References

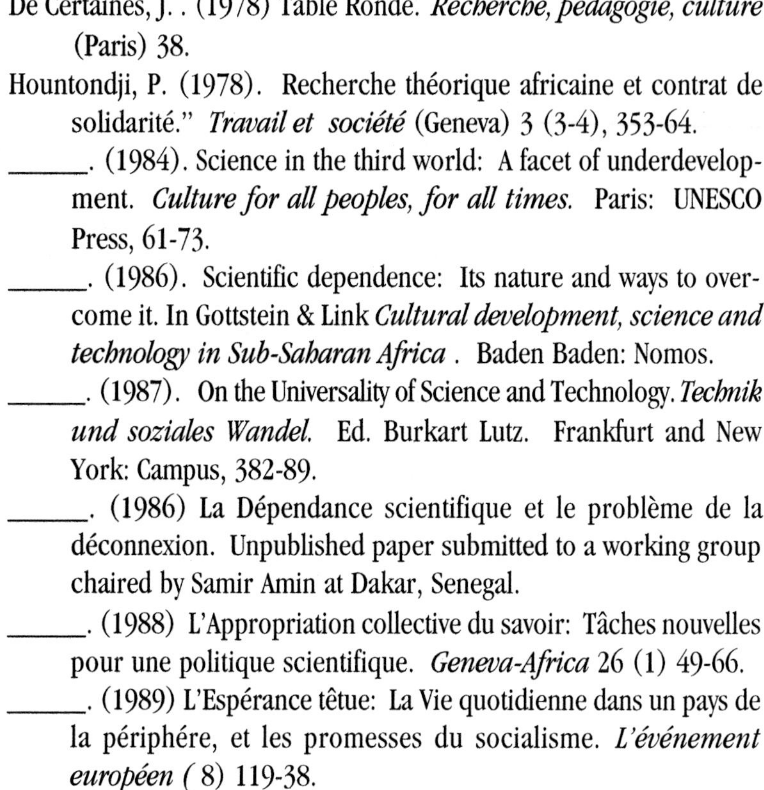

De Certaines, J. . (1978) Table Ronde. *Recherche, pedagogie, culture* (Paris) 38.

Hountondji, P. (1978). Recherche théorique africaine et contrat de solidarité." *Travail et société* (Geneva) 3 (3-4), 353-64.

______. (1984). Science in the third world: A facet of underdevelopment. *Culture for all peoples, for all times.* Paris: UNESCO Press, 61-73.

______. (1986). Scientific dependence: Its nature and ways to overcome it. In Gottstein & Link *Cultural development, science and technology in Sub-Saharan Africa* . Baden Baden: Nomos.

______. (1987). On the Universality of Science and Technology. *Technik und soziales Wandel.* Ed. Burkart Lutz. Frankfurt and New York: Campus, 382-89.

______. (1986) La Dépendance scientifique et le problème de la déconnexion. Unpublished paper submitted to a working group chaired by Samir Amin at Dakar, Senegal.

______. (1988) L'Appropriation collective du savoir: Tâches nouvelles pour une politique scientifique. *Geneva-Africa* 26 (1) 49-66.

______. (1989) L'Espérance têtue: La Vie quotidienne dans un pays de la périphére, et les promesses du socialisme. *L'événement européen* (8) 119-38.

CHAPTER 5

THE BABY ON THE BACK:
SCIENCE, TECHNOLOGY AND THE POLITICS OF PROGRESS IN AFRICA

Judi Wangalwa Wakhungu
Associate Professor of Science, Technology & Society and
Director of Women in the Sciences & Engineering Institute
Pennsylvania State University

Traditionally, new babies are welcomed with joyous celebrations. This was not the case, however, when African leaders met from July 9-11, 2001 in Lusaka, Zambia to introduce to the world their new baby – the African Union (AU). Skepticism teemed over this new birth that was conceived to replace the Organization of African Unity (OAU) formed in 1963, to assist African countries gain independence from colonial rule. Critics of the union say that Africa's history of coups, border disputes, disease, incompatible economies and ideologies make any sort of union an insurmountable task. Brushing aside criticisms, African leaders hope to model the AU after the European Union (EU) with a common African currency, trade and foreign policy, defense structure, and science and technology strategies. This chapter focuses on the latter issues and explores the role played by science and technology in establishing colonial and post-colonial development systems in Africa.

A Yoruba proverb tells us that, "the baby on the back does not know the distance to the market." This proverb provides a cogent description of the African science and technology baby as clinging onto the backs of former mother countries and therefore cannot determine, independently, the distance to the science and technology market. The notion that the innocent baby trusts that the mother is of the nurturing kind begs a study of how Africa's science and technology infrastructure was created.

Definitions

The terms "science" and "technology" are used variously. Science here will be defined as, the understanding of nature by employing experimentation and logical means. Technology, on the other hand, is the use of precise knowledge to manipulate nature in order to obtain specific results. Science in the purest sense and technology strictly defined, are nevertheless located at the extreme ends of a continuum in the spectrum of knowledge. These two extremes are often united in what is called the research and development (R&D) process, in which scientific research is conceived as leading to technological and economic development. But pure science does not always lead to technical advance, while new technologies can be invented without science. Additionally, technological challenges can lead to new scientific knowledge. Suffice it is to say that science and technology are in constant interaction with each other, and they affect wide-ranging social activities which are difficult to differentiate (Wad, 1988). A further distinction with regard to science and technology is historical. The extensive interactions increasingly characteristic of science and technology in Europe since the Renaissance define a kind of science and technology that is often called modern. But it is a mistake to think of science and technology as only modern phenomena. Science and technology in pre-modern, traditional, or indigenous forms are present in all human cultures. For example, science has always been in Africa where there have been significant achievements in astronomy, agriculture, mathematics, metallurgy, and medicine. Examples of historical centers of scholarship include, Alexandria in Egypt, Axum in Ethiopia, Benin in Nigeria, Lamu in Kenya, and Timbuktu in Mali (Asante, 1989; Mazrui, 1980).

Academic discussions about science and technology, both modern and pre-modern, have traditionally been sub-divided among specific disciplines, on the one hand, and into various policy perspectives, on the other. Scientists and engineers, philosophers, political scientists, historians, sociologists, and economists have unique concepts of science and technology (Wad, 1988). For example, while scientists are concerned with generating scientific ideas and expanding scientific knowledge, philosophers think about and reflect on scientific ideas. Historians study the social history of these ideas; economists focus on the dissemination of new technologies, understood as both products and processes. Collaborations among these disciplines are rare. Although the number of interdisciplinary research groups is growing, they remain the exception and not the rule. Examples of African interdisciplinary research groups include the African Academy of Sciences, African Center for Technology Studies, African Technology Policy Studies Network, and the Third World Academy of Sciences.

The result of this fragmented approach is that the role of science and technology in colonial and post-colonial development is observed through particular disciplinary and ideological lenses. This makes the issue of harnessing science and technology for improving the lives and condition of African people both problematic and elusive. Even the standard distinction between research and development need not always apply. What then is the most appropriate way of organizing science and technology, especially in underdeveloped regions such as Africa?

A national science and technology policy is generally thought of as incorporating several related elements. Ideally, it ought to have a general direction and an established set of priorities conducted under the state's legal and executive guidelines. These include research and development, the development of a cadre of scientific and technical personnel, and economic incentives to promote science and technology for social benefit. Distinctions are often made in terms of the functional areas and societal sectors. Functional areas include fields such as basic science, applied science, and industrial research, whereas societal sectors include areas such as communications, agriculture, energy, education, defense, and health (Forje, 1989; UNECA, 1993). Whether and to what extents such disciplines apply or ought to apply in African countries remain unclear.

Colonial Science, Technology, and Development

When thinking about the transition from colonial to post-colonial science and technology, scholars make a distinction between settler regions (such as Argentina, Australia, New Zealand, and North America) and non-settler ones (such as India and most of Africa) where nationals were colonized. The settler regions provided new markets and mechanisms for innovative research. Nationals of the latter were exploited for cheap labor, while their environment was exploited for its natural resources. For example, more scientific knowledge of African societies and environment was commissioned in order to pave the way for a sounder colonial policy and ultimately progress. This was the "science for development perspective." It was soon followed by the "development as experimental science perspective" when Africa was portrayed as a laboratory in which prospects for research and attendant experiments were high (Bonneuil, 2000; Merson, 2000).

Starting in the 1900s, these experiments took the form of prepackaged settlement schemes that redesigned African peoples' lives and engineered entire societies around the production of raw materials to fulfill the needs of the mother countries. These included the 1906 Gezira Scheme operated by the British in Sudan, the 1926 Office du Niger in French Sudan (Mali), the 1934 Terre Neuves Scheme of Senegal, the Sokoto Mechanized Rice Scheme (Nigeria) of 1949, and the 1964 Volta Dam project in Ghana. Other schemes such as Kenya's Swynnerton Plan and Ujamaa Villages in Tanzania, took an integrated approach involving changes in land use and tenure, soil conservation, agricultural techniques, village political organization, and health and educational programs (Bonneuil, 2000; Forje, 1989; Merson, 2000).

The schemes were designed and led by scientific and technical personnel spanning fields in agriculture, forestry, soil conservation, and geology. They exerted a great deal of influence as they helped the colonists master the African environments, pathologies, and societies. Legions of experts came to Africa, their scientific and technical expertise promising success to the settlement schemes. Scientific measures required that the lives of Africans who were forced to live in these schemes be constrained by disciplinary order; each reported to an African supervisor, who reported to a European inspector, who reported to European manager. African tenant farmers became prisoners of an organizational system in which they were simply factors of production (Bonneuil, 2000). This was the only way that "irresponsible" Africans could be prevented from destroying their environment and inhibiting the scientific experiments.

The trend of governing scientifically led to the need to systemize all branches of knowledge on Africa and merge scientific research, economic development, with good governance. One way of achieving this was to work with a cadre of social scientists who, together with the technical experts, could integrate science and technology into policymaking and planning, ultimately creating new scientific institutions that would enable better cooperation among colonial governments.

The first Pan-African Agricultural Conference was convened in 1929. This was followed by the 1935 Pan-African Health Conference. Two Congres de la Recherche Scientifique Coloniale were convened in 1931 and 1937 in Paris. In 1942, the Office de la Rechereche Scientifique Coloniale set up branches in all French colonies. Social science institutions were also established, starting with the International Institute of African Languages in London in 1926; the Institut Francais de Afrique Noire (IFAN) was founded in Dakar in 1936. These were followed by the 1937 creation of the Rhodes-Livingstone Institute in Lusaka, Zambia (Bonneuil, 2000).

After the war, the Scientific Council for Africa South of the Sahara was established in 1949. From the mid-1940s, mechanization of agriculture took precedence and Britain and France, impressed by the American and Soviet agricultural models, especially sought to use mechanical modes of production to increase African agricultural production. Therefore, planning and building laboratories for testing new varieties of crops and new crop rotations took precedence. By 1950, the number of researchers had grown to several thousand Europeans in the Belgian, British, and French colonies. But the number of development problems such as soil erosion and deforestation also increased. These were merely repackaged as technical problems that could be resolved with the appropriate technical solutions.

Land tenure and land ownership became a favored strategy of

social control (Nkrumah, 1965). The capture of African farmers as forced subjects of experimentation promised to enhance the scientific and technical knowledge of these new modes of agricultural production in Africa. Schemes were designed, especially in Kenya and Southern Rhodesia (Zimbabwe), to confine populations within less land in order to promote intensive cultivation. The promotion of monocrops (coffee, tea, rice, maize, peanuts etc.) eradicated the richness of local farming practices, deskilled African farmers, and transformed the landscape and people into uniform and controllable systems (Sachs, 1992).

Post-Colonial Science, Technology, and Development

Following de-colonization, most of the schemes initiated during the colonial era were continued after independence. Post-colonial African leaders assumed control of the fledgling research and development facilities created by the colonial masters. Training a cadre of scientists and engineers was highlighted. But Africa's reliance on import substitution schemes for the transfer of technology did not create an environment conducive to local innovation and the application of science (Forje, 1989; Nyerere, 1967).

Today, underdevelopment is still addressed in terms of what is scientifically and technically feasible in industrialized countries of the North, instead of what is socio-economically and culturally desirable in Africa; the capacity to formulate science and technology policies are overwhelming viewed as external to the African milieu, and the region as a whole is heavily reliant on foreign technologies (Hountoudji, 1990, pp. 6-15). These technologies are imported under unfavorable terms and at costs which cannot be economically sustained. For example, foreign aid is often tied to use of expensive donor services and technologies. These technologies are often either obsolete or ill-suited to the local conditions. Over-dependence on foreign technologies and expertise frustrates both the development of indigenous technologies and the innovative capacity for generating new technologies. In addition, the ability to adapt foreign technologies to the local situation is highly compromised (Deng, 1998; Ogbu, Oyeyinka, and Mlawa, 1995).

Serious discrepancies exist between the needs of national and socioeconomic development and the direction of scientific research, and many institutes conduct researches which are incompatible with the basic requirements of national economies. Strategies aimed at enhancing the technological situation in Africa have merely focused on providing a cadre of scientists and engineers. The result has been that, despite some worthy achievements in the fields of agriculture, entomology, and medicine in particular, the scientists and engineers have contributed little to the transformation of Africa's raw materials and upgrading of its products. Efforts to generate and nurture local demand for science and technology have been minimal. This has resulted in little connection between the generators of technology and the productive sector, and the liaison between policy-makers and R&D institutions is often diffuse. In the final analysis, African countries have been unable to exploit, judiciously, their own natural resources (AAAS, 1994).

Africa's contribution to global research and development (R&D) is 0.3 percent. This is the lowest in the world. Naturally, this does not bode well for Africa's share of the world trade which stands at roughly 2.5 percent. Africa not only maintains the lowest human resource contribution to R&D, but financially, the continent spends the least in R&D ventures, as well. The continent also suffers from a shortage of scientists and engineers. According to the 1998 UNESCO's *World Science Report*, in 1992, there were a total of 20,000 scientists and engineers in Africa. These represented 0.36 percent of the world's scientists. The shortage of science and technology personnel is due to a variety of factors, including limited higher education and research facilities, curricular which focuses on science and technology issues that are incompatible with national socioeconomic needs, and the brain drain.

Another factor that stunts science and technology development is that the private sector does not reinforce R&D, nor does it strengthen, deliberately, science and technology infrastructure. Additionally, financial institutions often have draconian policies and their provision for venture capital for new technologies is limited. Therefore, there is little or no insurance for entrepreneurs against risks for using unproved local expertise and technologies. In a nutshell, the critical role of science and technology to development continues to be sabotaged.

During the past several decades, international investments in science and technology in most African countries have decreased considerably. In addition, structural adjustment programs (SAPS) have replaced development policies, but with similar results. Almost all-new investment projects have been canceled, and the restoration of existing installations postponed. Several restrictions have been imposed on the importation of spare parts, equipment, technical assistance and the training of personnel both locally and overseas. The infrastructure is therefore unchanged; whereas in some areas the technical performance in some industries has deteriorated (AAAS, 1994).

More capital, in the form of debt service, is exported from Africa than it receives in the form of aid and other investments. The challenges for capacity building for science and technology in Africa are basically the challenges of an international economic environment in which African countries have limited leverage. As previously mentioned, most African countries not only rely on foreign technologies for the exploitation of their natural resources, but they are also heavily reliant on foreign advice as to what should be exploited, by whom, when, and with what technology.

Most African countries rely on the export of basic raw materials and minerals. However, the ability to transform and upgrade these commodities has been constrained by the declining prices of these commodities in international markets. Consider that 92 percent of

Africa's total export earnings are procured from the sale of primary commodities. Yet, between 1957 and 1992, the price of these commodities has fallen by over 50 percent. To exacerbate the situation and further reduce the continent's earnings, is the fact that the region is strained by repayment of external debts which have increased from US $185 billion in 1985 to US $275 billion in 1992, to $400 billion in 1996. Even though only half of the outstanding debts are being paid today, 40 percent of Africa's export revenue goes towards servicing debts. Furthermore, the official development assistance (ODA) decreased to US $19.7 billion in 1992, from US $28.2 billion in 1991. Due to these factors, African countries have been unable to invest in science and technology, nor have African governments been able to contribute one percent of their gross domestic product (GDP) to science and technology, as had been agreed to in the Lagos Plan of Action in 1980 (OAU, 1981).

Shortening the Distance to Science and Technology Market

There have been some worthy attempts to improve S&T (science and technology) policy and planning agencies in some African countries. Between 1979 and 1984, the number of African countries with Ministries of S&T increased from 9 to 17. While there are approximately 13 countries with a central science and technology agency, 5 with multisectorial science and technology coordination bodies, there are still several countries without a central science and technology body. The creation of science and technology agencies, however, is a clear indication that the importance of science and technology to socioeconomic development is being recognized (AAAS, 1994). However, there are still several obstacles we hope the new African Union can ameliorate. Consider that, because of policy disaggregation, the science and technology policy agencies are not linked to national research institutions, which are subsumed under other ministries. The science and technology portfolios have been relegated to ministries with other significant national problems, typically Ministries of Education. Ultimately, coordination of various research areas, in terms of program budgeting, setting priorities and program implementation becomes extremely difficult.

A study on the performance of Science and Technology Policy Institutions (STPI's) in several countries including Ghana, Kenya, Nigeria, Tanzania, Madagascar, Malawi, Senegal, Zimbabwe, Guinea, Gambia, and Sierra Leone was conducted by the United Nations Economic Commission for Africa (UNECA). The purpose of the study was to evaluate the functions, powers, organizational structures, and resources available to these national institutions; in all the cases, it was clear that the interpretation of S&T were too narrow, and that there was an urgent need for a major policy overhaul (UNECA, 1993). The study noted that African governments have tried to mimic industrialized countries, where S&T are construed as high-level R&D, that include training at tertiary and post-tertiary levels. The UNECA study recommended that, because of Africa's subordinate level in S&T, emphasis ought to be placed on the application of "of-the-shelf" S&T, as a starting point, with the concomitant education. African governments must put more emphasis on the R&D component so that research results can be commercialized. The UNECA study also noted that emphasis on the development side of the R&D equation is weak. Most of the funds allocated to S&T go towards research and high-level training whereas development of S&T receives limited resources.

Some African countries have also established national institutions in the form of Councils, Commissions, or Ministries, to coordinate S&T activities. Previously, these S&T bodies emphasized scientific research and were based on British or French models of Research Councils. For example, in the Francophone countries these are still in the form of Ministries of Scientific Research and Higher Education. As an outcome of the UNECA study, it now is recognized in many African countries that S&T policies should go hand-in-hand with fiscal, trade, industrial, and educational policies. It is now also recognized that, in the past, a crucial determinant of S&T project failure was that the cultural norms and practices of local people were treated as perfunctory. Yet these traditional practices (which include agricultural and traditional medical practices) must be regarded as assets, and as key determinants of success without which the impact of S&T policies on socioeconomic development will be minimal (Sachs, 1992).

In order to cope with the deteriorating socioeconomic conditions, African countries must use the African Union strategically as an instrument for S&T innovation; policymakers must use lessons learned from the colonial and post-colonial periods. The simplistic view of Africa as a less developed model of industrialized countries is ill conceived. Science and technology policies, imbued with values of industrialized countries, are not entirely conducive to providing the intellectual framework necessary for addressing the deteriorating socioeconomic conditions in Africa (Wakhungu, 1993). Since S&T policies are largely the responsibilities of governments, the low-level capacity of S&T capacity and the misuse of scarce resources can be attributed directly to governments. It is therefore incumbent on the African Union and African governments to facilitate the formulation and execution of clearly enunciated science and technology goals.

The African academic community should also assume a more active role in improving science, mathematics, and engineering throughout the curricular, in promoting the public's understanding of science and technology, and in demystifying existing views of science by highlighting the scientific basis of most traditional practices (Spurgeon, 1995). The research community's morale must be boosted by providing adequate financial resources and environments conducive to research. At the regional level, the African Union ought to provide support for institutions such as the African Foundation for Research and

Development (AFRAND), the African Technology Policy Studies (ATPS) Network, and the African Academy of Sciences.

Ideally, leadership of the African Union should provide financial and institutional incentives to practitioners and researchers. The educational system must be made more accessible, and guarantee scientific confidence in scientists and engineers so that they can contribute to national development. Innovative mechanisms to generate funds for the development and application of S&T should be encouraged and provided by regional institutions such as the African Development Bank (ADB), with the support of the African Union. African countries should also take advantage and keep abreast with the latest technologies in order to, for example, increase agricultural productivity, and boost industrial development. Bureaucratic controls that hamper entrepreneurship should be abolished.

Conclusion

Africa's colonial and post-colonial experiences places it in the same position as the baby on the back. Africa therefore lags behind the rest of the world in science and technology, and therefore faces tremendous challenges in S&T capacity building. The overall aim of science and technology policy for development is to improve standards of living of the people, by enhancing the capacity of African countries to help themselves. However, in Africa, science and technology were installed as instruments of domination, and both the colonial and post-colonial legacy, and the current political chaos stunted an already fragile S&T base. Reliance on European experts precluded broad African participation in even the limited R&D infrastructure created during colonialism. African countries were simply science and technology laboratories designed to be suppliers of raw materials and consumers of manufactured goods and foreign technology. This situation still exists today. African governments must therefore accord priority to developing a local S&T capacity as this is a prerequisite for the development of appropriate S&T policies. Although some form of international assistance will be required, the region cannot hope to solve its S&T problems by relying solely on the international community. African policy-makers must therefore assume a leadership role in ascertaining that the benefits of S&T are accrued locally.

Note

This paper is adapted from: Judi Wangalwa Wakhungu "Science, Technology, and Public Policy in Africa: A Framework for Action," Bulletin of Science, Technology, and Society, 21, 4, pp. 246-252, 2001. Reprint permission was granted by Sage Publications, Inc.

References

Asante, M. (1989). *Afrocentrity*. Trenton: Africa World Press. American Association for the Advancement in Science (AAAS). (1994). *Science in Africa: The challenges of capacity-building*. Washington, D.C. AAAS.

Bonneuil C. (2000). *Development as experiment: Science and state building in late-colonial and post-colonial Africa, 1930-1970, Osiris* 15, 258-281.

Deng, L. A. (1998). *Rethinking African development: Toward a framework for social integration and ecological harmony*. Trenton: Africa World Press.

Forje, J. W. (1989). *Science and technology in Africa*. London: Longman.

Hountondji, P. (1990). Commentary: Scientific dependence in Africa today. *Research in African literature*. 21, 3, 6-15.

Mazrui A. A. (1980). *The African condition*. Cambridge: Cambridge University Press.

Merson, J. (2000). Bio-prospecting or bio-piracy: Intellectual property rights and biodiversity in a colonial and post-colonial context. *Osiris* 15, 282-296.

Nkrumah, K. (1965). *Neo-colonialism: The last stage of imperialism*. London: Nelson.

Nyerere, J. (1967). *Freedom and Unity*. London: Oxford University Press.

Ogbu, O. M., Oyeyinka, B. O., & Mlawa, H. M. (Ed.). (1995). *Technology policy and practice in Africa*. Ottawa. IDRC.

Organization of African Unity (OAU). (1981). *The Lagos plan of action for the economic development of Africa 1980-2000*. Geneva: International Institute for Labor Studies.

United Nations Economic Commission for Africa (UNECA).(1993). *Report on the training seminar on integrating science and tech-*

nology, economic and development policies in Africa. Addis Ababa. UNECA.

Sachs, W. (Ed.). (1992). *The development dictionary: A guide to knowledge as power*. London: Zed Books.

Spurgeon, D. (1995). *Southern lights: Celebrating the scientific achievements of the developing world.* Ottawa: IDRC.

Wad, A., (Ed.). (1988). *Science, technology, and development*. Boulder: Westview Press.

Wakhungu, J. W. (1993). Underdevelopment and dependency: The case of Kenya's energy sector. *The bulletin of science, technology, and society,* 13, 6, 332-340.

______. (2001). Science, technology, and public policy in Africa: A framework for *action.* Bulletin of science, technology, & society. 21, 4, 246-252.

World Bank. (1989). *Sub-Saharan Africa: From crisis to sustainable growth*. Washington, D.C: The World Bank.

PART THREE

THE AFRICANA HUMAN CONDITION: EXPERIENCES AND SPACES OF LEARNING AND LIVELIHOODS

CHAPTER 6

INFUSING CRITICAL THINKING INTO COLLEGE AND UNIVERSITY COURSES IN KENYA:

A Needs Analysis via a Focus Group

Thomas O. Mwanika
Professor, Communications Studies Department
State University of New York at Cortland

Background

This chapter is based on the data from a larger SKEP (State University of New York (SUNY)-Kenya Educational Partnership) Project. It is therefore important that I provide some background information about that project.

The initiative for this project began in March 1997 when the author and his colleague, Dr. John Ogden, Director, Office of International Programs at SUNY Cortland, paid a two-week visit to Kenya. The purpose of the visit was to explore the potential for an educational partnership between the entire SUNY System and a consortium of Kenyan institutions of higher education, and to learn first-hand Kenya's professional and educational needs. We visited six public universities and colleges and three private universities and met with their Vice Chancellors or Principals and their faculty. Both of us took detailed notes of all meetings as well as of some informal discussions. Everywhere we went we were very warmly received and there was a lot of enthusiasm for the partnership idea.

Upon our return to SUNY Cortland, we compiled our observations into a document which we sent back to our Kenyan collaborators for their reviews and comments. Their comments were incorporated into the final document titled: "Post-secondary Educational Needs in Kenya" which was organized into three major issues: Youth Education Issues, Teacher Preparation Issues, and Teaching-Learning, Facilities, Equipment, and Materials Issues. The contents of each of those three issues were organized into three sub-sections: Context, Initiatives, and Action Goal. The "context" sub-section described the current status of the issue; the "initiatives" sub-section outlined the strategies for addressing the issue, and the "action goal" sub-section proposed the tasks with which to counter the issue.

One deficiency noted on teaching-learning is that the Kenyan education system prepares students for passing national examinations instead of providing them life-long knowledge and skills or preparing them for ways to earn a living. Without life-long knowledge and skills, the students are unable to relate their classroom knowledge to problems and to their personal experiences in the real world, and without a preparation on ways to earn a living, the graduates enter the job market without marketable skills.

The second pedagogical deficiency observed was that instructors in many Kenyan colleges and universities tended to concentrate inordinately on teaching subject matter content which they treated as isolated facts and discrete skills to be "learned." Teaching content *per se* is inadequate; as Paul (1990, p. 47) warns:

> We need to remember that all knowledge exists in and through critical thought. All the disciplines—mathematics, physics, chemistry, biology, geography, sociology, anthropology, history, philosophy, and so on—are modes of thought. We know mathematics, not to the extent that we can recite mathematical formulas, but only to the extent that we can think mathematically. We know science, not only to the extent that we can recall sentences from our science textbooks, but only to the extent that we can think scientifically. We understand sociology only to the extent the that we can think sociologically, history only to the extent that we can think historically, and philosophy only to the extent that we can think philosophically.
>
> When we teach each subject in such a way that students pass courses without thinking their way into the knowledge that these subjects make possible, students leave those courses without any more *knowledge* than they had when they entered them. When we sacrifice thought to gain coverage, *we sacrifice knowledge at the same time.* The issue is not shall we sacrifice knowledge to spend time on thought, but shall we continue to sacrifice both knowledge and thought for the mere appearance of learning, for mislearning, for fragmentary learning, for transitory learning, for inert, confused learning?

Indeed, teaching content *per se* encourages students to memorize domain-specific concepts, formulas, algorithms, and skills and to reproduce them "on demand" in tests which have nearly identical items (Paul, 1990). Consequently, students graduate generally without the language and structures for critical thinking, effective communication, or problem solving abilities since they do not have the understanding that "thought and language are inextricably connected" (Boyer, 1983), nor the understanding that "Thought is the key to knowledge. Knowledge is discovered by thinking, analyzed by thinking, organized by thinking, transformed by thinking, assessed by thinking and, most importantly, acquired by thinking" (Paul, 1990, p. xv). Subject matter content should be used as a format or channel for developing cognitive and problem-solving skills to be "used" throughout life (Bransford, et al., 1990; Paul, 1990).

Another pedagogical deficiency noted in Kenya's higher education system is that many instructors generally used one-way "didactic models" of instruction. Following Paul (1990, p. 20), these models are "ill-suited to the development of critical minds and literate persons" since students are,

> rarely encouraged to doubt what they hear in the classroom or read in their texts. Students' personal points of view or philosophies of life are considered largely irrelevant to education. In most classrooms teachers talked and students listened. Dense and typically speedy coverage of content is usually followed by content-specific testing. Students are drilled in applying formulas, skills, and concepts, then tested in nearly identical items. Instructional practices fail to require students to *use* what they learn when appropriate. Practice is stripped of meaning and purpose (Paul, 1990, p. 20).

Moreover, in using didactic models of instruction, students are not encouraged to relate what they learn to other subjects they study nor to problems and to their personal experiences in the real world. How can students make these connections?

In its report, *The Challenge of Connecting Learning*, the Association of American Colleges (1991, pp. 4-5) noted that learning is "a continuing exploration" in which "the role of faculty members is to provide structures and languages that enhance and challenge students' capacities to frame issues, to test hypotheses and arguments against evidence, and to address disputed claims."

One way to counter the above pedagogical deficiencies is to infuse critical thinking into university or college courses. But what is critical thinking? Unfortunately, there is no universal definition of critical thinking. Critical thinking is not a single skill. Rather, it is an amalgam of skills and concepts. As Paul (1990), the leading advocate of critical thinking in the modern world, states:

> ...because of the complexity of critical thinking—its relationship to an unlimited number of behaviors in an unlimited number of situations, its conceptual interdependence with other concepts such as the critical person, the critical society, a critical theory of knowledge, learning, and literacy, and rationality, not to speak of the opposites of these concepts—one should not put too much weight on any particular definition of critical thinking (pp. 30-31).

Although there are many definitions of critical thinking, the public and academic community generally agree that critical thinking is an important instructional outcome. According to Glaser (1941, pp. 5-6), one of the early leading proponents of critical thinking,

The ability to think critically,...involves three things: (1) an *attitude* of being disposed to consider in a thoughtful way the problems and subjects that come within the range of one's experience, (2) *knowledge* of the methods of logical inquiry and reasoning, and (3) some *skill* in applying those methods. Critical thinking calls for a persistent effort to examine any belief or supposed form of knowledge in the light of the evidence that supports it and the further conclusions to which it tends. It also generally requires *ability* to recognize problems, to find workable means for meeting those problems, to gather and marshal pertinent information, to recognize unstated assumptions and values, to comprehend and use language with accuracy, clarity, and discrimination, to interpret data, to appraise evidence and evaluate arguments, to recognize the existence (or non-existence) of logical relationships between propositions, to put to test the conclusions and generalizations at which one arrives, to reconstruct one's patterns of beliefs on the basis of a wider experience, and to render accurate judgments about specific things and qualities in everyday life.

The value underlying this composite skill is that a training in critical thinking improves students' communication (i.e., speaking, listening, reading, and writing) and computing skills. These skills enable students make more meaningful connections with disciplines and with their personal experiences. These connections are essential for leading a more productive life, earning a living, and a better understanding of the complex, highly interdependent, and ever-changing world (Paul, 1990; Howe & Warren, 1989; Ho, 1987, and Wilson, 1989).

This belief is buttressed by empirical evidence showing generally significant positive correlations between critical thinking and social and mathematical sciences (see King, et al., 1990), level of education (Campbell & Macey, 1988; Pascarella, 1989; Nelson, 1987, McMillan, 1987; Engeldinger, 1989), consumer education (Knapp, 1990), science education (Byrne & Johnstone, 1987), law education (Little, 1987), liberal education (Walters, 1986), and participation in democratic society (Kneedler, 1988).

The rest of this chapter reports the results from a focus group designed to determine Kenyan stakeholders' views of the value of infusing critical thinking in the teaching-learning process, and their views of the effective ways for infusing critical thinking into courses. This focus group was designed to address the *teaching-learning deficit* in the Kenyan system of higher education. Critical thinking was one of the eight focus group topics conducted in Nairobi and Nakuru, Kenya during the March 13-17, 2000 SKEP Project Conference. The *access deficit* was addressed by the focus group topics: (1) Meeting the Demands of Access to Higher Education, and (2) Structure and Function of Distance Learning Today. The *relevance deficit* was addressed by the focus group topics: (1) Education for Small Business Development, (2) Education for Natural Resource Management, (3) Education for Community Health (HIV/AIDS), (4) Linkages Between Higher Education and Business in Rift Valley Province, and (5) Linkages Between

Higher Education and Community Organizations in Rift Valley Province. A special focus group (number 9) was conducted among ten students and alumni of the Extramural Learning Center at Nakuru. This focus group was designed to elicit the participants' views about access to post-secondary education and the relevance of tertiary level education to the needs of the local community.

Methodology

Focus Group Choice

To assess accurately educational and professional needs in the three deficit areas noted above, it was necessary to focus on the stakeholders—the individuals who have direct interest in higher education in Kenya. It was also necessary to have an appropriate procedure for eliciting stakeholders' perceptions of the specific problems in those areas.

The project staff considered several procedures including personal interviews, mail and telephone surveys, and focus groups with stakeholders. The focus group procedure was chosen. This choice was informed firstly by the perspective of "symbolic interactionism." Blumer (1986, p. 2), who coined the term "symbolic interactionism," emphasized the importance of meaning in three premises: (1) "Human beings act toward things on the basis of the meanings that the things have for them;" (2) "The meaning of such things is derived from, or arises out of, the social interaction that one has with one's fellows;" (3) "These meanings are handled in, and modified through, an interpretive process used by the person in dealing with the things he encounters." Blumer (1986) sees people as "actors", not "reactors" in an interaction setting. People are able to act because they possess a self, and an individual has the ability to act toward self and an object.

This capacity to act implies that the individual can deal with problem situations. In addition, Blumer (1986, p. 14) recognized the importance of group action. What is seen as societal or group action is merely the extended process of many individuals fitting their actions to one another. A joint action of a group of people consists of an "interlinkage" of their separate actions, but group action is not a mere summation of the individual actions. Group action is based in individual acts. "The participants ...guide their respective acts by forming and using meanings." Goffman (1959), the leading proponent of symbolic interactionism, analyzes individual and group behavior using a theatrical "metaphor" with which he conceives an interaction setting as a "stage" and people in it as "actors." The actors perceive themselves relative to what others say or do in the group setting and they structure their performance to make impressions on the audiences in the group setting. According to Goffman (1959), what is real for a person emerges in that person's "definition of the situation." When faced with a situation, a person typically asks the question: "What is going on here?" The answer to this question is how the person defines the situation. The person's effort is directed toward making sense of the events in the situation and what the person constructs becomes that person's reality. Subsequently, the person structures his/her performances to project various aspects of the self and to make impressions on the audience. Goffman (1961, 1963, 1967, and 1971) uses the concept *face engagement*, to describe what occurs when people engage in focused interaction. In a face engagement, persons have a single focus of attention and a perceived mutual activity. In unfocused interaction people in public places acknowledge the presence of one another without paying attention to one another. In such an unfocused situation the individual is normally accessible for encounter with others. Once an engagement begins, a mutual contract exists to continue the engagement to some kind of termination. During this time a relationship develops and is mutually sustained. Face engagements are both verbal and nonverbal, and the cues exhibited are important in signifying the nature of the relationship as well as a mutual definition of the situation.

In its emphasis on meaning, interaction, attention, and the mutual influence between the individual and group, the symbolic interactionism perspective was informative about the nature of a focus group. Interaction is a prerequisite for a focus group and meaning and perception are both important in focus group interactions. According to Krueger (1994, p. 6), "...a focus group is a carefully planned discussion designed to obtain perceptions on a defined area of interest in a permissive, non-threatening environment. It is conducted with approximately 7 to 10 people by a skilled interviewer. The discussion is comfortable and often enjoyable for participants as they share their ideas and perceptions. Group members influence each other by responding to ideas and comments in the discussion." Also, based on the Hawthorne studies (Wren, 1987) which showed positive effects of attention and social and group influences on worker productivity (the Hawthorne effect), we expected that all the focus group members would be active in contributing to the discussions since the training of moderators emphasized open and non-threatening discussion environment, and not allowing anyone to monopolize the discussion or to be judgmental.

Other theoretic considerations made in selecting the focus group procedure included a variety of orientations subsumed under the field of "group dynamics" (Cartwright & Zander, 1968). These orientations included Lewin's (1951) "field theory" which asserts that behavior is a product of a field of interdependent determinants of "life space or social space," "interaction theory" (Bales, 1950; Homans 1950; Whyte, 1951) in which a group is conceived as a system of interacting individuals, "system theory" (Newcomb, 1950) which is based on the view that a group is a system of "interlocking positions and roles." System theories place major emphasis on various kinds of "input" and "output" of the system.

In addition, the selection of the focus group method was informed by empirical studies on the effects of groups on individual performance. The literature indicates that individual performance is significantly enhanced by the presence of others than in "alone" condition (Allport, 1920; Dashiell, 1930) and arousal, activation, or drive all have as a consequence the enhancement of dominant responses (Spence, 1956).

Finally, the choice of the focus group procedure was also influenced by cost and validity considerations. Compared to other data gathering procedures such as mail and telephone surveys and personal interviews, the focus group method is relatively inexpensive (Krueger, 1994). This feature was attractive given phone and transportation problems in Kenya plus the project's budget constraints. The focus group procedure was also found to be more valid than other procedures since the stakeholders' responses (perceptions and opinions) to predetermined open-ended questions are obtained directly and "in a permissive, non-threatening environment" (Krueger, 1994, p. 6).

Selecting Participants

The focus group participants had to be stakeholders—those individuals with legitimate interest in the problems of access, relevance, and quality of higher education in Kenya. They included college or university students, faculty and administrators plus representatives from women's organizations and the business community. All the vice-chancellors and principals of Kenyan partner institutions were invited, and they in turn invited their faculty and staff to attend the SKEP Project conference in Nairobi and Nakuru. Similarly, leaders of various women's organizations and representatives of private businesses were invited. At the Nairobi part of the conference, there were nearly 100 people including seven faculty and staff members from SUNY partner institutions. When the conference opened, individuals were asked to sign up to attend one of six focus group topics scheduled at Nairobi (three focus groups were held at the Nakuru part of the conference).

Focus Group Composition

The focus group on infusing critical thinking had 13 participants. This number included one moderator from SUNY Cortland and a second moderator and a rapporteur, both faculty members at the University of Nairobi. The rest of the participants (10) were faculty and staff members from various Kenyan public and private universities and colleges plus one private attorney.

Training Materials

The project director (from SUNY Cortland) developed a "moderator's guide" which outlined the guidelines for focus group methodology, purpose, goal, procedures, and strategies, and the roles of focus group moderators and rapporteurs. The second set of materials was a one-page handout titled "Infusing Critical Thinking" which provided information designed to focus the discussion. It contained a brief statement about the context of traditional teaching, specific questions for discussing critical thinking, and cue materials to stimulate focused discussion as shown in the plate below.

Staff Training

Using the materials described above, this focus group's second moderator and the rapporteur were trained by the project director (from SUNY) who was assisted by the project co-director (from SUNY) and project director (from Kenya). For the moderator, this training emphasized particular guidelines on: (1) asking key questions (and probes when necessary), (2) proper listening, (3) use of cue materials, (4) controlling body language that may communicate approval or disapproval, and (4) keeping an accurate and complete record of participants' responses. Finally, the training also emphasized the significance of conducting a smooth discussion, not allowing anyone to monopolize the discussion, and not allowing anyone to be judgmental. The discussion environment had to be open and non-threatening.

For the rapporteur, the training emphasized guidelines on: (1) proper listening, (2) taking accurate and complete notes of the participants' responses or comments, (3) noting the key words and main ideas, and (4) noting the frequency or extensiveness of comments. The rapporteur was also required to re-write (for completeness) and compile the notes immediately after the focus group session, and give these notes to the project director.

Data Analysis

The information recorded by the rapporteurs was supplemented with the notes taken by the two moderators. This became the master document report of participants' responses. The responses were word-processed using MS Word 97. The word-processed document was then imported into *WinMAX 98: Software for Qualitative Data Analysis* which facilitated the coding and retrieving of text segments for analysis.

Results

The results from the analyses are presented in four exhibits below.

Exhibit 1: Participants' views of the value of critical thinking.

POSITIVE VIEWS	NEGATIVE VIEWS
1. Critical thinkers are the hope for changing Kenya	1. Too much questioning can produce a student skeptical of everything
2. Produces creative thinkers	2. Students may become arrogant about their abilities
3. Produces inquisitive thinkers	3. Students become a nuisance to the teacher
4. Produces independent thinkers	4. Students may become egocentric
5. Enhances students' self-esteem	5. Students may become unable to relate to the social environment
6. Expands knowledge base beyond syllabus	6. Students may become repulsive
7. Enables students to detect fallacies and misleading information in communication	7. Students may fail to fit into a traditional authoritarian society
8. Enables students to create and evaluate options	8. Reduces efficiency as it allows the decision making process
9. Enhances relevance and value of subject matter	
10. Makes students appreciate the subject matter more	
11. Allows students to reflect on subject matter	
12. Provides life long knowledge and skills	
13. Enhances students' understanding of themselves and their environment	
14. Creates synergy for different views	
15. Fosters dynamic classroom environment	
16. Fosters humility	
17. Makes learning more interesting	
18. Encourages participation	
19. Helps students judge between right and wrong	
20. Encourages students reflect and consider all issues	
21. Encourages students respect others	

Exhibit 2: Participants' views of the value of critical thinking to the instructor

POSITIVE VIEWS	NEGATIVE VIEWS
1. Teacher becomes a participant in learning	1. Threat for possible loss of status and prestige
2. Learning enhanced through constructive criticism	2. Teaching critical thinking takes time
3. Adds "Why?" question to the usual "Who?", "What?", "When?", "Where?" and "How?" interactions	3. Teacher may be forced to return to the traditional lecture or dictating methods in order to cover the syllabus
4. Distinguishes between true intellectuals and mere scholars	4. Possible loss of control of the class
5. Teacher becomes aware if monologue, didactic or dialogue model of thinking is being used	5. Students may ask difficult or vulgar questions embarrassing the teacher
6. Teacher and student enjoy academic exchange	6. Loss of position as guardians and possessors of knowledge
7. Gives opportunity to student to comment on lectures	7. May feel inadequate to respond to student questions
8. Gives opportunity to students to engage and question the teacher	
9. Teacher also asks questions	
10. Forced to prepare for classes better once students start asking "Why?"	
11. Must be a critical thinker to produce critical thinkers	
12. Ability to maintain an atmosphere conducive to free exchange	
13. Ability to detach from contributions to encourage every student to share their viewpoints	

Exhibit 3:
Participants' views of critical thinking skills unique and common to the instructor and students

SKILLS FOR TEACHER

1. Asking open-ended questions
2. Facilitating discussion
3. Emphasizing key words
4. Designing case studies
5. Encouraging students to ask questions
6. Differentiating between debate and discussion and using them appropriately
7. Professional devotion (teaching is no longer "just a job")
8. Having empathy with students
9. Assisting shy students give their views
10. Having pedagogical patience
11. Guiding students to resources
12. Creating student-oriented syllabi and course outlines
13. Designing every lesson with purpose & measurable & achievable objectives
14. Knowing research on critical thinking
15. Fostering a supportive and non-threatening environment
16. Asking self-reflective questions after each lesson
17. Using the learning triangle when interacting with students: Knowledge, Comprehension, and Understanding
18. Helping students become aware of presuppositions & assumptions, and evaluate them for usefulness

SKILLS FOR STUDENTS

1. Not taking anything for granted
2. Recording & presenting group views
3. Supporting ideas with rational thinking
4. Making linkages and connections between knowledge
5. Identifying and evaluating choices for decision-making
6. Public speaking skills
7. Relating general knowledge & life experiences to the topic of discussion

COMMON SKILLS

1. Analysis
2. Synthesis
3. Evaluation
4. Communication
5. Listening
6. Open-mindedness
7. Question-asking attitude
8. Respect for divergent opinion

Exhibit 4:
Participants' views of the ways to infuse critical thinking skills into courses

WAYS FOR INFUSING CRITICAL THINKING INTO COURSES

1. Design learning experiences (e.g., contrary case studies) that help students examine assumptions and presuppositions
2. Design value clarification exercises
3. Design learning materials dealing with issues of real concern to students
4. Use materials that are relevant to the life experiences of students
5. Walk the street looking for links to students' lives
6. Ask students to consistently journal their personal response to different learning experiences
7. Understand that critical thinking is more in the delivery method rather than being a topic in the course outline
8. Use role playing exercises
9. Encourage open-ended discussions

Discussion

First, the stakeholders' views of infusing critical thinking into college and university courses is positive. Exhibit 1 shows that the stakeholders see critical thinking as an effective means for changing Kenya and for producing students who are creative, inquisitive, and independent. They feel that critical thinking enhances students' communication skills, self-esteem, participation, and humility. Critical thinking also improves students' perception of themselves and the environment, and respect for different views and for others. In addition, the participants feel that critical thinking expands students' knowledge base, provides students life long knowledge and skills, fosters a dynamic classroom environment, makes learning more interesting, and enhances relevance and value of subject matter. At the same time, however, the stakeholders are concerned about the negative consequences of teaching critical thinking. Exhibit 1 shows that the participants feel that teaching critical thinking may produce students who become skeptical of everything, arrogant, a nuisance, egocentric, repulsive, unable to relate to the social environment and to fit into a traditional authoritarian society. They also feel that teaching critical thinking reduces efficiency as it slows the decision making process.

Secondly, these stakeholders see the values of critical thinking that are unique to the instructor. On the positive side, the participants feel that critical thinking makes the instructor a participant in learning, forces the instructor to provide constructive criticism and to encourage question asking and open and free dialogue; enables the instructor to distinguish between monologue (didactic) and dialogue models of thinking, and forces the instructor to prepare for classes better once students start asking "Why?" On the negative side, the participants felt that teaching critical thinking may make the instructor feel threatened by possible loss of status, prestige, control of the class, and the inability and embarrassment to answer difficult and vulgar questions. Moreover, the instructor may be forced to return to the traditional lecture and dictating methods in order to cover the syllabus since teaching critical thinking takes more time.

Thirdly, the participants distinguish between critical thinking skills unique and common to the instructor and students. This is a very important distinction given that critical thinking skills are traditionally perceived to be the same for the instructors and students. The participants' views of critical thinking skills unique to the instructor (see Exhibit 3) generally fall in four dimensions: *communication, environment, lesson plan, and professionalism.*

In the communication dimension, the critical thinking skills include: Asking open-ended and self-reflective questions; facilitating discussion and distinguishing between debate and discussion; emphasizing key words; using the learning triangle (knowledge, comprehension, and understanding); helping students become aware of presuppositions and assumptions, and evaluating them for usefulness. The critical thinking skills in the environmental dimension include having empathy with students; assisting shy students to give their views; encouraging students ask questions; fostering a supportive and non-threatening environment, and using a systems approach in the classroom. In the lesson plan dimension, the critical thinking skills include designing case studies; creating student-oriented syllabi and course outlines, and designing every lesson with purpose and measurable and achievable objectives. Finally, in the professionalism dimension, the critical thinking skills include professional devotion (teaching is no longer "just a job"); having pedagogical patience; knowing research on critical thinking, and guiding students to resources.

The participants' views of critical thinking skills unique to students (see Exhibit 3) include: Not taking anything for granted; recording and presenting group views; supporting ideas with rational thinking; making linkages and connections between knowledge; identifying and evaluating choices for decision-making; public speaking skills, and relating general knowledge and life experiences to the topic of discussion. The participants' views of critical thinking skills common to both the instructors and students include: analysis, synthesis, evaluation, communication, listening, open-mindedness, question asking attitude, and respect for divergent opinions.

Finally, the participants felt that there are effective ways for infusing critical thinking skills into college and university courses. It is important to note that most of the methods they provided center on student experiences (see Exhibit 4). These methods include: using learning experiences such as contrary case studies that help students examine assumptions and presuppositions; using value clarification exercises; using learning materials dealing with issues of real concern to students, and using materials that are relevant to the life experiences of students. The participants also suggested the use of role playing exercises and encouraging open-ended discussions, and asking students to consistently journal their personal response to different learning experiences. However, the participants warn that instructors must understand that critical thinking is more of a delivery method rather than a topic in the course outline.

It is important to note that the views expressed in this focus group were by college and university faculty and staff only and not by students since this focus group did not have students. Thus, students' views of the value of critical thinking remain unknown. Future studies will therefore need to involve students since students are the primary beneficiaries of the courses enhanced with critical thinking.

The second area of concern is implementation. Although the SKEP Project partners jointly outlined the methods for incorporating critical thinking into courses during their November 27 – December 1, 2000 conference at SUNY Cortland, the application of any of those methods may be delayed given that Kenya's educational priorities have shifted from SKEP Project's initial goals to the upgrading of a teacher's college into a four-year college.

Some challenges for instructors who decide to infuse critical thinking into their courses may be noted. One challenge will be to reconceptualize and restructure or redesign the content of their courses to maximize the impact of these courses on students. The second challenge will be to develop appropriate materials for infusing critical thinking effectively such as those in Exhibit 4. The third challenge will be the instructors' transformation of their traditional pedagogical practices by, for example, a shift away from one-way didactic models to focused discussions and open-ended questioning. The fourth challenge will be in evaluating student outcomes. Traditionally, to evaluate whether or not students have learned the content, many instructors use tests that generally rely on the so-called "objective" tests such as multiple-choice, true-false, or matching. However, these tests encourage students to reproduce factual information and discrete skills in which they have been dinned. These exams also impose unrealistic boundaries that deprive students of their freedom to think critically and argue creatively their answers to exam questions dealing usually with complex issues. The challenge will be the shift away from these exams to alternatives such as essay tests, portfolios, and demonstration projects. Finally for instructors using instructional technologies, the challenge for them will be the selection and use of materials appropriate for infusing critical thinking effectively and compatible with the technology in use at the same time.

Finally, there are also challenges at the national level for infusing critical thinking into the curricula. One challenge will be whether to use "the process approach" in which critical thinking is taught as an independent course or "the content approach" in which critical thinking is taught within established courses (ERIC, 1988). The second challenge will be the development and production of materials appropriate for infusing critical thinking at various school levels and the distribution of these materials to those schools. To develop "critical consciousness" among school and college graduates, it is important that such materials not only facilitate the teaching of content but must also be centered on the values which the Kenyan society wants in its graduates. Curricular "centeredness" in the education of a Black child in the United States was recently emphasized by Asumah and Perkins (2001, p. 81) when they stated that "The embodiment of an African-centered curriculum is a textbook, course catalog, subject guide, lesson plan, specification charts, school board policy or community and the state regulations that *reflect the needs, culture, learning experiences, and the future* place the African American society holds in the United States and worldwide. Consequently, an African-centered curriculum is about *structuring schoolwork in our learning institutions to improve the overall performance of the students, schools and the community*" (emphasis is mine). The third challenge will be in how to meet the demands for critical thinking by new teachers, current teachers, and college/university professors. The demand by new teachers may be met directly through the enhanced curricula at the teacher training colleges while those of the present teachers and college/university professors may be met through faculty development programs. The challenge will be the financial investment necessary to pay for the trainers, in-service training, training materials, and ancillary expenses.

Acknowledgments

I wish to acknowledge the support of USAID/ALO for the grant No. HNE-A-00-97-00059-00 which made this project possible. I thank Dr. George Jones (United States International University), SKEP Project Director/Kenya and Dr. John Ogden (SUNY Cortland), SKEP Project Co-director, for their contributions to the SKEP Project, conference plans and staff training for the focus groups. I also wish to thank Dr. Katherine Getao and Dr. Samuel Ruhiu, both at the University of Nairobi, for serving as focus group co-moderator and rapporteur respectively. There are many others who contributed to the success of this project. However, it is impossible to name all them. Suffice to say I am indebted to all of them. Notwithstanding the contributions of the many individuals, any flaws in this manuscript are mine.

References

Allport, F.H. (1920). The influence of the group upon association and thought. *Journal of experimental psychology*, 3, 159-182.

Association of American Colleges (1991). *The challenge of connecting learning.* Washington, D.C.: Association of American Colleges.

Asumah, S. N. & Perkins, V. C. (2001). *Educating the Black child in the Black independent school*. Binghamton, NY: Global Publications.

Bales, R.F. (1950). *Interaction process analysis.* Cambridge, Mass.: Addison-Wesley.

Beyer, B.K. (1985). Critical thinking: What is it? *Social education.* 49, 270-276.

Blumer, H. (1986). Symbolic interactionism: Perspective and method Berkeley: University of California Press.

Boyer, E. L. (1983). High school: A report on secondary education in America. Princeton, N.J.: The Carniegie Foundation for the Advancement of Teaching; Also, New York: Harper & Row.

Bransford, J. D., Sherwood, R. D., Hasselbring, T. S., Kinzer, C. K., and Williams, S. M. (1990). *Anchored instruction: Why we need it and how technology can help.* In D. Nix and R. Spiro (Eds.). *Cognition, education, and multimedia: Exploring ideas in high technology.* Hillsdale, N.J.: Lawrence Erlbaum, 115-141.

Byrne, M. S. & Johnstone, A. H. (1987). Critical thinking and science education. studies in higher education. 12, (3), 325-39.

Campbell, D. E & Macey, J. R. (1988). Critical thinking: Its relationship in education and training. Paper presented at the Conference on Technology and Training in Education (Biloxi, MS, March 7-11).

Cartwright, D. and Zander, A. (1968). *Group dynamics: Research and theory*, 3rd edition. New York: Harper & Row, Publishers.

Dashiell, J. F. (1930). An experimental analysis of some group effects. *Journal of abnormal and social psychology*, 25, 190-199.

Engeldinger, E. A. (1988). Bibliographic instruction and critical thinking: The contribution of the annotated bibliography. *RQ*, 28, (2), 195-202.

ERIC Digest 3-88, ED297003, (1988). (ERIC Document Reproduction Service).

Glaser, E. M. (1941). *An experiment in the development of critical thinking*. New York: Bureau of Publications, Teachers College, Colombia University.

Goffman, E. (1959). *The presentation of self in everyday life*. Garden City, NY: Doubleday.

______. (1961). *Encounters: Two studies in the sociology of interaction.* Indianapolis, IN: Bobbs-Merrill.

______. (1963). *Behavior in public places*. New York: Free Press.

______. (1967). *Interaction ritual: Essays on face-to-face behavior.* Garden City, NY: Doubleday.

______. (1971). *Relations in public*. New York: Basic Books.

Ho, H. H. (1987). *Methodology and critical thinking*. EDRS.

Homans, G.C. (1950). The human group. New York: Harcourt, Brace.

Howe, R. W & Warren, C. R (1989). *Teaching critical thinking through environmental education*. Columbus, Ohio: ERIC Clearinghouse for Science, Mathematics, and Environmental Education.

King, P. M, et al. (1990, Winter). Critical thinking among college and graduate students. *Review of higher education.* 13, (2), 167-186.

Knapp, J. (1990). The profits of consumer education. *Advancing the consumer interest.* 2, (2), 26-29.

Kneedler, P. E (1988). *Assessment of the critical thinking skills in history -- social science*. Social studies. Review. 27, (3), 2-93.

Krueger, R. A. (1994). *Focus groups: A practical guide for applied research.* 2nd edition. Thousand Oaks, CA: Sage Publications.

Lewin, K. (1951). *Field theory in social science.* New York: Harper.

Little, T. H. (1987). Law-related education. *Michigan social studies journal.* 1, (2), 65-68.

McMillan, J. H (1987). Enhancing college students' critical thinking: A review of studies. *Research in higher education.* 26, (1), 3-29.

Morgan, D. L. (1997). *Focus groups as qualitative research.* 16, 2nd edition Thousand Oaks, CA: Sage Publications.

Nelson, J. L (1987, Fall). Critical thinking in social education: The genocide example. *Social science record.* 24, (2), 60-62.

Newcomb, T.M. (1950). *Social psychology.* New York: Dryden.

Pascarella, E. T (1989). The development of critical thinking: Does college make a difference? *Journal of college student development.* 30, (1), 19-26.

Paul, R. (1990). *Critical thinking: What every person needs to survive in a rapidly changing world.* Rohnert, CA: Center for Critical Thinking and Moral Critique, Sonoma State University.

Reinard, J. (1998). *Introduction to communication research.* 2nd edition. Boston, Massachusetts: McGraw-Hill.

Spence, K.W. (1956). *Behavior theory and conditioning.* New Haven, Conn.: Yale University Press.

Walters, K. S (1986). Critical thinking in liberal education: A case of overkill? *Liberal education.* 72, (1), 1-7.

Wilson, J. K (1989). *L.A.N.D critical thinking workshop with applications for develop-mental students.* Charles Stewart Mott Community College, Flint, Michigan.

Whyte, W.F. (1951). Small groups and large organizations. In J.H. Rohrer & M. Sherif (eds.), *Social psychology at the cross-roads.* New York: Harper.

Wren, D. A (1987). *The evolution of management thought.* New York: John Wiley.

CHAPTER 7

AFRICAN AND AFRICAN-CENTERED EDUCATIONAL MODELS:

Critical Linkages of Theory and Praxis

Ranahnah A. Afriye
Graduate Student
Cornell University

Introduction

When discussing African-centered educational principles, as they were defined during the U.S. independent black school movement of the early 1960's, there is often little connection drawn between the pedagogical principles that have existed in Africa since pre-colonial times and those that exist today within some African educational models in the United States. It is important that such comparisons be made in order to 1) ascertain some underlying principles for an indigenous African educational model and 2) situate African-centered curriculum and theory within a continuum of educational structures that have existed from ancient times to the present. This chapter explores this connection and gives some points of comparison between educational models of the African continent and those of the African-centered school movement in the United States.

Indigenous Pedagogy in Contemporary Africa

There are numerous published materials on this topic, although few scholars have endeavored to analyze the full body of resources that are currently available through literature and oral history (Occitti, 1992, p. 2). A few authors have conducted comparative surveys of African education, and have outlined some pervasive general characteristics. Abdou Moumouni has defined the following characteristics of "traditional education" that he has identified among numerous ethnic groups throughout the African continent:

> 1. The great importance which is attached to it, and its collective and social nature.
> 2. Its intimate tie with social life, both in a material and spiritual sense.
> 3. Its multivalent character, both in terms of its goals and means employed.
> 4. Its gradual and progressive achievement, in conformity with the successive stages of physical, emotional and mental development of the child
>
> (Moumouni, 1968, p. 15).

Pierre Erny further delineates the aims and core values of African education as generally characterized by the orientation from the " . . .

'I' centeredness to 'We' centeredness, from individualism to communalism. For self-centeredness is a prominent feature of a child and an immature adult . . . . Traditional education is, therefore, a lifelong journey of preparation for communing and fusing with the whole of life—that is, community life" (Moumouni, 1968, p. 114).

A.B. Fafunwa conducted a comparative survey of education in Africa and summarized the following "cardinal goals of indigenous African education":

- To develop the child's latent physical skills.
- To develop character.
- To teach respect for elders and those in positions of authority.
- To develop intellectual skills.
- To acquire specific vocational training and to develop a healthy attitude toward honest labor.
- To develop a sense of belonging and to encourage active participation in family and community affairs.
- To understand, appreciate and promote the cultural heritage of the community at large (cited in Tedla, 1995, pp. 114-115).

In *The Child and His Environment in Black Africa: An Essay on Traditional Education,* Pierre Erny (1981) describes the rites and practices of African education, among various ethnic groups, as constructing a complex matrix of social integration. There are essentially two fundamental levels, both vertical and horizontal, by which the child is integrated into society. The vertical linkage is constructed intergenerationally, situating each individual in a social order with deference given to one's elders and the responsibilities of mentorship assigned to younger generations. The horizontal level is intragenerational, existing within an age group. Youth are thus socialized and taught to cement relationships along fraternal lines. The age groupings are essential in forming the linkages of kinship and marriage, which will assure the longevity of the ethnic group (Erny, 1973, p. 182). The parameters of these age groups consist of those born within a variable time (depending on the specific practices of each ethnic group), generally seven years. Although specific age groupings differ, there are four age phases that are represented; roughly corresponding to infancy, childhood, adolescence, and adulthood, age phases tend to be marked by group rites or modified changes in socialization practices.

The age set serves the essential function of integrating each individual into alignment with their peers, as well as socializing each generation into the ethnic group's values and "cultural memory." It is equally important that these age groups provide a devise to demarcate psychophysical development stages. The appropriate level of knowledge and skills that correspond to these stages are taught, and one is expected to assume the responsibilities that go with one's age level (Tedla, 1995, p. 116).

Many of the aforementioned general characteristics are exemplified in the formal educational system of the Poro and Sande societies of West Africa. The influence of the Poro and Sande stretches from northern Liberia to Sierra Leone and the borders of Guinea, encompassing numerous ethnic groups (Scanlon, 1964, p. 15). The Poro is the decentralized system of education for males, while the Sande serves the females. Each group is responsible for providing youth with the preparation and instruction for both horizontal and vertical integration into the larger society. As previously discussed, educational systems or "initiation schools" (Scanlon, 1964, p. 15) facilitate social cohesion within the peer group, while also cementing relationships with the elders (and ancestral spirits) who are the leaders or facilitators of the schools' activities (Okpaku, Opubor, Oloruntimehin, 1986, p. 121).

Historically in the Poro schools, boys are initially placed in one class where they are all taught the laws and customs of their ethnic group; they are later divided into specific groups according to age, aptitude, and the position in society that they intend to occupy. The subject matter ranges from the use of medicinal herbs to cultural history; folklore and storytelling serve to inculcate social mores among youth (Scanlon, 1964, p. 23). Physical aptitude is particularly important, and these skills are honed through games and sports such as canoeing, hunting, and wrestling. Boys are also responsible for the construction of the buildings that are used for the initiation period (Okpaku et al 1986, p. 122).

The teachings of the Sande society include training in medicinal practices, such as the proper identification and use of healing herbs. Girls are also taught agricultural skills (farming and harvesting), housework, and numerous artistic pursuits including dancing and singing (Okpaku, Opubor & Oloruntimehin, 1986, p. 122).

Within both societies, aptitude tests are one of the initial activities, testing the cognitive and analytical abilities of the young men and women (Okpaku, Opubor, & Oloruntimehin, 1986, p. 123). The opening and closing of the formal schooling period is ceremoniously marked by circumcision at its inception or in its initial stages (Okpaku, Opubor & Oloruntimehin, 1986, p. 122), and renaming at the end of the course to symbolize students becoming new beings (Okpaku, Opubor & Oloruntimehin, 1986, p. 124).

This description of the Poro and Sande societies supports the comparative data for an indigenous educational model that was provided by Erny, Moumouni, and Tedla.

Education is conducted first in the context of the family, and later in the context of the ethnic group or societal institutions. The second phase is one of apprenticeship and of participation in-group tasks. Initiation rites often follow group socialization practices where individuals are placed on the fringe of their normal environment, in "initiation schools," for the sake of rigorous socialization for a variable period of time.

Education in this form continues throughout the life of an individual, as they are guided through rites of passage, leading to adulthood, responsibilities as social elders, and subsequently to death and spiritual transformation to the vilified role of *ancestor*: "Among the Bambara, a person normally passes through a whole chain of societies of initiation until with the last one — and thanks to the rites involved––he has reached a true transformation in God who assures him of immortality at the end of his spiritual journey and mystical ascension" (Erny, 1981, p. 8). As Pierre Erny notably remarks,

> The pedagogy which is directed to the child. . .must be situated in this vaster and more complete totality, embracing the whole life and marking its stages. . .These facts make us see that basic to any education whatsoever, there is a particular way of perceiving and understanding man-his genesis, his development, his presence in the world, the goals he is called upon to pursue (Erny, 1981, p. 8-9).

From this foundation, some of the key elements of an indigenous African educational model can be extrapolated. One of its most pronounced elements is the dual purpose of the educational process that has been identified in all of the textual references that we have examined. As Jomo Kenyatta states in *Facing Mount Kenya*,

> The striking thing in the Gikuyu system of education, and the feature which most sharply distinguishes it from the European system of education, is the primary place given to personal relations. Each official statement of educational policy repeats this well-worn declaration that the aim of education must be building of character and not the mere acquisition of knowledge (Kenyatta, 1962, p. 117).

There is a clear synthesis of cognitive (knowledge based) and affective (establishing interrelationship between the individual and group) educational mechanisms. "Affective education attempts to create more powerful channels of nurture and integrates the youth's feelings and values with his or her intellectual development (Okpaku,

Opubor, Oloruntimehin, 1986, p. 110)."

This is an important observation for our purposes, because this holistic integration of cognitive skills and social/ spiritual orientation was also a key element found in the ancient African educational systems of Kemet and Ethiopia (Bekerie 1998; Carruthers & Karenga 1986; Hilliard 1998; James 1992). The realization that the individual is a cog within an integrated whole, that is, the *community*, is essential. Contained within this assumption is the equally valued belief that each individual's actions and health reflect the well being of the larger body. There is a prevailing sentiment of community responsibility perpetuated in the indigenous African educational model, which is inextricably linked with individual cognitive and intellectual development.

Education for Liberation in the United States: The Black Independent School Movement

The inception of the independent Black school movement, as an organized endeavor of African-American educators, resulted from the efforts of four conferences: California Association for Afro-American Education and Nairobi College Workshop (August, 1970), First Congress of Afrikan Peoples (September 1970), the First NYC African American Teacher's Convention (April, 1972), and the Founding Session of the Council for Independent Black Institutions held in June 1972 (Doughty, 1973, 89). In the developments of these meetings, an agenda for independent black institutions (IBIs) was articulated which would shape the future formation of independent black schools throughout the U.S.

The first of these conferences, attended by representatives from more than twenty independent black educational institutions, was held at the California Association for Afro-American Education and Nairobi College Workshop in August 1970 (Doughty 1973, p. 87). The establishment of a national Pan-African[3] school system was proposed, and characteristics for membership in this system were defined. It is important that we refer to these designated characteristics in order to ascertain the educational objectives that underpin the independent black school movement that would later materialize:

1. Black people would need to be in exclusive control of the decision-making process.
2. Primary emphasis should be placed on developing financial resources from within the black community; however, funds could be obtained from any source. Exogenous funding should only be received based on the self-defined parameters of the IBI (Independent Black Institutions).
3. The institution must subscribe to the ideology of Pan-Africanism and Black Nationalism.[4]
4. All staff are required to be of African ancestry and, finally,
5. The institutional activities must be directed toward serving the needs of black people (Doughty, 1973, p. 106).

The idea for creating a national umbrella organization to coordinate the activities and objectives of independent Black Schools was not proposed until 1972, during the Independent Black Schools Workshop of the First New York City African-American Teachers Convention. At this point, the educators and school representatives in attendance decided to create a Council for Independent Black Institutions (CIBI), appointing Kasisi Jetu Weusi, headmaster of the Uhuru Sasa Schule, as one of the founding organizers. CIBI became the organizing body for the majority of IBI's in the United States, particularly aimed at educating youth from kindergarten through grade 12.

In regards to the philosophy, curriculum, and content of Independent Black Schools, there were four governing principles (consistent with those of the Nairobi College Conference) which underscored all of the independent initiatives of CIBI's member organizations: 1.

Maulana Karenga's Kawaida Theory, 2. Black Nationalism, 3. Black Power, and 4. Pan-Afrikanism.

By reviewing the policies that were designed to govern the nascent independent black schools, we can clearly ascertain the prevailing ideology of the schools' founders. The educational institution served the purposes of both social and individual development. As Mwalimu Shujaa comments,

the number of African-American parents who are looking at schooling in its broader social context are also growing. By assigning dual priority to academic preparation and cultural awareness, these parents are demonstrating the capacity

to differentiate schooling and education. These parents' decisions to enroll their children in African-American independent schools are efforts to obtain schooling that is more closely attuned to the values and beliefs they are developing within their own families. The school, therefore, is used by parents to extend the educational foundation begun at home (Shujaa, 1996, p. 374).

Schools were community organized or often founded by community members who had been dissatisfied with the inadequacies of mainstream schools (Kifano, 1996, p. 209). Parents were viewed as the foundation of the new institutions; they were not merely fundraisers, but also policymakers, implementers, and evaluators (Doughty, 1973, p. 199). Within the independent black schools, the definition of "parent" was prescribed by the extended family structure, giving responsibility to all those involved in the work of the school (Doughty, 1973, p. 199). The school was thus redefined as an integral agent in African-American community development, in promoting cultural affirmation, the construction of a Pan-African identity, and economic self-determination.

To examine the content and purpose of a case study institution, the New Concept Development Center in Chicago, Illinois, is to provide a more detailed portrait of a Black independent school of this era.

Founded in 1972, the school began as a Saturday school program for African-American children from 2-12, eventually becoming a full time day school in 1974 for kindergarten through third grade (Lee, 1992, p. 162). The program emerged from the efforts of a group of individuals, many of them parents, who had been working with the independent black publishing company, Third World Press, since 1967.

Carol Lee (Safisha Madhubuti), one of the founding members of this school, describes their objectives as follows:

> Our goal was to develop an educational institution within Chicago's Black community that would teach African American history and culture as well as imbue the values of Black self-love and cooperation among the children it served. Moreover, it was envisioned that this institution would operate independent of resources and influences from outside the Black community (Lee, 1992, p. 162).

NCDC's academic program consisted of two parts: a pre-school level for youth aged 2-5 and primary level for youth aged 6-8. Each of these larger groups was broken into smaller divisions based on the academic level of the child. The curriculum for all youth included the following:

1. *Communications*- language, reading and composition skills, beginning in kindergarten;
2. *Mathematics*- basic operations and problem solving;
3. *Culture*- identity and values, geography and social studies;
4. *Science*- with emphasis on problem solving, hands-on investigation and thinking skills.
5. *Kujichagulia (Self-Determination) Skills*- for younger children; this includes cutting, buttoning, zippering, etc; for older children, skills included sweeping, setting the table, brushing teeth and other personal hygiene skills.
6. *Physical Development*- classes stressed coordination, strength,

endurance, and cooperation. Team sports are also included;

7. *Cultural Arts-* includes foreign language instruction (Kiswahili, French, and Spanish), music and crafts (Smith, 1984).

Lee refers to NCDC's curricular content as "reflective of the Kemetic proposition that moral social practice is essential to human development... [uniting] academic excellence and positive character development as co-partners in the education of youth" (Smith, 1984, pp. 168-171). The courses that were taught aimed to reinforce youth's community identity, establishing linkages to the history and culture of African people of the continent and diaspora.

In addition to subject matter, NCDC encompassed a social component that was central to the school's structure and operation. The school itself was attached to the Institute of Positive Education, a non-profit community service institution. Under the auspices of IPE, the New Concept Development Center and its community (students, teachers, parents, administrators) actively participated in a self-sustaining unit that linked education to economic production. Educational materials (curricula, worksheets, etc.) were produced at the school and shared within the Council of Independent Black Institutions network.

IPE's complex program structure provided a varied array of goods and services to the local community. It is noteworthy that the Institute of Positive Education's economic and educational ventures were synthesized into a fresh food co-op, tutorial services, summer camp, youth programs, NCDC's elementary school, educational aids and publications, a working farm, community programs (lectures and seminars), and a seasonal magazine on issues of importance to the black community.

Parents were active members of the school community; many volunteered as teachers or staff while others participated in fundraising activities through the parents' association. As described by one of the school's founders, Carol Lee, upon enrollment, the rigor of parents' role in the NCDC educational community was clearly stated: "expected social relations were made clear. . . to ensure that families become and remain supportive of their children's physical, social, and moral development (Lee, 1992, p. 173)."

As Mwalimu Shujaa states in his book, *Too Much Schooling Too Little Education*, one of the functions of the U.S. school system has been to effect a gradual destruction of the cultural identity of African-Americans (Shujaa, 1994, p. 30). However, the African-centered model of schooling differs greatly from this miseducation of African Americans. Instead, a unique union of academic excellence, economic self-sufficiency, and cultural competence characterizes schools such as NCDC; this has been a formula for their successful socialization of African-American youth.

Conclusion

A salient element throughout the educational systems that I have described is the role that education plays within the community itself. Education in the context of indigenous African society overtly encompasses two primary objectives; it is a purveyor of social values, imbued with the philosophy and ethos of its formulators, along with its functional purpose of vocational and social preparedness. More specifically, the educational institution is responsible for providing students with substantive knowledge of culture, history, and virtue. By virtue, I refer to the instilling of a prescribed value system or spiritual tradition in the foundational principles of the school.

As examined in the examples of the Poro and Sande societies, African indigenous pedagogy purposefully situates the individual within a matrix of social integration. Through a phased process of education––first within the family, then in the "initiation school", and culminating in to a period of apprenticeship— the student is expected to become a productive member of society, capable of not only vocational proficiency, but also the continuity of cultural traditions. The social matrix that has been mentioned throughout this study is essential as it shapes the identity of youth in an overt manner. Cultural identity and social responsibility are values that are systematically relayed within the educational structure.

It is a significant testament to cultural survivals to note the reaffirmation of these educational traditions within the black independent schools in the U.S. Although limitations of space does not allow for a fuller exploration of the content of NCDC's curriculum, there are some clear linkages that can be established. The fundamental character of the IBI's was based on community involvement and control, self-reliance, and cultural identity. This is a key point of parallel. What made these schools so unique is that they were created by members of the black community (often parents) for the nurturing of Black youth and the fostering of a positive African identity. Parents and community members participated in the school, while the school offered services for the greater community. This practice fostered the creation of an extended family network between individuals who were internal and external to the institution.

As mentioned earlier, a key component of the independent black school was to counter European hegemony. The recognition of African subjugation by the structures of European indoctrination was central to the construction of the ethos that pervaded the Black independent school. This is a characteristic that is unique to these institutions, and should be understandable, in light of the unique social and historic context of the African-American population.

Elleni Tedla succinctly proposes the essential role that reflection on indigenous African educational models offer to the future of African education. Some of her words on the topic are worth quoting at length here:

> Africans need to ground the framework of their education on the posi-

> tivity of indigenous education and thought. Unless they build on Africa's cultural and historical roots, they will continue to marginalize and lock out the vast majority of African people who follow the traditional way of life. In order to empower Africa and its youth with the wisdom teachings of the ancestors, it is important to use a language that does not depreciate African experiences. . . . The viewing and measuring of other people's cultures must stop. New educational frameworks that are grounded in the positive aspects of Africa's cultural heritage should be created. Only in this way can Africans wrestle with the educational problems they are faced with as a result of colonialization and modernization (Tedla, 1995, p. 111).

It is essential for educators to develop their comprehension of an African educational tradition in order to prescribe a formula for educating African-American youth that is reflective of this African cultural ethos. We must ascertain the applicable elements of indigenous African education towards the creation of an African-centered educational model whose underlying precepts serve the specific needs (historical, geographic, cultural, and economic) of the varied populations throughout the continent and within the African diaspora.

References

Bekerie, A. (1998, March). Knowledge, Language, and Writing Systems: The Case of Ethiopia. *Africa Notes*, Cornell University: Institute for African Development, PAGE.

Bowers, M. A. (1984). *The Independent Black Educational Institution: An Exploration and Identification of Selected Factors that Relate to Their Survival*. Doctoral Dissertation, Atlanta University, Atlanta, GA.

Carruthers, J. & Karenga, M. (1986). *Kemet and the African Worldview*. Los Angeles: University of Sankore Press.

Doughty, J. (1973). *A historical analysis of Black education: Focusing on the contemporary independent Black school movement.* Dissertation, Ohio State University.

Erny, P. (1973). *Childhood and cosmos: The social psychology of the Black African child.* Washington, DC: Black Orpheus Press.

——. (1981). *The child and his environment in Black Africa: An essay on traditional education.* Nairobi: Oxford University Press.

Hilliard, A. (1998). *SBA: The reawakening of the African mind.* Gainseville: Makare Publishing.

James, G. (1992). G.M., *Stolen legacy*. Trenton: Africa World Press.

Kenyatta, J. (1962). *Facing Mount Kenya*. New York: Vintage Books.

Kifano, S. (1996). Afrocentric education in supplementary schools: Paradigm and practice at the Mary McLeod Bethune Institute. *Journal of negro education*, 65 (2).

Lee, C. D. (1992, Spring). Profile of an independent Black institution: African-centered education at work. *Journal of negro education*. 61 (2).

Moumouni, A. (1968). *Education in Africa*. New York: Praeger.

Ocitti, P. J. (1992). *An introduction to indigenous education in Sub-Saharan Africa*. The Hague: Centre for the Study of Education in Developing Countries.

Okpaku, J., Opubor, A. & Oloruntimehin. (Eds.). (1986). *The arts and civilization of Black and African peoples. Black civilization and pedagogy*-Lagos, Nigeria: The Centre for Black and African Arts and Civilization (6).

Scanlon, David G. (Ed.). (1964). *Traditions of African education.* New York: Teacher's College, Columbia University.

Smith, A.(1984). *Theory and praxis: A case study of Kawaida theory and the institute of positive education.* Ithaca: Cornell University, Master's Thesis.

Shujaa, M (Ed.). (1996). *Beyond desegregation: The politics of quality in African-American schooling.* Thousand Oaks, California: Corwin Press.

———. (1994). *Too much schooling, too little education.* Trenton: Africa World Press.

Tedla, E (1995). *Sankofa: African thought and education.* New York: Peter Lang.

Woodson, C. G. (1990). *The miseducation of the negro.* Trenton: First Africa World Press.

CHAPTER 8

IDEAL SPACES AND MULTICENTERED PLACES OF THE PLANTATION HOUSEHOLD

Lori Lee
Doctoral Candidate
Department of Anthropology
Syracuse University

Space defines landscape, where space combined with memory defines place.

Lucy Lippard

House and Household

Recent anthropological research has brought a renewed focus to using house or household as the unit of analysis. The terms 'house' and 'household' evoke images and conceptions of family. The term household in this essay is used in its anthropologically derived sense, to refer to individuals who are not necessarily consanguinely related nor living under one roof, but rather are identified as a unit by other means. More specifically, Fox-Genovese's definition of household is utilized as a heuristic device. She defines household as "units that pool economic resources or income" (1988, p. 86). She is careful to highlight, however, the importance of the ways in which household boundaries are drawn and the ways social change impacts the fluidity of those boundaries; differential contributions to the resource pool are also significant for understanding power relations within the household unit, which are correlated to those that exist in the society at large. Using this definition, households are revealed as micro-manifestations of contemporary social relations. The architectural form of the buildings that comprise the household represent the ideal, from the perspective and temporal framework of those who instructed them to be built. Yet the ideal rarely matches the real, as will be demonstrated by examining the experiences of those who lived within the built environment of plantation households.

Plantation Household

In *The House of Seven Gables*, one of Hawthorne's main characters remarked:

> We shall live to see the day, I trust, when no man shall build his house for posterity...It were better that they should crumble to ruin, once in every twenty years, or thereabouts, as a hint to the people to examine into and reform the institutions which they symbolize.

Houses are often built to last, and rarely offer an opportunity to evaluate the embedded changing social ideals in this manner. However, some structures are built to be temporary. One example of this type of historical structure was the cabin built for agricultural field slaves. These cabins were moved periodically, to provide proximity to the ground currently under cultivation. In some cases these cabins were consequently rebuilt every seven to ten years. Yet, the form of the structure changed very little over time, throughout the eighteenth century until the second decade of the nineteenth century (Vlach, 1993b). This lack of change in house form is as revealing of social attitudes as changing house forms. For those who ordered the cabins to be built, white slaveholders, the conception of 'slave' also remained fairly monolithic during this time period.

The slave house was one component of the built environment of a plantation household that was created according to the parameters set by the white slaveholder. Slave houses should not be examined as distinct slave households, independently of the broader plantation household of which they were an integral part. Understanding the ideology that is reflected in slave housing necessitates understanding the ideology of the broader plantation system. The antebellum southern slaveholding plantation was chosen as the locus for this analysis of domestic space.

Fox-Genovese defines a plantation household as a "slaveholding household that contained twenty or more slaves" (1988, p. 32). Slaveholding plantations were diverse, and it is not my goal to present them as monolithic or homogeneous. The size of the plantation household, the number of buildings associated with it, and the form that these took all depended on a number of temporal, regional, and socio-economic factors. While acknowledging this diversity, I will not attempt to address its breadth in this brief essay. Rather, I will analyze the buildings of a 'typical' plantation household, using Thomas Jefferson's Monticello as a model.

I chose the plantation household for a number of reasons. First, the plantation household extends beyond the boundaries of a single building to encompass many buildings and activity areas. Second, plantation households often existed in relative isolation, requiring, as they did, vast tracts of agricultural land. This degree of isolation and distance provides analytical, though not impermeable, boundaries for the household unit. Each household comprised a microcosm of southern society and conversely each was connected to the global marketplace via capitalism. I will analyze the plantation system as an organization of space; place provides the social parameters that give dimensions to space. Asking who owns, uses, and creates these spaces, how they change over time, and how social parameters transform them into places, will reveal the imagery of the plantation household as a multilocal, multicentered space.

Theory

The concept of multicenteredness was developed by Lucy Lippard. She writes that:

> The notion of multicenteredness is an extension of the often-abused notion of multiculturalism. Most of us move around a lot, but when we move we often come into contact with those who haven't moved around, or who have come from different places . . . .Each time we enter a new place, we become one of the ingredients of an existing hybridity, which is really what all "local places" consist of. By entering that hybrid, we change it; and in each situation we may play a different role. . . .S/he remains the same person, and may remain an outsider in both cases, but reciprocal identity is inevitably altered by the place, by the relationship to the place itself and the people who are already there. Sometimes the place or "nature" will provide nourishment that social life cannot (1997, p. 6).

Lippard uses this concept to explore multiple senses of place, or multilocality. She applies this concept to contexts very different from plantation households. Yet, this conception is useful to think through the complexities that exist in the contested landscape of plantation households. Some individuals, both black and white, entered the plantation household by being born into it or marrying into it, others by being sold into it. Each of these individuals, to a greater or lesser degree reciprocally altered and was altered by the place. Giddens and Bourdieu's structuration and practice theories, respectively, explicate this general process. The work of these authors, as well as the structural analysis of Deetz and Glassie, inform this essay. Structural analysis is used to interpret the architectural layout of the plantation household, followed by an analysis of the lived-experience using the concept of Lippard as a conceptual framework.

Architecture and Ideology of the Plantation Household

It merits reiterating that slaveholding plantations were very diverse in nature. However, for our purposes here, I have chosen one plantation, Monticello, as an example. I do not intend to suggest that this plantation is representative of all or even most slaveholding plantations, but it did have the full complement of buildings required for the self-sufficient functioning of a slave holding plantation that were found on a number of plantations. Additionally, this historical example is well documented. The architectural layout of Thomas Jefferson's Monticello aids in assessing the contemporary ideology of Southern U.S. slaveholders.

Looking at the architectural layout of Monticello, we're first drawn to the 'great house' or 'big house' that Jefferson built as a home for his family. The lure of this house is intentional. The landscape is designed so that 'the big house' is at the center; it is meant to be the focal point.

The house itself is symmetrical, built in a Georgian/Palladian style. The wings on the house both enhance this symmetry and emphasize the house's centrality. Much has been written about the Georgian style and its ideological correlates (e.g., Deagan, 1982; Deetz, 1996; Glassie, 1975). The reflection of ideology in architecture and other material culture remnants has been the focus of a branch of archaeology known as cognitive archaeology.

The goal of cognitive archaeology is to get at the cognitive maps of individuals (and the collective) through the analysis of material remains and/or written sources. The primary goal is to get at *how* they were thinking, not *what* they were thinking. James Deetz is the most widely cited practitioner of cognitive archaeology. Deetz' work demonstrates that insight can also be gained into the cognitive systems of the historic period through the use of material remains.

Deetz (1996) traced changes in the form and decoration of 18th and 19th century Anglo-American ceramics, gravestones, houses, and artifacts. Changes in the style of architecture reflect movement along the continuum between binary opposites, according to his work. Particularly, the shift from public to private, communal to individual, emotion to intellect, and nonsymmetry to symmetry are expressed in changing form and structure. These shifts parallel changes in ceramics and other artifacts analyzed by Deetz (Deetz 1993; Deetz 1996; Glassie 1975). Changes in artifact styles that correspond with transitioning ideologies support Donley-Reid's (1990) conception of active objects that are structured by behavior and the reciprocally structured behavior. In a broader context, Deetz (1988) interprets these stylistic changes as reflections of the shift from the medieval worldview to the Georgian worldview.

The medieval mindset was characterized by "an organic, informal, and unstructured pattern of organizing the material world. Houses were asymmetrical and grew in response to need rather than plan. Existence was corporate and privacy was not highly valued" (Deagan,

1982, p. 169). This cognitive model shifted in the mid-eighteenth century to "a new cognitive model known as the Georgian mindset, and characterized by an emphasis on the individual, separation of components, and tripartite symmetry" (ibid). An additional example that captures this change in ideology is the novel fascination with "whiteness" that coincides with this shift.

Whiteness in this sense refers to the color of choice for architecture and artifacts. The structuralists ground this fascination in an attempt to create a *cultural* veneer that masks the *natural* earthtones that were the stylistic choice under the medieval paradigm. However, within the plantation household setting, this can also be further interpreted as an increasing emphasis on 'whiteness' as it relates to skin color and ethnicity. In the late antebellum era, there were changes in the plantation landscape. These changes reflected changes in the ideology, or mental landscape, of the plantation owners. As war became more imminent, boundaries were challenged and transgressed. Boundaries are most apparent in times when they are threatened. The lines drawn between black and white were being etched deeper in the prelude to legislated segregation. In this time frame, the plantation household was a contested, multilocal space embedded with the conflicting cultural values of whites and blacks.

Monticello

Returning to the Monticello architectural layout, one recognizes not only that the architecture makes the house central, but the landscape as well. Jefferson chose a natural elevation and enhanced it through cultural modification. Jefferson made explicit, in both written records and architectural designs, that the main house was to be central and that the housing for the servants and the enslaved were to be hidden from view of the main house. At Monticello, the servants and the enslaved were housed in the south wing along Mulberry row, and in the field slave quarters at a distance from the main house. Within the main house itself, Jefferson very carefully designed stairways and passageways, and modified dumbwaiters to minimize the visible presence of servants and the enslaved within the home (Epperson, 2000). The Georgian design and the special attention given to spaces of the enslaved and servants emphasized control and privacy; both are themes of the Georgian mindset. They also emphasized the aesthetic over the practical, a nuance of the shift in value placed on culture over nature.

The main house is a symbol of the power and domination of the 'master', control over the 'natural' elements, including the enslaved. The enslaved were considered property, not unlike livestock. Often, their quarters would be placed adjacent to those reserved for livestock, further emphasizing this conceptual synonymity in the minds of slaveholders. Each architectural element, including distance and elevation, emphasized that the landowner/slaveholder was central and in control and the enslaved/servants were peripheral and 'invisible.' This was the slaveholder's ideal writ large. Yet the lived-experience posited a different perspective.

Lived-Experience of the Plantation Household

I chose to analyze the Works Progress Administration's Oklahoma Slave Narratives as a source for gaining insight into the lived-experience of the enslaved. The narratives that were analyzed consisted of one hundred and thirty interviews. I use the W.P.A. narratives in conjunction with archaeological and historical evidence to flesh out the skeleton created by the architectural evidence.

Based on architectural evidence alone, an archaeologist might determine that the main house on a plantation was the home of the 'elite' class, while the homes of the enslaved were homes of workers who were of a lower class. The main house was more complex and ornate; it was much larger, and it had much more internal complexity than houses for the enslaved. Houses that are uniform in size, such as those of the enslaved, suggest an egalitarian, relatively monolithic socioeconomic class to an archaeologist. These contrast starkly with the main house. What is being represented is the planter's ideal. For the planter, the enslaved were a fairly monolithic group that fit neatly into the category of 'property.' Slave houses were most commonly one-room cabins of approximately ten by ten feet, or duplexes shared by two families (Vlach, 1993b); the following are some descriptions of housing provided to the former slaves:

> "We lived in a one-room log hut" (p. 23). "The Perryman slave cabins was all alike—just two-room log cabins, with a fireplace . . ." (p. 30). "I remember the old slave cabins, just alike, setting in a row . . . the cabins was only one room, without windows, facing the south, with a fireplace in one end" (p. 45). "two room cabins built of logs, but the back cabin was just a shed that everyone called the lean-to"(p. 53).

As it can be clearly seen, slave houses were typically made of log or small frame and they were commonly placed in rows, at some distance from, but within view of, the main house (p. 53). Vlach suggests that these "linear plans and the insistent repetition of geometric shapes gave each [slave] quarter a regimented appearance intended to remind slaves of the strict rules of conduct that their masters sought to establish" (1993a).

Though plantation owners or overseers typically dictated the location and sizes of slave houses, it is probable that individuals had freedom to organize the space around and within their houses. Archaeological evidence reveals that yard space was an important living space utilized by the enslaved. Some people enclosed these spaces with fences. Fences create boundaries that separated "within from without" (Heath, 1999); they created a sense of personal space, or place. Not unintentionally, the preferred yard space was on that side of the house that was out of the view of the main house (Heath, *p.* 44); this removed the activities of the inhabitants from the panoptic view of the slaveholder. This 'panoptic view' is not an imposition of the twentieth century retrospective observer. Jefferson's library contained Jeremy Bentham's *Panopticon* as well as an autographed copy of Bentham's *Essays on Political Tactics* (Epperson, 2000). Historical documentation and Jefferson's architectural plans indicate that he planned to build an observatory tower on his plantation. It was, however, never built. Such a building was necessary on most plantations, where the houses for the enslaved were in view of the main house at a distance but one could never be certain whether or not one was being watched from within, thus creating the panoptic effect without additional buildings.

In addition to yard space, many enslaved had gardens or 'provisioning grounds,' which were intended to provide subsistence:

> Every slave had a patch of his own. . . . What he made on that patch belonged to him. . . . Every slave can fix up his own cabin anyway he wants to, and pick out a good place with a spring if he can find one (Baker and Baker, 1996, p. 226).

Personal garden plots are mentioned by a number of individuals: "All the slave families had a garden spot for they own self, take out what they need whenever they need it" (p. 53). These gardens and yard spaces provided 'autonomy' for the enslaved. The enslaved were allotted 'free' time to work these gardens; it is ironic that much of the 'free' time was actually spent on working. However, as these citations indicate, personal gardens provided a sense of ownership and private property that challenged the conception of enslavement. Though the slaveholders owned the spaces, the enslaved owned their own places within them. The slave quarter cabins thus provide evidence for multilocality. These spaces served different purposes for the slaveholder and the enslaved; they were at once places of enslavement as well as the locus for slave initiative.

Though the life of enslaved individuals was severely restricted by slaveholders, the archaeological record also provides evidence of autonomy in the form of material items. One individual mentioned a lock: "Slaves would have a little party; all the niggers [sic] would gather at one of the cabins and lock the door so the patterollers couldn't get in" (Brown and Brown, 1996, p. 425). Further evidence of autonomy is provided by objects that have been interpreted to have African religious significance, such as the hand charms found at the Hermitage and the cache of artifacts from the Levi Jordan plantation that Brown has interpreted to be a root-doctor's tool kit (Wilkie, 1995, p. 141). These artifacts reveal that some enslaved individuals were able to self-direct certain aspects of their own lives, even if it was at times done secretly.

Another element of private space was found inside some slave cabins in the Upper South, including Monticello. These were subterranean storage pits popularly known as 'root cellars.' Some of these pits were simply dug into the earth; others were lined with clay or brick. Heath (1999) notes that these structures are significant for understanding slave houses, because, unlike the buildings themselves, these spaces were actually designed by their inhabitants (p. 37).

Archaeologists disagree about the primary function of these spaces. Some argue that they were primarily places of storage, while others argue that their primary use was to hide things from the view of the slaveholder. A contemporary document from Poplar Forest, Thomas Jefferson's working plantation, complained that one of the enslaved laborers was taking all of the vegetables from the garden and then "carries them to his cabin and buries them in the ground" (Heath, 1999, p. 37).

Archaeological excavations of root cellars reveal many types of artifacts, including those that are suggested to have had African-American religious significance, such as pierced coins, quartz crystals, and Native American stone artifacts. It seems that these spaces were utilized for storage, illicitly or not, of personal belongings. This challenges the status of the enslaved as property, because property cannot legally *own* property. Root cellars were one means of converting a slave house into a home, a space into a place that became the center, with the inclusion of the yard space, in the lives of the enslaved.

Slave houses were not the only buildings in the plantation household where the dominance and centrality of the slaveholder was challenged or decentered. This process occurred daily in innumerable small and large ways. In some buildings it had more visibility than in others. Most conspicuous were the kitchens and smokehouses, but it also occurred within the main house. Slaves worked in the kitchens and smokehouses, buildings rarely entered by mistresses of plantation households. This nearly exclusive use of space transforms these buildings into slave places as well. Fox-Genovese expresses the relative gendered knowledge of these buildings: "As most slaveholding women knew, female house servants, notably cooks, were likely to know a great deal more about their craft than most mistresses—and frequently more about children, medicine, and life as well" (1988, p. 137). Slave 'mammies' were a hallmark of the plantation south. Not only did enslaved women know more about children in general, but also more about the children of the slaveholders than the slaveholders themselves, because the care of all children was entrusted to the enslaved.

Given that knowledge is power, this superior knowledge of enslaved women subverted, in some ways, the power of slaveholding women. The house has been traditionally interpreted as the sphere of women. The kitchen or hearth is seen to be central to that sphere. Slave women controlled these environments, placing them within this center. This power was not only a veneer in some cases but also had real exclusionary effects, as exemplified by one mistress who enjoyed cooking but complained about being frequently denied access to the kitchen by the cook.

Drawing on roots from their African past and charting routes for the American future, African-Americans had a definite impact on the landscape of the plantation south. John Vlach's (1993b) study of the southern shotgun house, for instance, establishes its origins in the compounds of West Africa, its creolization in French Haiti and New Orleans and its spread through the American South in the nineteenth century. Thompson contends that the American porch reflects another African influence, brought by slaves from the Kongo and Angola. Today, according to Prussin, when black people move into a white neighborhood, they often add front porches, turning the street "into a wholly different cultural situation, with dialogues crossing streets, porch to porch" (cited in Lippard, 1997, p. 30). Reciprocally, the plantation south had an impact on African-Americans. After emancipation, many African-Americans continued to build houses that were similar to those they lived in during the period of slavery, even when their economic status was elevated. They also used those same skills they were encouraged to cultivate under slavery, such as carpentry, artisanry, and domestic skills, to enter the job market after emancipation.

The plantation south had further repercussions for the maintenance of African-American culture and identity. The most pervasive, described in W.P.A. narratives, involved constructions of race and status. Several informants labeled diverse groups of whites as "poor white trash." For example, Hal Hutson commented, "All of us niggers [sic] called all the whites 'poor white trash.' The overseer was nothing but poor white trash. . ." (Baker and Baker, 1996, p. 206). With statements like this one, former slaves were altering the status of the whites they discussed and creating a status hierarchy, which placed these whites below their own status. This highlights the fact that identity is a relationship, with each variable of identity defined in relation to someone or something else. These relationships are understood in relation to oneself, by placing self in relation to others. Class and status do not exist without these relationships.

The household itself exists in relationships to larger social systems in which it is entrenched and these also impacted identity construction. Chaney McNair stated that, "Back in Fort Scott where I worked, there's this little girl, beautiful girl with long curls. I wondered why God made me black and ugly and this little girl so white" (McNair, p. 276). Ms. McNair was defining her self-conception in relation to the other child. Race, in the form of physical attributes, was the yardstick often used in the plantation South to define class and status. Several individuals made statements about skin color and its marked associations in the slave narratives. Della Fountain commented, "Father finally had to whup Joe to make him know he was black" (Fountain, p. 157), indicating that Joe was not acting in a way that was acceptable for someone who was black, and he had to be reminded of his status. As the statements of the formerly enslaved reveal, the behavioral correlates of ethnic markers were incorporated differentially by individuals. The built environment, some forms of material culture, and the slaveholders themselves served as agents that reminded each individual, daily, of his/her ideal place within the spaces of plantation culture. Yet, the lived experiences of the enslaved highlight the 'real' that complemented, challenged, and transmogrified the ideal, consequently decentering the built environment from the hierarchically arranged ideal spaces into inhabited, multicentered, multilocal places.

Conclusion

Plantation households provide an interesting inversion of those roles and spaces that were traditionally considered to be male and female, black and white. Racial slavery largely denied the gendered differences of field slaves and enslaved children. However, house slaves were elevated to a different status and their gender was taken into account. As demonstrated, female slaves were at the active core of the traditional female sphere—the kitchen. Yet, equally significant female slaveholders were active in the household management, which in this context included family business, as business was based on home production. This task was traditionally associated with men. Men were the titular and symbolic heads of the household, yet most of them were absent, frequently on business that took them away from the home. Thus, roles within the home were intertwined; the roles of the enslaved and slaveholders were enmeshed, creating a multilocality within the home.

The main house was not only a center for the slaveholding family, but also for house slaves who either lived, or spent most of their time, in it. But this centrality itself was transitory, based on context. Center depends on perspective and perspective changes with context. There are work centers, living centers, religious centers, family centers, etc. All household members, black and white, experienced these various centers differentially in the constructed spaces and places of the plantation household. Traces of these spaces and places are found occasionally in the form of extant buildings. Additional traces are detectable through archaeological means and in historical documents.

One's interpretation of a center is related to context. The contradictions embedded in the buildings of the plantation household are manifestations of the complex social relationships between slaveholders and the enslaved on a small scale and between blacks and whites, north and south on a larger scale. A peopled place, such as a plantation, does not necessarily represent a community. Rather, peopled places represent groups of individuals who share a common space, psychology, community, and history. As the collective nature of the plantation household suggests, the external worlds of the enslaved and the slaveholders were not independent spheres. However, the fact that individuals shared a space, does not imply that they shared either a sense of place or centeredness.

Social space exists not just in the external world, but internally—in the mind, as well. Levine (1977) cites a slave spiritual: "Got one mind for white folks to see, 'nother for what I know is me; He don't know, he don't know my mind" (p. 6). This duality, or double consciousness, hints at the different mental landscapes of antebellum blacks and whites, parts of which they attempted to hide from the surveillance of the other. In the space of the mind, as in the physical world, existed places that were exclusive to whites and blacks. Yet, just as in the external realm, there were many places that were shared by both. The worldview of each group impacted the other through daily interaction and relationships. It has been said that, "space speaks." In the spaces of the plantation household, spaces spoke multivocally and in numerous dialects. In some spaces, the dialect was pidgin, a language that was native to neither group but rather developed as a means of communicating between and within groups. In other spaces, the dialects were variants of Anglo-American, European, Native American, African, or African-American. These dialects, in the discourse of space, reflected the shared and unshared aspects of the mental landscapes that were forged in the vast space of the plantation household. These ideologies influenced the everyday lives of the inhabitants. Through actual, lived experiences, these individuals reciprocally impacted the ideals of the plantation household.

References

Anthony, C. (1976a). The big house and the slave quarters. Part I. Prelude to new world architecture. *Landscape,* 20, 8-19

——. (1976b) The big house and the slave quarters. Part II. African contributions to the new world. *Landscape,* 21, 9-15.

Baker, T. L. & Baker, J. (1996). *The WPA Oklahoma slave narratives.* Norman: University of Oklahoma Press.

Bakhtin, M. (1981). *The dialogic imagination.* Austin: University of Texas Press.

Chapman, W. (1991). Slave villages in the Danish West Indies. In *perspectives in vernacular architecture IV.* Carter, T. (Ed.). Columbia: University of Missouri Press:

Deagan, K. (1982). Avenues of inquiry in historical archaeology. *Advances in archaeological method and theory.* 5, 151-177. Schiffer, M. (Ed.). New York: Academic Press.

Deetz, J. (1996). In *Small things forgotten.* New York: Anchor Books Doubleday.

_____. (1993) *Flowerdew hundred.* Charlottesville: University Press of Virginia.

_____. (1988). Material culture and worldview in colonial Anglo-America. *The recovery of meaning.* Washington and London: Smithsonian Institution Press, 219-233.

______. (1967). *Invitation to archaeology.* Garden City: Natural History Press.

______. (1965). *The dynamics of stylistic change in Arikara ceramics.* Illinois Studies in Anthropology. Urbana: University of Illinois Press.

Donley-Reid, L. (1990). A structuring structure: the Swahili house. In *Domestic architecture and the age of space.* Kent, S (Ed.). Cambridge: Cambridge University Press.

Epperson, T. (2000). Panoptic Plantations. In *Lines that divide.* Delle,

J.; Mrozowski, S.; and Paynter, R. (Eds.). Knoxville: University of Tennessee Press.

Fox-Genovese, E. (1988). *Within the plantation household.* Chapel Hill: University of North Carolina Press.

Glassie, H. (1975). *Folk housing in middle Virginia*. Knoxville: University of Tennessee Press.

Heath, B. (1999). *Hidden lives*. Charlottesville: University Press of Virginia.

Levine, L. (1977). *Black culture and Black consciousness*. New York: Oxford University Press.

Lippard, L. (1997). *The lure of the local*. New York: The New Press.

Morton, P. (1996). (Ed.). D*iscovering the women in slavery*. Athens: University of Georgia Press.

Refrew, C. & Ezra Z. (1994). *The ancient mind: Elements of cognitive archaeology*. Cambridge: Cambridge University Press.

Vlach, J. (1993a). Not mansions . . . but good enough: Slave quarters as bi-cultural expression. In B*lack and White: Cultural interaction in the antebellum south.* Ownby, T. (Ed.). Oxford: University Press of Mississippi.

_______. (1993b). *Back of the big house*. Chapel Hill: University of North Carolina Press.

_______. (1990). *The Afro-American tradition in decorative arts*. Athens: University of Georgia Press.

Wilkie, L. (1995). Magic and Empowerment on the Plantation. *Southeastern archaeology*. 14 (2), 136-148.

CHAPTER 9

GETTING TO WORK IN SPITE OF THE ODDS:
COMMUTING PATTERNS OF AFRICAN AMERICANS IN ROCHESTER AND BUFFALO

Ibipo Johnston-Anumonwo
Associate Professor and Acting Chair
Geography Department
State University of New York at Cortland

Differences in the residential, employment, and household characteristics of African Americans and European Americans are well documented, but racial differences in the journey to work are still not well known. Compared to the past, there are now more studies about the commuting behavior of African Americans, but the specific impact of the exodus of jobs to suburban locations on African American men and women who live in inner cities is still understudied. One study of Buffalo, NY examined racial differences in commuting, but it focused only on women (Johnston-Anumonwo, 1995). In a follow-up study, men were included in the analysis (Johnston-Anumonwo, 1997), but both sets of inquiries concentrated on employment characteristics and ignored household characteristics which are likely to feature significantly for female workers.

The purpose of the present study is to examine the question of racial differences in locational access to jobs in Rochester, New York and draw parallels with the previous findings for Buffalo, New York. While presenting new data for Rochester, the study retains the critical inquiry on whether suburban employment imposes longer commute times on African Americans (Blacks) than on European Americans (Whites), but extends the inquiry to see if presence of children in the home affects workers' commute lengths. The results for Rochester strongly complement those for Buffalo and are consistent with the spatial mismatch hypothesis, which posited that African Americans suffer from distant suburban employment.

Following a review of the background literature of the journey to work for African Americans, a brief description of the study areas and data is provided, and then the findings are presented. The study's findings highlight the fact that African American men, and especially women, endure relatively long commutes to get to work in spite of transportation, locational and socioeconomic hindrances.

The Journey to Work for African Americans

Inquiries about racial disparities in employment accessibility are central to the spatial mismatch hypothesis (Kain, 1968). When it was first proposed in the 1960s, the hypothesis emphasized that employment opportunities are expanding in suburban locations, but because of continuing segregation of Blacks in inner cities, there exists a spatial mismatch, such that Black inner city residents face difficulties in reaching the growing job opportunities in suburbs (see Holzer, 1991). There has been little change in the residential segregation of Blacks between 1960s and now (Darden, 1990; Denton, 1994; Massey and Hajnal, 1995). This is true for the two Upstate New York counties selected for this study: Monroe County and Erie County (with Rochester and Buffalo as their respective central cities). Monroe County was 4.1 percent black in 1960 and 10.1 percent black in 1980, but 97.5 percent of the county's Black population in 1960 lived in the Rochester central city and in 1980, 87.7 percent did. A similar and even sharper pattern of disproportionate representation of Blacks in the central city prevails in Erie County. Erie County was 7 percent black in 1960 and 10.1 percent black in 1980 with 94.7 percent and 92.4 percent of the Black population respectively living in the central city in both time periods (U.S. Dept. of Commerce, 1963; 1983a; 1983b).

Early research on the effect of the exodus of jobs to suburban locations on the workplace accessibility of inner city African Americans rarely included female workers even though African American women have historically had high levels of labor force participation. Studies on the journey to work of female workers highlight two key trends. First, Black women have longer travel times than White women. Second, unlike White women who typically have shorter commutes than White men, the journey-to-work time of Black women is generally as long as that of Black men. For example, McLafferty and Preston (1991) report that in 1980, African American women in metropolitan New York spend ten minutes longer on the average for their home-to-work trip than European American women. Other studies report longer commuting times for African American men than European American men as well (e.g., Greytak, 1974; Ellwood, 1986; Leonard, 1987). The research finding that being Black is associated with longer work-trip times can readily be attributed to racial differences in the use of a private automobile, but racial differences in other locational and socioeconomic variables that are known to affect journey-to-work time are also relevant.

The journey-to-work literature is replete with findings that workers who use public transportation usually spend a longer time getting to work than those who use a private car. Similarly, those earning high incomes have longer work-trip times than those who have low incomes (e.g., U.S. Department of Commerce, 1979, 1982; Hanson & Johnston, 1985; Pisarski, 1987; Gordon et al., 1989; Dubin, 1991; Cooke & Shumway, 1991; Ihlanfeldt, 1992; McLafferty & Preston, 1992). The evidence about the role of child status on commuting time is mixed. But in a study on women's work-trip time across racial groups, Preston et al. (1993) found that Black mothers had longer work trips than White mothers.

Although the spatial mismatch hypothesis specifies the growing trend of workplaces in suburban locations, there are still very few empirical inquiries of the impact of suburban workplace destination on the commuting behavior of African American men and women. One study of race and commutes in Detroit found that in 1980, Blacks who worked in the Central Business District worked closer to home than Whites, but for suburban destinations Blacks commuted longer than Whites (Zax, 1990). This different commuting pattern, according to Zax, suggests that racial residential segregation restricts Black suburbanization and contributes to longer commutes for Blacks who have to work in suburban Detroit.

But disagreement persists about whether or not African American workers in U.S. metropolitan areas are more distant from centers of employment than European Americans are. This paper reports on an empirical inquiry about the question of the spatial mismatch of African Americans resident in Monroe County (Rochester) and Erie County (Buffalo) New York. Using data from the 1980 census, the study investigates whether African American working men and women in Rochester and Buffalo experience greater commuting difficulties than European Americans while taking into consideration racial differences in key factors that affect work-trip length—namely, automobile use, location, income and child status.

In Rochester and especially in Buffalo, the majority of African Americans still live in segregated neighborhoods. In fact, Buffalo remains a city with one of the highest levels of racial residential segregation in the United States *(USA Today,* 1991). Both Rochester and Buffalo are representative examples of cities that experienced massive de-industrialization starting in the 1970s when manufacturing jobs slumped in the urban economy and moved out of the central city to the suburbs. The prevalent trend was one of job decentralization. Thus, one can expect to find evidence of journey-to-work constraints for inner city African American residents of Rochester and Buffalo.

A specified set of research questions is examined. Do African American men and women in Rochester and Buffalo spend a longer time commuting than European American men and women? Does unequal access to private automobiles lead to differences in the journey-to-work time of African Americans and European Americans? If differential access to private automobiles is responsible for longer commute times among African Americans, then there should be no racial difference in the work-trip times of private auto users. Is location of the workplace responsible for any racial difference in commuting? Lastly, is there any difference in the commute times of African American and European American workers with similar income and child status?

Description of the Data

The range of factors necessary for a full understanding of racial disparities in commuting means that detailed data about working individuals are preferred. The Public Use Microdata Samples (PUMS), which is a database with information on individuals' socioeconomic characteristics and their locational and work-trip attributes, meets this requirement. The 1980 five percent Public Use Microdata Samples (PUMS) for Monroe County and Erie County, New York is used for this study. In 1980, for the first time, the census included information on journey-to-work time, i.e., the time spent traveling from home to work. Travel time, the actual number of minutes spent from home to work as reported by the respondent, is thus the measure available for work-trip length. The travel mode is the means of transportation that the worker uses to get to work e.g., public transportation or private automobile. Because of budget cut backs, the Census Bureau processed only half of the responses about the journey to work for the 1980 census, so the sample sizes are small.

While socioeconomic and demographic information provided in the PUMS is quite detailed, detail information about location is not provided in these public use data sets in order to protect the confidentiality of respondents. Only two very broad locational categories are available for this study—central city location and non-central city location. In other words, locations outside the census-designated central city limits are classified simply as non central city locations (i.e., suburb). Income, the worker's annual salary in 1979, is divided into two categories: (a) below $10,000 or (b) $10,000 and above. Child status is also divided into two categories by focusing on the presence of children in the home: (a) households with no children and (b) households with school-aged children. The Census Bureau specifies race as White, Black, etc. based on respondents' self-classification (U.S. Department of Commerce, 1983c). Only White and Black employed males and females who are sixteen years old and older are selected for the study.

The five percent PUMS is used so that the study would include a large number of Black workers in these two predominantly White Upstate New York counties. In the Monroe County sample, there are

3,755 European American (White) men, 261 African American (Black) men, 2,769 European American (White) women and 282 African American (Black) women. In the Erie County sample, there are 4,876 European American (White) men, 304 African American (Black) men, 3,551 European American (White) women and 321 African American (Black) women. These then are the four race-sex groups that constitute the basis of the comparisons in the study. Racial differences in journey-to-work time are assessed using simple t-test statistics. Only racial differences that are significant at 95 percent level of confidence and above are reported. The results are presented next starting with racial differences in means of transportation used for the work trip.

Findings

African Americans Rely More on Public Transportation

African American workers in Rochester and Buffalo used public transportation more than European Americans did in 1980. Indeed, a much higher proportion of African American women than European American women used public transportation for their work trip. In Monroe County, 24.8 percent of African American women used public transportation compared to 7.8 percent of European American women, while 12.3 percent of African American men used public transportation compared to only 3.9 percent of European American men. In Erie County 33.6 percent of African American women used public transportation compared to 9.9 percent of European American women, while 11.8 percent of African American men used public transportation compared to only 4.1 percent of European American men. This greater reliance of African Americans on public transportation conforms with well documented patterns, and it is expected to increase their average work-trip time since public transportation is typically a slower and more time consuming mode of travel.

African Americans Spend More Time for the Work Trip

When average work-trip times are examined, the work trips of African American men and women in Monroe County and Erie County are longer than for European American men and women (see Tables 1 and 2 for racial differences in commuting time in Rochester and Buffalo respectively). African American men in Rochester spend 21.4 minutes versus 19.4 minutes for European American men, while the African American women spend 24.4 minutes versus 17.4 minutes for European American women (t-values are significant at p=<0.01). This means that African American women in Rochester spend 7 minutes longer on the average for their work trip than European American women counterparts. There is also a significant racial gap among women in Buffalo where African American women spend 22.8 minutes versus 18.1 minutes for European American women.

Since more African Americans use public transportation, and since research consistently confirms the pronounced lengthening effect of public transportation on workers' commute times (e.g., U.S. Department of Commerce, 1982; Taylor & Ong, 1995; McLafferty & Preston, 1992), one should make allowance for this, and examine only workers with the same mode of travel. For the remainder of the study, all comparisons about racial differences in work-trip time are restricted to respondents who use a car.

When the work-trip times of private automobile users are compared, there are no remarkable racial differences among men in Rochester and Buffalo, or among women in Buffalo; while the racial gap among women in Rochester reduces to four minutes: i.e., 20.9 minutes for Black women and 16.8 minutes for White women (note however, that this reduced difference is still statistically significant p=<.01, —Table 1).

The disproportionate use of public transportation by African Americans therefore accounts to a large measure for their relatively longer travel times. Greater dependence on public transportation does not however offer complete explanation for continuing longer work-trip times of many African Americans because, when the samples are examined further by workplace location or by income and child status, significant racial differences persist in the commuting time of some auto users. In spite of the use of a private automobile, some African Americans spend a longer time than European American counterparts. The continuing racial differences in travel time among auto users with similar locational and socioeconomic profiles are reported below. First, we look at workers with the same workplace location.

Some African Americans Spend a Longer Time than European Americans with the Same Workplace Location

If a work trip begins and ends in the same area, it is likely to take a shorter time than if the trip starts in one area and ends in another area. For instance, trips that start in the central city and end in the suburbs may take longer than those that begin in the central city and end in the central city. That is, intra-area trips typically take a longer time than opposite direction trips (Hanson & Johnston, 1985; Johnston-Anumonwo, 1995). Racial differences in geographic location of the home and workplace are likely to contribute to racial gaps in commute times, so it is more accurate to compare workers with the same home and work location.

Primarily because of insufficient sample sizes for African Americans who reside outside the central cities of both Rochester and Buffalo, and precisely because the spatial mismatch hypothesis is concerned with the situation of inner city workers, I restrict the remaining comparisons on location effects to respondents with central city homes.

African American male and female auto users who live in the central city and whose workplaces are in Rochester central city, spend longer times than European American counterparts. In Buffalo, African American male auto users whose workplaces are in the central city also spend a longer time than European American men with central city workplaces. According to the findings then, African American respondents who reside and work in central city locations are seen to spend a longer time than the European Americans.

African American Women with Suburban Work Destinations Spend a Longer Time Getting to Work

When the focus is on those workers with non-central city destinations (i.e., reverse commuters) for both study areas, it is only among women that a very large and significant racial gap in commuting time is observed. African American women residing in Rochester and who commute to work locations outside the central city spend almost eight minutes longer than European American counterparts (26.6 minutes compared with 18.9 minutes). In Buffalo, African American female reverse commuters spend almost six minutes longer than European American counterparts (26.1 minutes compared with 20.3 minutes). It appears that unlike Black men, Black women bear a bigger cost for work trips to non-central city destinations when compared to their White counterparts. Generally therefore, the African American women auto users with work destinations in the *suburbs* of Monroe County and Erie County spend considerable time commuting to work. In addition, some other African American women spend considerably longer time getting to work as discussed next.

Low Income African American Women and Working Mothers Spend a Longer Time Getting to Work

The two socioeconomic factors examined are income and the presence of children in the household. The common expectations are that low wage earners will be less able to afford long commutes, and workers with high levels of domestic duties will try to meet time pressures by avoiding time-consuming commutes. African American and European American workers usually differ in income level and household composition. African American workers should have shorter commutes if their lower incomes disallow long commutes, or if they have greater domestic obligations, such as household responsibilities associated with children, that places more demand on their time.

First, racial disparities in work trip length of workers in the two income groups are examined. African American low income female workers in Monroe County spend a longer time for their work trip than European American low income female workers (22.2 minutes versus 15.3 minutes—significant at p=<.01 in Table 1). There are no other significant racial disparities among workers with similar income levels. The substantial racial difference in commute time among Monroe County's low-income women (seven minutes) is noteworthy. It indicates that these Black women are enduring relatively long commutes to low-waged jobs.

For child status, the commute times of workers in households without children are compared with those in households with children (school-aged children). Significant racial differences are observed only among women. African American mothers in Monroe County spend five minutes longer time than European American mothers (20.6 versus 15.4 minutes (significant at p=<.01); and African American mothers in Erie County spend almost four minutes longer time than European American mothers (19.7 versus 16.0 minutes [significant at p=<.01 in Table 1]).

This set of findings runs contrary to common expectations that those workers earning low incomes or with household responsibilities for children will have shorter commutes. In spite of the constraints, low-income African American women in Monroe County and those with children in both counties put up with longer commutes than their European American counterparts.

Keeping in mind that since these comparisons are conducted only for auto users, the findings show that even when access to an automobile is not a hindrance, many African American workers (especially female workers) in Rochester and Buffalo still bear a bigger time cost than European Americans. Also, with the widest racial gap being observed among women, the results counter the welfare queen stereotype of Black women since the women in the analysis are all employed. Lastly, although the time differences may appear small, the time cost for African American workers is not trivial. For instance the cumulative time of the two-way work trip is quite considerable, and it amounts to time lost from other tasks. In the final section below, I elaborate on the implications of these findings.

Conclusions and Discussion

According to the findings of this study, African Americans in Monroe and Erie counties as a group do have longer commutes than do European American workers. As expected, the reason lies largely in the greater reliance of African Americans on public transportation. Once travel mode is taken into account, the racial difference in commuting time among most auto users is negligible. Taylor and Ong (1995) also note that among workers who have access to automobiles, there is a reduced racial gap in travel time.

By failing to conduct race-specific and sex-specific comparisons, many previous studies masked continuing significant differences among subgroups of workers, and by ignoring the impact of workplace location on the duration of the work trip, racial disparities in locational access to jobs are understated. Hence, one main contribution of this study is to demonstrate that taking into account the workplace location provides a clear assessment of the existence and nature of commuting difficulties that African Americans face when they live in central cities and/or work in suburbs.

Most of the African Americans in both counties do work in the central cities. And while the observed racial disparities are less pronounced among men, Black men who live and work in the central cities still spend about three minutes more for their work trip than do White counterparts, but note that the average trip length is under 20 minutes. Among women in Rochester, Black women with intra-city trips also spend a longer time than the White counterparts. But the more striking finding for African American women is the substantially longer commuting time of reverse commuters (approximately 26 minutes). Indeed, a central line of inquiry in the study is the specific impact of suburban employment on the commutes of African Americans. The need to work in suburban destinations (i.e., outside the central city) of Rochester and Buffalo in 1980 imposes a disproportionate commuting time burden on inner city Black women than on White women. This study thus provides support of a spatial mismatch in Black women's geographical access to employment in Monroe and Erie counties in 1980. It validates the early conclusions of McLafferty and Preston (1991) that many African American women experience a very insidious form of spatial mismatch and face significant transportation and locational barriers in traveling to work.

The longer times spent by Black women may be expected to decrease if Black women have more access to private automobiles. However, the longer commutes of African American women who reverse commute suggest that it is reasonable to speculate that as employment opportunities continue to expand in suburban locations and not in central city locations, African American women (even those who use a car) are still likely to suffer the inconvenience of significantly longer commutes to suburban workplaces than European American women.

There is reason to believe that concerns about spatial mismatch remain current in U.S. cities. For example, a recent study presents evidence of spatial mismatch as well as evidence of the negative treatment of Blacks by suburban police officers and White residents as testimony of the multiple barriers facing African Americans in gaining access to employment opportunities in suburban Detroit. Similarly, in

Buffalo, the current validity of both an automobile mismatch and a spatial mismatch for African American women proved tragically true in the case of a Black woman who was killed while crossing an expressway in suburban Buffalo on her way to the shopping mall where she was employed. This particular case had racist underpinnings because the management of the suburban mall seemed to have pursued explicit policy decisions preventing buses coming from inner city Buffalo from stopping at the mall.

One should note that the results for these two Upstate New York cities corroborate those of other cities. For example, Cooke and Shumway's (1991) analysis of 1980 PUMS data for three large Midwest cities—Chicago, Cleveland and Detroit—revealed that central city residents experience constrained access to employment. If more jobs were available in central cities, there would be less need to reverse commute to reach suburban jobs. Alternatively, if Blacks had unhindered access to suburban housing, the racial disparity in locational access to jobs would be lessened. It is inaccurate to minimize the importance of locational access to Black employment outcomes, and it would be premature to abandon inquiries about the possible role of location in the mismatch of workers and jobs.

Apart from difficult access to suburban work destinations, the study also finds evidence of other travel time constraints for Black women. Specifically, in Monroe County, it is the low income Black women who have relatively long commutes, while in both Monroe County and Erie County, it is African American mothers who have relatively long commutes. It is clear from the study that not all African American women face the constraints of long journeys to low-paying jobs, and not all African American mothers have very long travel times. But the emerging profile of some Black women who combine parenthood with wage earning and endure long commutes to suburban destinations suggest that policy makers need to recognize the efforts of these workers and reward their diligence with remunerative job opportunities.

It is essential to stress that like all studies that use commuting data, this study understates the general problem of access to jobs since it excludes the unemployed, many of whom are unemployed probably due to locational constraints. However, the use of journey-to-work data, and the focus on travel time in particular is appropriate. Time is a resource. In some instances, time is money, therefore lost time is lost money. Much of the extra time that African Americans in Monroe and Erie counties spend longer than European Americans range from 3 minutes to over 6 minutes. Using simple calculations, this can be extrapolated into between 6 minutes and 12 minutes per day, or between 30 minutes and 60 minutes a week, or between 25 and 50 hours a year—-the equivalent of about a week. Cast in this light, the longer commute times of African Americans can be interpreted as constituting a race tax burden.

In conclusion, this analysis of work trips in Rochester and Buffalo complements as well as expands the empirical literature on racial differences in the commuting patterns of American urban residents. The study has shed additional light on analyses about differences in commuting by highlighting the significance of several factors—race, gender, means of transportation, residence, workplace location, income, and presence of children—in the job access constraints of groups of African Americans. These factors have to remain central in upcoming analyses of other more up-to-date data particularly for informing contemporary policy debates such as welfare reform. For now, the evidence from Rochester and Buffalo about the journey to work of African American workers in spite of transportation, location, income or household responsibility constraints strongly counters prevailing stereotypes of welfare dependent African Americans.

References

Cooke T. J. and J. M. Shumway. (1991). Developing the spatial mismatch hypothesis: Problems of accessibility to employment for low wage central city labor. *Urban Geography* 12, 310-323.

Darden, J. T. (1990). Differential access to housing in the suburbs. *Journal of Black Studies* 21, 15-22.

Denton, N. A. (1994). Are African Americans still hypersegregated? In *Residential apartheid: The American legacy*. Bullard, R. D.; Grigsby, J. E. III and Lee, C. (Eds.) 49-81. Los Angeles: Center for Afro-American Studies, University of California.

Dubin, R. (1991). Commuting patterns and firm decentralization. *Land Economics* 67, 15-29.

Ellwood, D. T. (1986). The spatial mismatch hypothesis: are there teenage jobs missing in the ghetto? In Freeman, R. B. and Holzer, H. J. (Eds.). *The Black youth employment crisis,* 147-187. Chicago: University of Chicago Press.

Gordon, P., Kumar, A. & Richardson, H .W. (1989). The spatial mismatch hypothesis: Some new evidence. *Urban Studies* 26, 315-26.

Greytak, D. (1974). The journey to work: Racial differences and city size. *Traffic Quarterly*, 28, (2), 241-256.

Hanson, S., & Johnston, I. (1985). Gender differences in work-trip length: explanations and implications. *Urban Geography* 6, 193-219.

Holzer, H. J. (1991). The spatial mismatch hypothesis: What has the evidence shown? *Urban Studies* 28, (1), 105-22.

Ihlanfeldt, K. R. (1992). Intraurban wage gradients: Evidence by race, gender, occupational class, and sector. *Journal of Urban Economics* 32, 70-91.

Johnston-Anumonwo, I. (1995). Racial differences in the commuting behavior of women in Buffalo, NY, 1980-1990. *Urban Geogra-*

phy 16, 23-45.

______. (1997). Race, gender, and constrained work trips in Buffalo, NY, 1990. *Professional Geographer* 49, 306-317.

Kain, J. (1968). Housing segregation, Negro employment, and metropolitan decentralization. *Quarterly Journal of Economics* 82, (2), 175-97.

Leonard, J. S. (1987). The interaction of residential segregation and employment discrimination. *Journal of Urban Economics*, 21, 323-346.

Massey, D. S., and Z. L. Hajnal. (1995). The changing geographic structure of black-white segregation in the United States. *Social Science Quarterly* 76, (3), 527-42.

McLafferty, S., and V. Preston. (1991). Gender, race and commuting among service sector workers. *Professional Geographer* 43, 1-15.

______. (1992). Spatial mismatch and labor market segmentation for African American and Latina women. *Economic Geography* 68, 406-31.

Pisarski, A. (1987). *Commuting in America*. Westport, CT: Eno Foundation.

Preston, V., S. McLafferty, and E. Halmilton. (1993). The impact of family status on black, white and Hispanic women's commuting. *Urban Geography* 14, 228-50.

Taylor, B. D., and P. M. Ong. (1995). Spatial mismatch or automobile mismatch? An examination of race, residence and commuting in US metropolitan areas. *Urban Studies* 32, 1453-73.

U.S. Department of Commerce. (1963). *U.S. Census of Population: 1960, Volume 1, Characteristics of the Population, Part 34, New York*. Washington, DC: U.S. Bureau of the Census.

U.S. Department of Commerce. (1979). *The Journey to Work in the United States: 1975*. Current Population Reports P-23, Special Studies, 99. Washington, DC: U.S. Bureau of the Census.

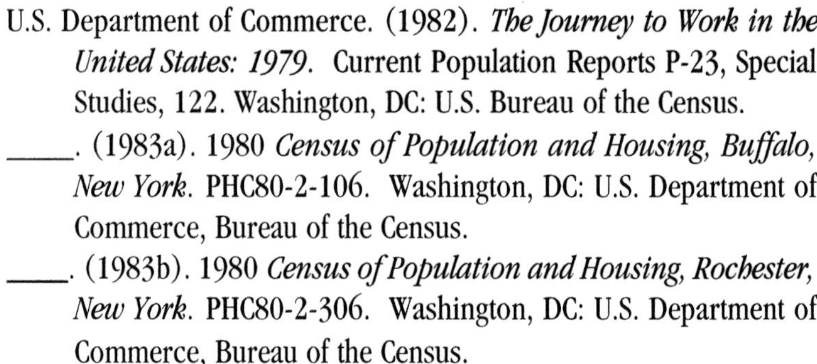

U.S. Department of Commerce. (1982). *The Journey to Work in the United States: 1979*. Current Population Reports P-23, Special Studies, 122. Washington, DC: U.S. Bureau of the Census.

_____. (1983a). 1980 *Census of Population and Housing, Buffalo, New York*. PHC80-2-106. Washington, DC: U.S. Department of Commerce, Bureau of the Census.

_____. (1983b). 1980 *Census of Population and Housing, Rochester, New York*. PHC80-2-306. Washington, DC: U.S. Department of Commerce, Bureau of the Census.

_____. (1983c). *Census of Population and Housing, 1980: Public-Use Microdata Samples, Technical Documentation*. Washington, DC: U.S. Bureau of the Census.

U.S.A. Today. (1991). By the numbers, tracking segregation in 219 metro areas. November 11, 3a.

Zax, J. F. (1990). Race and commutes. *Journal of Urban Economics* 28, 336-348.

TABLE 1

AVERAGE WORK–TRIP TIME (MINUTES) MONROE COUNTY, 1980

		Black Men	White Men		Black Women	White Women	
Full Sample	N	261	3755		282	2769	
Travel Time		21.4	19.4	**	24.4	17.4	**
Auto Users Only	N	201	3421		197	2394	
Travel Time		19.9	19.3	ns	20.9	16.8	**
Work Location							
Central City Residence to Central City Workplace	N	114	529		107	380	
Travel Time		17.5	14.7	**	18.0	13.9	**
Central City Residence to Suburban Workplace	N	35	206		48	142	
Travel Time		22.3	20.4	ns	26.6	18.9	**
Income Status							
Low Income (<$10,000)	N	41	599		82	1261	
Travel Time		18.6	16.5	ns	22.2	15.3	**
High Income (=>$10,000)	N	154	2641		108	1047	
Travel Time		20.5	20.0	ns	20.1	18.5	ns
Child Status							
No Child in Household	N	53	1284		49	959	
Travel Time		20.6	19.5	ns	20.2	17.9	ns
Child Present	N	63	1089		76	778	
Travel Time		21.5	19.1	ns	20.6	15.4	**

** - difference is significant at 95 percent level of confidence or higher.
ns - difference is not significant.

TABLE 2

AVERAGE WORK–TRIP TIME (MINUTES) ERIE COUNTY, 1980

		Black Men	White Men		Black Women	White Women	
Full Sample	N	304	4876		321	3551	
Travel Time		22.5	20.9	ns	22.8	18.1	**
Auto Users Only	N	241	4442		186	2924	
Travel Time		22.0	20.9	ns	18.5	17.1	ns
Work Location							
Central City Residence to Central City Workplace	N	121	596		133	477	
Travel Time		19.7	16.4	**	16.1	15.4	ns
Central City Residence to Suburban Workplace	N	88	373		34	173	
Travel Time		24.6	24.0	ns	26.1	20.3	**
Income Status							
Low Income (<$10,000)	N	66	889		99	1902	
Travel Time		19.5	17.7	ns	17.6	16.0	ns
High Income (=>$10,000)	N	168	3335		79	906	
Travel Time		22.3	21.9	ns	19.2	19.7	ns
Child Status							
No Child in Household	N	88	1803		60	1281	
Travel Time		22.5	20.8	ns	18.8	18.0	ns
Child Present	N	72	1438		78	936	
Travel Time		21.4	20.9	ns	19.7	16.0	**

** - difference is significant at 95 percent level of confidence or higher.

ns - difference is not significant.

CHAPTER 10

DEHUMANIZATION OF AFRICAN WOMEN:

An Analysis of Widowhood Practices Among the Igbos of Nigeria

Davidson C. Umeh
Associate Professor
John Jay College of Criminal Justice
City University of New York

Introduction

The death of a spouse is a very stressful event. When a spouse dies, a partner loses a best friend, a companion and a confidant. The stress of the loss of a husband is increased by the rituals of widowhood practices in Africa. Women in African society are deprived of basic human rights through widowhood practices. According to Thomas et. al. (1988, p. 225) the loss of a spouse is consistently rated as one of the most stressful of life's events. This psycho-physiological response is due to the realization of the vacuum created by the departure of one's partner.

The Igbo people have a set of mechanisms that glorify men to the detriment of the self-esteem and self-image of women. The patrilineal custom in Igbo society and the emphasis on the importance of husbands have helped to encourage the oppression of women. In support of the concept of the importance of husbands in Igbo society, Okoye (2000, p. 3) identifies the following beliefs through such statements as *"di bu ugwu nwanyi," "mma nwanyi bu di," and "agbala nwe nwanyi bu di ya,"* which could be literally translated as "marriage is the dignity of womanhood," "a woman's beauty is her husband," and "the god that owns a woman is her husband." Okoye further emphasizes that it is marriage alone that confers a measure of status on women. Hence, when a man dies, Igbo culture strips the widow of self-esteem as shown through widowhood practices. In this cultural construct, women accept many dehumanizing rituals expected of them by the society at the death of their husband. It is, therefore, essential that, rather than blame women for their roles in enforcing the harmful widowhood rituals on other women, we must sympathize and work with the women to re-educate the entire society.

There is evidence of several efforts made in Nigeria to alleviate various devastating health problems that affect the members of the community. Okafor (1997, p. 105) states that the Federal Government of Nigeria adopted a multi-sectorial approach in an effort to prevent HIV/AIDS. The government involved the non-governmental and private organizations in the process of HIV/AIDS education and prevention programs. Yet, there is no concerted effort to address many of the social, physical, emotional, mental and spiritual health issues that emanate from widowhood practices. For example, the problems of widows in

Igbo society have been ignored and swept under the carpet for centuries. The apathy and nonchalance to the ordeals of widows in Igbo society are influenced by the fear of discussing issues about death. Okafor (1993) states that men and women exhibit the same characteristics of avoiding discussion on death and that the subject of death is treated as a taboo (p. 271). The myth of men's superiority to women is another major factor in the inhumane treatment of women in African societies. Tobrise (1998) states that Nigeria, for example, represents a terrain of diverse cultures and traditions as regards to women (p. 4). As a result, women have for long been "scapegoats" of cultural practices. The idea of female marginalization in African cultures, on the one hand, is borne out of the age-long men's control of women and myths about female inferiority. Prevailing cultural and traditional rituals, which imprison wives when the husband dies, have devastating implications on the health of the widows.

There is an overwhelming number of widows in Nigeria, Zambia, Kenya, as well as other nation-states—hence the need for urgent attention to this issue. Chen (1995) states that in Asia and Africa, widowhood affects many women at younger ages as compared to women in the developed world (p. 100). In many countries in these regions, up to 20-25 percent of women aged 45-59 are widowed, and in some countries up to 5 percent of even younger women, aged 20-44, are widows. This data is not surprising because of the age disparity between men and their wives in Africa. It is common for older men to marry women as young as fifteen years of age.

The ordeal of widows in Igbo society is bound in culture and traditions. Culture is the total way of life of a group of people. Culture influences people's behavior, music, language, beliefs, education and other forms of thoughts and practices. Cultural beliefs prescribe the rules and regulations that control acceptable behavior in a given society. In the present era, among many of Igbos of Nigeria, women are highly educated and competent; yet there is a conflict between the proscribed cultural expectations and their western world views. Ayisi (1989) states that in Southern Africa, women are often caught in a conflict between tradition and modernity, with widows particularly being the victims of customary practices which deprive them of human dignity (p. 65). Legal efforts to protect women's rights must be initiated and supported, along with attempts to change cultural attitudes.

Culture is dynamic and it is supposed to keep pace with developments in the society. Cultural changes and progressive attitudes are mainly dependent on the custodians of the culture. However, significant persons in Igbo society appear not to be interested in making changes to improve the lot of women, especially widows. According to Meena (1992), culture has been used to justify the subordinate position of women in the household, a factor which discriminates against women, as regards to property ownership (p. 10). Culture has also been used to justify the existing unequal division of labor. Some cultural norms, with regard to age at marriage and marriage rights, have also limited women's participation in formal schooling. African states have claimed that African culture is dynamic and change-oriented. When it comes to issues of gender inequity, African cultures seem to be static and protecting a culture of oppression.

In assessing the cultural expectations of the women in the event of the death of a spouse, one wonders why men are not expected to go through similar rituals in the event of their wives' death. Henderson (1972) states that, on the death of a woman, the mourning period for her husband is expected to be brief and relatively burdenless (p. 229). This is another example of the asymmetrical relationship between husband and wife. A wife's funeral duties are quite different from that of a husband's rites. The only justifiable reason appears to be that men are the custodians of the culture and they effect changes that maintain male superiority over women in the status quo. Korieh (1998) contends that across the world, women are denied equal rights before the law in the name of culture or tradition and are targeted because they protest against unacceptable practices and campaign for change in the society (p. 20).

Widowhood Practices

Widowhood practices are the rituals a woman undergoes from the time of the husband's death to a period of three months to one year. Korieh (1996) defines the practice as sets of expectations as to actions and behavior of the widow, actions by others towards the widow, and rituals performed by, or on behalf of the widow, from the time of the death of her husband (p. 19). Widowhood practices are similar in most Igbo communities with little variations from one group to the other. Okoye (1995) identified the following factors that influence widowhood practices in Africa: cosmology, religion, illiteracy, low concept of women, male dominance, *umuada* (daughters of the lineage), female passivity, inheritance and marriage laws of the land, the extended family system, and poverty (p. 129). Women are expected to perform dehumanizing rituals to pay their respect to the dead husband. Korieh (1996) confirms that widowhood throughout Africa is a period of hardship and deprivation that includes varying degrees of physical seclusion and calls for purification (p. 3).

Levirate

The levirate custom of widow inheritance is the co-habitation of a widow with her brother-in-law as a substitute for her deceased husband (Kirwen, 1979). A widow in Igbo society in this 21st Century is still expected to be inherited by her brother-in-law or any close relation. The distressing part of the custom is that the widow is not even consulted in arriving at the decision. Nwapa (1970) argues in her novel,

Idu, that the custom of widow inheritance adds insult to injury to a grieving widow who could be still very much in love with her deceased spouse.

At the present era, the practice of wife/husband selection by parents is outdated. Young men and women often date and get to know each other before marriage. But prerogative of choice is negated when the spouse dies and the widow is left to accept whoever the family assigns to her. Arranged marriages by parents and family members have been shown to be problematic for the couple because of a lack of understanding and love for each other. A case in point is a young Turkish man, Bunyamin, who respected the parents' wishes and married a young woman, Sorgul. When he felt dissatisfied with his marriage and considered divorce, Bunyamin stated that he was living his life for his parents to satisfy them but he saw that he needed to live for himself and could not do that without leaving Sorgul the wife (*New York Times*, 2000, p. A10). The predicament of Bunyamin who was forced to marry Sorgul can be likened to the widow in Igbo society who must succumb to any man arranged to inherit her. The man selected may sometimes be very much below the social and educational status of the widow and she may not love him. But all these do not really matter because as an Igbo adage states: *"Nwoke Adi Njo,"* that is, a man is never ugly. Widows in a levirate arrangement are sad and distressed, but they have few recourses because they have to accept the traditional practice of Igbo people or risk ostracization.

The practice of levirate among the Igbos is established to protect the widow and her children. However, Blair et. al. (1997) pointed out that the tradition of requiring widows to be inherited by the surviving brother or another male relative of the deceased husband for protection, home and comfort for the widow's children is now often practiced mainly to get access to the wealth and property left by the deceased (p. 75).

Marriage in Igbo society is a bond between members of a lineage. When a man dies, the wife and children belong to a lineage. Kirwen (1979) states that custom of levirate arises in the context that marriage involves both individuals and their lineages; marriage is both a personal and social contract. Therefore, the bride is both the wife of an individual and the lineage. The disappointing circumstance in the plight of the widow is that the initial reasons of protection and care in the levirate custom is no more practiced by the men. Rather, levirate is seen as an opportunity to subdue the widow and take away all her husband's belongings from her. Levirate has left women penniless and in precarious economic situations in which they could not take care of themselves or their children. Aphane et. al. (1995) states that the practice of levirate opens avenues for the deceased husband's relatives to have access to property that the widow acquired with the husband. Levirate also denies the widow the right to choose a man of her own, should she desire to remarry (p. 45).

The levirate practice exposes women to the possibility of HIV/AIDS infection; the men who inherit the widows are sometimes married to other women and have mistresses in the society. The issue of wife inheritance is physically, emotionally, spiritually, mentally, and socially problematic. Women feel violated when relationships are contracted without asking for their opinion and consent. The widow finds herself in a stressful dilemma, left to the whims and caprices of her husband's family.

Isolation

At the confirmation of a husband's death, the widow in Igbo society is immediately isolated and confined to the family compound. She is forced to dress in old, ragged clothes and seated on the floor. The widow does not move out of the compound for the necessary economic activities to sustain her and the children. She does not communicate with the public or participate in social activities. Throughout the mourning period, the widow is seen as unclean and sympathizers cannot shake hands with her. Instead, they leave gifts of money on the floor for her. After the official burial and funeral ceremony is completed, the widow spends from three to twelve months at home, in mourning for her husband. The widow depends on her family and friends to help her through these difficult times for economic survival.

Widows in some cultures are made to sleep on the same bed with the corpse of the husband; others are expected to sit by the deceased corpse until he is buried. During the mourning period, widows do not take a bath or groom themselves. Such attention is believed to be disrespectful to the dead. Widows are also not allowed to cook any food; they can only eat the food given to them by members of the husband's family. Owen (1996) emphasized that rituals concerning the physical appearance of widows, and restrictions on their diet and lifestyle exist in many cultures, and that there seems to be an almost universal wish, patriarchal in origin, to de-sex the widow, to emphasize her celibacy, to make her look undesirable, whereas a widower normally has no such obligations as a way of showing regret for the death of a wife (p. 16).

A widow already feels a sense of isolation and loss upon the death of her husband; the mandated isolation rituals that further keep her away from other people in the community are socially unhealthy. Bowling (1988-89) believes that close interpersonal relationships buffer individuals against the negative impact of stressful life events (p. 136). Communication is very essential as a medium to express one's needs and feelings. But during this period of isolation, the widow is not allowed to express herself. The old, ragged clothes that the widow is forced to wear as she sits on the floor are socially and emotionally degrading. Nevertheless, the widow has to hide her pride and abandon her personal decorum and accept her burdens in the name of culture. The widow is not allowed to bathe, clean her surroundings, or wash her clothes during this period. These rituals have far reaching health implications and often result in the growth of micro-organisms capable of causing various diseases and even death. Korieh (1996) states that any widow found washing and bathing during this period is punished because she is assumed to be beautifying and grooming herself to attract men (p. 24).

Good nutrition is essential for health. But the widow is not allowed to cook. Her eating at this time is dependent on the "good will" of friends and family members. In this tightly controlled environment, the widow may not be fed and she is not allowed by custom to cook for herself. Prolonged undernourishment during mourning period often leads to nutritional deficiency.

Forced Crying

Widows cry uncontrollably to indicate the loss of the spouse and the deep pain felt from the husband's death. Basden (1966) states that when death is announced, there is an outburst of wailing, the women particularly cry to give full vent to their grief (p. 270). Sometimes a wife or a mother will rush from the house, heedless of direction, waving arms, and beating her breasts as she bemoans her loss. At such times, a woman will roam aimlessly throughout the village for hours crying at the top of her lungs. Eventually, after possibly being out all night, she struggles back to her hut, physically and mentally exhausted. Widows have to cry at specific times of the day as a way to publically mourn their dead husbands. The widows that do not comply to crying out loud as required, are suspected of lacking concern over their husband's death. Some widows suffer a lot during a spouse's illness. Hence, when he dies, they are already so emotionally and mentally exhausted that they hardly can cry as a sign of their grief. However, this sign of a lack of outward exhibition of emotional distress will be used against her as a show of disrespect for the husband. Individuals have different ways of expressing grief; forcing widows to cry may not indicate remorse; it may not accomplish the objective of making the widow feel deep pain and hurt.

Cleansing Ceremony

At the expiration of the mourning period, the widow undergoes a cleansing ceremony before she is readmitted to the community. The cleansing ritual is performed to wash away the evil spirits and the bad omen associated with the loss of a husband. The cleansing ceremony in some Igbo communities includes the expectation that the widow will have sexual intercourse with a male relative of the husband; the expectation for the widow to visit the market place dressed in rags is termed "*Izu ahia Mkpe*" (first market outing after the mourning of the husband). The widow is expected to walk naked in the night, escorted by a man to the stream to take a ritual bath. Okoye (2000) explains that men exploit these women sexually (p. 16). Some men take advantage of the naked widow in the tradition of *'Iwalu ya nku"* (breaking firewood for her). This is the act of a man having sex with the widow, the first time since the death of her husband, six months to a year ago. Aphane et. al. (1995) state that this behavior exposes the widow to HIV/AIDS and other sexually transmitted diseases (p. 11). The widow cannot be accepted in Igbo community until she completes the cleansing ceremony. Ritual cleansing is, therefore, a significant step to readmit widows into the Igbo community and officially end the mourning period for the husband. Widows sometimes succumb to these rituals in order to ensure their continued membership in their families for the fear of death or ostracism. Another factor is that widows may want to maintain cordial relations with their deceased husbands' families.

The Shaving of the Hair

The widow's hair is shaved immediately after the burial of her husband. Hair shaving is performed by the *umuada*. Hair shaving can be done with a blunt razor blade as punishment by the *umuada*, if they do not like the widow. Korieh (1995) states that the *umuada* retains great influence over what happens in the family in which they were born, and in some cases this means tyrannical power over the women married by their brothers, particularly at the death of any of these brothers (p. 20).

Women in every culture revere their hair. They make great efforts to groom their hair for good hygiene and healthy appearances. Good hair on the head brings pride to women. Pride and happiness are destroyed when the widow is forced to cut her hair at the death of the husband. The impact of this must have devastating emotional and psychological effects on the health of the widow; a widow should not be punished/forced to be bald upon the demise of her spouse.

Proof of Innocence

Widows must also prove their innocence of any crime or complicity in their husbands' deaths to appease their husbands' relations. Different ethnic groups perform different rituals to ascertain the innocence of the wife. According to Okoye, in her play *When the Man Dies* (1997), some ethnic groups expect widows to drink the bath water used to wash the husbands' corpses (p. 68). This unhealthy ritual is practiced in some Igbo communities especially when foul play is suspected for the death of the man. Other customs expect the woman to jump over the husband's casket; others may make the widow sleep on the grave of the dead husband. All these rituals are done to avenge the man's death on the wife, as if wife were always responsible for the death of a spouse.

The basic human tenet of law assumes that everyone is innocent until proven guilty. But widows in Igbo society do not have this right. Immediately a man is pronounced dead, the members of his family will subject his widow to all sorts of rituals to test her innocence of any crime or compliance in the husband's death. This accusation with no foundation could be spiritually and emotionally devastating and unhealthy for the widow. Aphane et. al. (1995) states that in some instances, the deceased husband's relatives accused the widow of having used black magic or witchcraft to precipitate the death of her husband (p. 26). She is forced to sleep by the husband's grave, sleep on the same bed with his corpse and, to crown it all, she is required to drink the remains of bath water used for washing the husband's corpse. Okoye (1995), amazed at this ritual, asks the community to really "consider the culture of making a widow drink the water used in washing the corpse of her dead husband. How viable is such an institution in the present day health hazard, posed by infectious and contagious diseases" (p. 238)? The bath water of any human being is filled with micro-organisms capable of causing diseases, and this ritual amounts to poisoning the widow to punish or even kill her because her husband died.

Economic Deprivation

Women are expected to mourn their husbands' death from three months to a year, depending on the ethnic group. During this period, the women do not trade or seek an income unless they are lucky to get help from family members and friends. This long mourning period places women in precarious positions economically, especially those who do not have relations to help them financially.

A lack of economic power is responsible for poor health. People without money do not have the resources to seek medical attention when they are ill. Widows who lose their source of economic sustenance due to prolonged mourning are upset because they know they have the obligation to provide for their children and cannot do so. In Muslim areas, Islamic laws have specific rules that a husband has the obligation to take care of his wife and children. Even though the widow is assigned some part of the husband's estate upon his death, the share may not be enough to care for her and her children. Schildkrout (1986) states that widows usually inherit one–quarter or one–third of the husband's estate and is guaranteed residency rights in her husband's compound without threat of eviction by the deceased's blood relatives. These rituals seem to cater more to the dead than to the living, especially the widow and her children.

Rights of Inheritance

Women do not have the right to inherit land or property according to traditional Igbo laws and custom. On the death of a husband, the relations of the husband take over all the properties and belongings of the family, whether the items were bought by the wife or not. Igbo culture asserts that the husband owns the wife and all her property. Whatever property is given to the woman is dependent on the good will of the man's family. The inability to inherit any of the husband's property is worse if the woman does not have a male child. Ayisi (1989), relating the experience of a widow in Southern Africa, states that just a few days after the death of the husband, her in-laws took most of the possessions that she and her husband had bought together which included the car, refrigerator, camera, clothes, hi-fi system and records. In such circumstances, a woman cannot seek redress in the legal system because Africa has two legal systems the customary and general court laws with conflicting interpretations (p. 66). Under the customary law, a woman has no right of inheritance to the husband's property in the event of his death.

Widows are disinherited of all the properties owned by the couple with no concession given for those items purchased together or solely by her. In some cases, acquisition may involve physical struggle. The widow finds herself physically assaulted and emotionally challenged by the actions of her husband's family. The psychological and emotional impact are felt more when the woman knows that she was really the bread winner in her husband's household. There is no way around this because tradition and custom state that the husband owns the wife, as well as her property.

Code of Dress

The widow has a prescribed attire during the mourning period. The widow will have to dress in black throughout this time. Religious organizations have helped to provide the option of having widows dress in white clothes. Assigning special attire to widows is like labeling the individual with the scarlet letter "A" in Nathaniel Hawthorne's novel. In *The Scarlet Letter*, the "A" symbolizes a badge of shame which a woman convicted of adultery was once compelled to wear in Puritan America. Buchi Emecheta (1976) in her novel, *The Bride Price* stresses that before Ma Blackie could guess that her husband was dead, she was stripped of her clothes and given an older, torn set to put on. A place on the cement floor was cleared for her to sit and cry and mourn for her dead husband.

A widow's code of dressing is a constant reminder of the husband's death. This practice is emotionally unhealthy. In some ethnic groups, mourning may be from one to two years. During this period the widow, because she is constantly dressed in black, stands out in the crowd. People often stop her on the way to find out the circumstance of the husband's death. Such gestures of goodwill, rather than relieve stress, often recreate memories about the deceased and develop new emotional stress for the widow. Igbo society has yet to develop healthy, positive strategies that will help the widow forget and overcome her grief in the shortest period of time.

Suggestions For Change

An analysis of retrogressive widowhood practices leads one to believe that the tradition sets the widow up to literally die with the husband. It may be more appropriate to compare the inhumane treatment meted out to African widows at the death of their husbands to what is experienced by Hindu widows in India who are burnt with the husbands' corpses¯the only difference being that the former action is covert while the latter is overt.

The Igbos have a very rich culture which must be preserved. But, at the same time, they must identify and discontinue those cultural practices that are harmful to the health of all citizens. At present, widowhood practices in Igboland are not in line with worldwide health policies for the 21st century. Chen (1995) states that the growing evidence on widowhood issues argues for a full review of the legal and cultural practices contributing to the special deprivations of widows, particularly where widows are likely to have dependent children (p. 103). Widows clearly experience special difficulties and deprivations connected with the restrictions imposed on their lifestyles and the persistence of negative social attitudes toward them. Given that the social ideals of support and protection for widows are less widely reflected in practice than the social rules restricting widows, it is important to pay attention to widowhood as a particular cause of deprivation and to undertake public action and policies in support of widows. Culture is dynamic and necessary changes can be made in any culture without destroying the basic fabric of the society. Changes can be made when active sections of the society—women, men, religious organizations, and the government—commit themselves to restore the human rights of everyone.

African Women in Transition

A careful assessment of the practices indicate the important role women play in perpetuating these harmful widowhood practices. One wonders why women precipitate violence against women. To bring about changes in widowhood practices in Igbo society, women must be at the forefront of the crusade against retrogressive cultural norms. Igbo women play a significant role in upholding the culture of the society. The *umuada* is a very strong organization in the Igbo community. One may wonder why the *umuada* are the very ones who perpetuate the observance of widowhood rituals on fellow women instead of protesting against the inhuman treatment meted out to their sex. The answer to women on women violence in the Igbo community is based on illiteracy, jealousy, and hunger for power by women in the rural communities in Igboland. There is a dichotomy between the women who live in the cities and those who reside in the rural areas. There is the envy for those women who live in the cities with all the modern amenities that do not exist in the villages. Hence, there seems to be distress and competition between rural and city women. Traditional functions, such as burial ceremonies which are performed in the rural villages, become opportunities where rural women can get at those living in the cities. Harmful widowhood practices give an opportunity for rural women to exact their *quasi* power over other women. Widowhood practices could be eradicated in the nearest future if all Igbo women (both those in rural and city communities) join forces against this cruel and oppressive tradition. By organizing a re-education campaign for the women, particularly the leaders of the *umuada* who are very instrumental in upholding the cultures of the community, tension will be reduced among women. An organized effort will encourage women to speak up for their rights and condemn the cultural norms that dehumanize women. Recent national education programs in Nigeria, such as the former "Better Life for Rural Women" initiative organized by Mrs. Maryam Babangida, in the 1980s and 1990s, made women and men more aware of the need to stand up for a better and improved quality of life.

In the 21st century, women need to develop a united front to stand up for dignity and justice. Babangida (1988), citing the accomplishment from a united effort by Nigeria army officers' wives, states: "I remember when an officer, whose wife was my friend, took a second wife" (p. 41). She complained to all her friends living in the barracks, and we all came together and planned a strategy which we used in chasing the second wife out. When the officer got word of our plan after his second wife had left, he came to our house to complain to my husband. But we all ended up laughing about it."

The Role of Men

Men too are the custodians of the Igbo culture. It is very important to educate them on the negative health effects of widowhood practices. Effective methods of reaching the men is through the age grade societies where dialogue can be conducted on the issue. A gradual approach must be used in introducing the topic because it is a sensitive issue which aims to remove men's power over women. Treating widows like human beings should not be a threat to the status quo. The health educator should approach the subject matter from the angle of the health implications of the rituals and develop communication strategies that can be applied to explain to the men the dehumanizing effects of the practices on their own mothers, wives, sisters, daughters and female kith and kin.

Religious Organizations

Religion plays a significant role in the life of Igbo people. Animism, Christianity and Islam, which are the major religions of Africans, are silent about the atrocities of widowhood practices. The Christian religion has changed the dress code from black to white. However, this is a token gesture which ignores the real problems. Islam has prescribed rules about widowhood practices but again widows are yet to be treated with dignity when they, too, are bereaved. The clergy and other significant persons in religious organizations must be made aware of the need for drastic changes in the rituals that are very harmful to the widow's health and the family. Successful alliances with the religious bodies will be helpful in the campaign to bring about change in the society.

The Role of Traditional Rulers

The traditional rulers are responsible for governance in the local communities. Responsible governance for all citizens demands that the traditional rulers see the abuse of widows as a crime and enact relevant laws to prosecute the offenders. Additionally, traditional rulers have to initiate awareness programs for the better treatment of widows in the villages. Both preventive measures and corrective strategies must be employed to end the tyranny of widows. The health educator must design appropriate information on the need for change in widowhood practices for the traditional rulers and their counselors.

The Power of Laws

African rulers can play a significant role in changing the rituals widows are expected to perform. The government can pass laws and enact policies that will eliminate the prescribed practices. Even though the general and customary laws are different, support in the form of a general law from the government will act as a catalyst to stimulate local governments to pay more attention to addressing widowhood practices in their communities. Zambia has already taken the lead in this direction by passing a law which states that the deceased's property will be divided up, giving 20 percent to the widow or widower, 50 percent to the children, 20 percent to the deceased's parents, and 10 percent to other dependents (Ayisi, 1989, p. 66). Changing the law is a giant step in the right direction. However, the main emphasis should be on changing the attitude of the people in general on issues about widowhood practices. The need for laws to prevent wife inheritance by close relatives is most important in these times of HIV/AIDS epidemic in African communities. Blair (1997) identifies a Luo community in Kenya that required widows to be married by one of the surviving brothers or another close male relative of the deceased husband (p. 52). This practice of wife inheritance has caused a proliferation of HIV/AIDS infections. Schoofs (1999) observed in his field research that there are homes in Africa where all the males have died from HIV/AIDS due to widow inheritance.

Conclusion

Charmaz (1980) states that the problems and dilemmas facing those who confront death are not so different in kind from those experienced in ordinary circumstances. Each individual makes unique contributions to the social order. One's death means not only the cessation of his contributions, but also the partial death of all those for whom the deceased is significant. The widow is, therefore, not only faced with the loss of her husband but also the burden of caring for the children and dealing with the family members and other people in the society, who are ready to take advantage of her because her husband is no longer around to protect her. With these predicaments facing the widow, Igbo society has to change its attitudes towards widows and create a supportive environment to help them deal with their loss with dignity, rather than shame. The cultural change in widowhood practices is overdue. Lastly, widowhood practices are infringements on the human rights of women, and there is an urgent need to rectify this anomaly.

References

Aphane, D., Gwaunza, E., Kasonde-Ngandu, S., Kidd, P., Matashane, K., Mvududu, S., & Temba, E. (1995). Picking up the pieces: Widowhood in southern Africa. Women in law in southern Africa research. *Trust* (WLSA) Working Paper No. 13.

Ayisi. R. A. (May/June 1989). Protect the widow. *Africa Report*. p. 65.

Babangida, M. (1988). *The home front: Nigerian army officers and their wives*. Ibadan, Nigeria, Fountain Publications.

Basden, G. T. (1966). *Among the Ibos of Nigeria*. London, Frank, Cass and Co.

Blair, C., Ojakaa, D., Ochola, S. A. and Gogi, D. (1997). Barriers to behavior change: Results of focus group discussion conducted in a high HIV/AIDS incidence area of Kenya. In D. C. Umeh (Ed.). *Confronting the AIDS epidemic, cross-cultural perspectives on HIV/AIDS education*. Trenton, NJ: Africa World Press.

Bowling, A. (1988-89). Who dies after widow(er)hood? A discriminant analysis. *Omega*, 19, (2).

Charmaz, K. (1980). *The social reality of death: Death in contemporary America*. MA: Addison-Wesley Publishing Co.

Chen, M. A. (1995). *Why widowhood matters. Women: Looking beyond 2000.* New York: United Nations Publications.

Crossette, B. (2001, February). In India and Africa, women's low status worsens their risk of AIDS. *New York Times*, A9.

Emecheta, B. (1976). *The bride price*. New York: George Braziller.

Greenberg, J. S., Dintiman, G. B. and Oakes, B. M. (1998). *Physical fitness and wellness*. Boston: Allyn and Bacon.

Henderson, R. N. (1972). *The king in every man.* Yale: Yale University Press.

Inset, P. M. and Roth, W. T. (1998). *Core concepts in health*. CA: Mayfield Publishing.

Kirwen, M. C. (1979). *African widows.* Maryknoll, New York: Orbis

Books.

Korieh, C. J. (Spring 1996). *Widowhood among the Igbo of eastern Nigeria*. M.A. Thesis in History. Bergen, Norway: University of Bergen.

_______. (1998, April/May). Looking to the 21st Century: What's Happening to Women? 20-21. *African Profile. U.S.A.*

Meena, R. (1992). Women and sustainable development. *Equal Opportunity International*, 11, (6).

_______. (2000, December). New danes face divide from their old cultures. *New York Times*, A1 &10.

Nwapa, F. (1970). *Idu.* London, Heinemann.

Okafor, J. O. (1997). AIDS campaign in Nigeria: The efforts of the federal government. In Umeh, D. C. (Ed). *Confronting the AIDS epidemic: Cross-cultural perspectives on HIV/AIDS education.* Trenton, NJ: Africa World Press.

Okafor, R. U. (1993). Death education in the Nigerian home: The mother's role *Omega*, 27, (4), 271-280.

Okoye. P. U. (1995). *Widowhood: A natural or cultural tragedy*. Enugu, Nucik Publishers.

_______. (1997). *When the man dies*. Enugu, Nucik Publishers.

_______. (2000). *Harmful widowhood practices in Anambra state: The new millenium strategies for eradication*. Enugu, Nucik Publishers.

Owen, M. (1996). *A world of widows.* New Jersey: Zed Books.

Schildkrout, E. (1986). Widows in Hausa society: Ritual phase or social status? In Potash, B. (Ed.) *Widows in African societies: Choices and constraints,* 131-152. CA: Stanford University Press.

Schoofs, M. (Dec. 7, 1999). How sexism spreads AIDS in Africa. *The Village Voice*. XLIV, (48), 67-73.

Thomas, L. E., DiGiulio, R. C. and Sheehan, N. W. (1988). Identity loss and psychological crisis in widowhood: A re-evaluation. *The International Journal of Aging and Human Development.*

Vol.26(3), pp. 225-239.

Tobrise, M. 1. E. (1998). *Women and development: A cultural imperative.* lbadan. Humanities Research Centre.

Umeh, M. (Forthcoming 2002). Should wills become an option for married couples? Revolutionizing the laws of succession in African society. *Africa Today.*

PART FOUR

AFRICANA LITERATURE AND THE HUMAN CONDITION

CHAPTER 11

NNEKA OR 'MOTHER IS SUPREME':
POWERFUL FEMALE IMAGERY IN *THINGS FALL APART* AND FEMINISM IN THE NEW MILLENNIUM

Cindy Mathieson Ibechem
Assistant Professor
Department of Anthropology
Hartwick College

> Feminism is often equated with radical feminism and with hatred of men, penis envy, nonacceptance of African traditions, a fundamental rejection of marriage and motherhood, a favoring of lesbian love, and an endeavor to invert the power relationships of the genders.
>
> - Susan Arndt -

> A man belongs to his fatherland when things are good and life is sweet. But when there is sorrow and bitterness he finds refuge in his motherland. Your mother is there to protect you. She is buried there. And that is why we say that mother is supreme.
>
> -Chinua Achebe-

Introduction

A unified vision of feminism is necessary in the future. Such a goal will be achieved only after feminists, through consultative discussion, strive to re-evaluate the nature, constitution and purpose of the discourse. Since the turn of the new millennium, there have been multiple debates over what to name the new baby (*new feminism*) and who, in fact, should name her.

Choosing a name for a new feminism may be an important starting point, yet it leaves the question about how to find a unified vision for the discipline unanswered. Perhaps we should begin by locating the community(ies) where new feminism will reside. In fact, she may have multiple homes, like an Igbo child who is welcomed by several mothers in her family's compound. After establishing where the new feminism lives, it will then be easier to speak about possibilities for her rearing, maturation and future career.

After the new feminism finally comes of age, she will be able to help with a number of projects, including: 1) evaluating descriptions and the inclusion of women in ethnographic accounts; 2) examining the portrayal of female characters in novels written by African men; 3) providing analyses of African women's novels; and, 4) presenting critiques of female scholars' works.

My endeavor in this chapter will be to discuss the second project mentioned above. I am examining the construction of images of women in Achebe's (1994) classic novel, *Things Fall Apart*, and re-evaluating the roles of Okonkwo's mother and other strong female figures in the text. Further, I propose a feminist anthropological reading of the novel that utilizes ethnographic analyses, highlights African cultural values and ideas about women's power and acknowledges sub-cultural ideologies in the context of hegemonic subordination (Afigbo, 1972; Amadiume, 1987; Asante, 1987; Collier, 1974; Foucault, 1978; Green, 1964; Hebdige, 1999; Ifeka-Moller,1975; McCall, 1996, 2000; Mead, 1960; Njaka, 1974; Okonjo, 1976; Rosaldo & Lamphere, 1974; Uchendu, 1960).

The first half of this endeavor is a discussion that considers the following issues: 1) the multiplicity of feminisms; 2) public versus private spheres and symbolic analysis of women and power; 3) historical and social construction of gender identity, and, 4) gender, race, class, age-status, religion and marriage.

The second half involves an examination of female imagery in Achebe's (1994) novel. It begins with an evaluation of Okonkwo, the tragic hero of the novel, and his relationship to the women in his community (Boyce Davies, 1986; Ibechem, 2000; Jeyifo, 1993; Njaka, 1974; Uchendu, 1965). The sections that follow involve consideration of powerful women, female religious symbols, oracles, priestesses and goddesses.

The section prior to the conclusion briefly explores what I have termed *secondary female imagery*. The conclusion offers some comments about female imagery in the novel, Igbo culture as presented by Achebe, women's power and feminism in the new millennium.

A Discussion of Feminism(s)

Partly as a result of American women's quest for equality with men, the Women's Liberation Movement was born. During the 1960's and early 1970's, the movement stimulated a lot of academic discussion and highlighted the difference between feminism's experiential base and its analytical component. Among early feminist anthropologists, it catalyzed a cross-cultural examination of gender relationships (Ortner, 1974; Rosaldo and Lamphere, 1974; Sanday, 1974). For example, Ortner (1974) examined the relationship between women and men, suggested that females were considered symbolically closer to nature, white men were equated with culture; the implication here is that in the United States, culture (men) dominated or tamed nature (women). Rosaldo and Lamphere (1974) used the phrase sexual asymmetry to describe a universal state of inequality between men and women and concluded that all societies seemed to value male over female roles. Further, they were dissatisfied with the high percentage of androcentric or male-centered ethnographic accounts (in the field of Anthropology), stating that only a few had taken women's perspectives into consideration.

Aside from these, however, anthropologists in writing about human culture have followed our own culture's ideological biases in treating women as relatively invisible and describing what are largely the activities and interests of men. In order to correct that bias, to alter our conceptions of the female, and to understand their source, what we need are new perspectives. Today, it seems reasonable to argue that the social world is the creation of both male and female actors, and that any full understanding of human society and any viable program for social change will have to incorporate the goals, thoughts and activities of the second sex (Rosaldo and Lamphere, 1974, p. 2).

In her examination of female status in the public domain, Sanday (1974) noted that female power and authority is highest in societies where women and men contribute equally to subsistence. While early feminist anthropologists, such as Rosaldo and Lamphere (1974), started with the assumption of universal female subordination, they also acknowledged women's informal influence and power in many societies.

Mead's 1960 observation that sex roles are not genetic but acquired through cultural learning, emphasized the idea of gender plasticity. Her observation raised an important question that stimulated further research. "Perhaps the first question that arises in an anthropological study of women is whether there are societies, unlike our own, in which women are publicly recognized as equal to or more powerful than men" (Rosaldo and Lamphere, 1974, p. 2). Consequently, early feminist anthropological scholars catalyzed investigations into the nature of women's power and authority in multiple cultures (Collier, 1974; Rosaldo and Lamphere, 1974; Sanday, 1974).

While present scholarship has largely discredited the idea of universal "sexual asymmetry", the above authors helped pave the way for future consideration of the following issues, including: 1) the significance of symbolism involving women; 2) historical and social contexts of gender relationships; and, 3) the holistic consideration of gender, race, class, age-status, religion, and marriage. Several important trends in symbolic analysis have included consideration of females in public and private societal spheres and evaluations of women's power and protest actions such as the Igbo Women's War of 1929 (Collier, 1974; Hewlett, 2001; Ifeka-Moller, 1975; Lamphere, 2001; Leacock, 1978; Ogunyemi, 1996; Ortner, 1979; Sanday, 1974, 1981; Van Allen, 2001).

Symbolism Involving Women and Their Power: Public Versus Private Spheres, and The Igbo Women's War

Hewlett (2001), Lamphere (2001), Leacock (1978), and Sanday (1978) have all contributed to the analysis of symbolism involving women by re-examining female status in relation to public and private spheres. Hewlett (2001) proposed that the household unit among the Aka (of the Central African Republic and northern Congo-Brazzaville) could best be described as public, while the sphere outside the home should be called private, i.e. a reversal of the original dichotomy. Lamphere (2001) concluded that the concept of public and private realms had its limits and probably more accurately reflected Western perspectives and household dynamics than universal tendencies. Leacock (1978) criticized the idea that a public/private dichotomy existed in all cultures, stating that a clear delineation between the spheres was harder to observe among hunter-gatherers and some farming populations, than it was in state level societies.

Sanday's (1978) research supported Leacock's (1978) conclusions in noting that clear-cut distinctions between public and "familial spheres" (private spheres) did not exist among the matrilineal Iroquois, or the Ashanti. Further, she observed "scripts for female power" in cultures where female deities worked alongside with or "dominated" a "male principle" (Sanday, 1978, p. 33). She described the Iroquois and Ashanti as having gender relationships that were essentially "separate and equal." Sanday (1978) states that

> When the female creative principle dominates or works in conjunction with the male principle, the sexes are either integrated and equal in everyday life (as they are, at least in theory, among the Balinese, and in practice among the Semang and the Mbuti) or they are separate and equal (as among the Iroquois and the Ashanti) (p. 33).

Symbolic analyses of female protest actions have highlighted women's agency and the differing interpetations of "key symbols" such as the Igbo Women's War (*Ogu Umunwanyi*) of 1929 (Ifeka-Moller, 1975; Ogunyemi, 1996; Ortner, 1979; Van Allen, 2001). Ifeka-Moller (1975) noted that participants in the Women's War were wearing greenery (such as palm fronds), which signified that they were in a state of taboo that prohibited people from disturbing them. Cultural confusion was evident when British colonial authorities didn't understand the symbolism, and sent colonial soldiers with rifles to forcibly confront women who were carrying cooking pestles. Unfortunately, soldiers fired at the women during their protests in Utu Etim, Abak and Opobo, killing 50 women (Afigbo, 1972). No British soldiers were injured.

Ogunyemi (1996) indicated a different interpretation for female participation in the Women's War. She translated *Ogu Umunwanyi* as the Women's Struggle, rather than the Women's War stating that the word "struggle" implied continuity, whereas the term "war" relegated female action to a series of past events. She stressed that Igbo women's protest actions did not begin or end with the Women's War. Therefore, she chose to refer to the War as one action in a series that demonstrated Nigerian women's struggle for liberation and empowerment.

Van Allen's (2001) analysis of the Women's War highlighted the fact that there were conceptual differences between the female participants and the British colonial administrators. While Igbo people referred to the event as *Ogu Umunwanyi* (the Igbo Women's War), colonial authorities described it as the Aba Riots. Different names for the same event contrast female agency (the Igbo Women's War) with hysteria and lack of control (the Aba Riots), respectively. In essence, Van Allen's (2001) analysis illustrates the idea that a "war" (Igbo interpretation) is generally a powerful event in which community support is apparent, whereas a "riot" (British colonial interpretation) is an unplanned, mass outburst. It is clear that hierarchical gender relationships, introduced by British colonists must have clashed with existing Igbo systems of "gender parallelism," where men and women had equally important, yet differing roles in society (Amadiume, 1987; Okonjo, 1976; Silverblatt 1987). Thus, the conflicting accounts of the Igbo Women's War highlight the importance of understanding indigenous concepts of female power.

Abu-Lughod (1990), Ibechem (2000), Landsman and Krasniewicz (1992) and McCall (1996, 2000) have all stressed indigenous women's perspectives in ethnographic accounts. Abu-Lughod's (1990) concept of female power incorporates the following considerations, including:

1) women's ability to determine their own actions and influence others; 2) analysis of systems of power within the community; and, 3) historical process. Her research among Bedouin women highlights women's subversion of power through daily acts of protest. She found that women defied rules or restrictions enforced by male community elders by maintaining a female-segregated sphere, resisting arranged marriages and engaging in sexually explicit discourse. Flipping Foucault's (1978) maxim, "Where there is power, there is resistance" (pp. 95-96); Abu-Lughod (1990) stated instead that, "Where there is resistance, there is power" (p. 42). She links her definition of female power to "systems" in the community.

Highlighting indigenous concepts of female power both aid our understanding of differing cultural systems and contribute toward developing definitions that move beyond Western descriptions. Western conceptions of power, like our ideas about feminism, are influenced by the experiential components of our social systems, cultural traditions and beliefs. "With a Western conception of power, people are easily separable from society and family as isolated (portable) individuals" (Ibechem, 2000). In contrast, I found that women's power is rooted in connectedness to both marital and natal families, female organizations and the community. During interviews with women in Umuneke, I observed that,

Powerful women exhibit strength of character while actively demonstrating their willingness to maintain peace in the village. Powerful women are also industrious and resourceful; they are community builders and display leadership qualities. A powerful woman (*nwanyi dike*) is able to mobilize her fellow women to action, utilizing good judgement and treating everybody fairly; she loves people but does not play favorites. She is a good mother (*ezigbo nne*). As Mrs. Ester Egwim of Ofodim stated, "She is a woman that maintains peace and harmony in her family and others; she gathers together and doesn't scatter" (Ibechem, 2000, p. 272).

The endeavor to delineate indigenous concepts of female power is aided by a new approach to anthropological research that McCall (2000) termed "heuristic ethnography" (p. 9). Heuristic ethnography encourages the "open exchange of ideas" between researcher and subject, thus shrinking the gap between "lived experience" and "formalized discourse" (pp. 18-19). Importantly, a heuristic approach to studying other societies includes indigenous ideas or "interpretive frameworks" in the analysis of cultural concepts such as power (Landsman and Krasniewicz, 1992). Consideration of the interplay between indigenous systems of power, interpretive frameworks, and historical account(s), will aid in the delineation of feminist theories that transcend Western definitions.

Historical and Social Construction of Gender Identity

Leacock (1978), Rapp (2001) and Silverblatt (1987) have all contributed to historical and cross-cultural understanding of gender relationships. These scholars have examined women's status in relation to the advent of colonialism and the rise of state level societies. They both noted that, with the advent of colonialism and the rise of the state, the status of women generally suffered. In contrast, gender relationships in pre-colonial and pre-state societies were typified by parallel male/female roles. Rapp (2001) states that,

The evidence also suggests a general pattern concerning political organization. Prior to colonial penetration, gender relations in indigenous cultures appear to have been organized along essentially parallel and complementary lines. Men and women had distinct but equally significant roles in production, distribution, and ritual activities (p. 304).

Silverblatt's (1987) analysis of gender relationships among Andean (Quechua) women of Peru, illustrate historical changes from "gender parallelism," to "gender distinction" (after Incan conquest) and then "gender hierarchy" (after Spanish colonization).

While the above anthropological scholars have examined gender relationships from historical and cross-cultural perspectives, their analyses are not representative of the main body of Western feminist theory. Therefore, many African, African American, diaspora, and international feminists have argued that feminism is predominantly a white, Western middle-class preoccupation that doesn't necessarily support the idea of universal sisterhood (Amadiume, 1987; hooks, 1984; Hill Collins, 1989; Ogunyemi, 1996; White, 1992). Critiques of the relationship between race, class and gender, challenge current feminist theoreticians to be more inclusive of intercultural, international and sub-cultural perspectives. In essence, African, African American, diaspora and international feminist experiential perspectives highlight an unmet need for diverse examinations of cultural practices in relation to women's status.

Gender, Race, Class, Age-Status, Religion and Marriage

Amadiume (1987) and Oyewumi's (2000) consideration of gender identity in Nigeria add both inter-cultural and international feminist perspectives to the body of theoretical discourse. Based on her research in Nnobi, Amadiume (1987) noted the difference between Igbo (West African) and Western gender identification. She states that Igbo gender construction is flexible, while Western identification is rigid and equates biological sexual status with social roles. As Igbo gender construction is neither rigid nor linked to biological sexuality, women are free to "marry" wives, and daughters are considered more or less "male" depending on the context. For example, a barren woman may marry another woman who will have children for her, and a "male daughter" may inherit land in the absence of a son.

Oyewumi (2000) stresses that there are experiential and conceptual differences between Nigerian (African feminists), like herself, and white Western feminists; she illustrates this by establishing a connection between Western family values and white feminist discourse. She states that "the woman in feminist theory is a wife-the subordinated half of a couple in a nuclear family-who is housed in a single family home" (Oyewumi, 2000 p. 1094). In contrast, Nigerian feminists frame their discourse from the conceptual/experiential context of "African family arrangements," where gender parallelism, polygamous marriage and extended family households exist. Further, most African kin systems privilege the mother/child bond over that of the husband and wife. Oyewumi (2000) states that "the most important ties within the family flow from the mother to the child and connect all children of the same mother in bonds that are conceived as natural and unbreakable" (Oyewumi 2000, p. 1098). Therefore, while African women may view themselves primarily as mothers and secondarily as wives, Western women usually privilege the romantic relationship between husband and wife over that of mother and child. In short, Western family values, experiences and conceptual frameworks are not everywhere applicable.

While analyses by Amadiume (1987) and Oyewumi (2000) stress cultural distinctions in gender identity construction, black feminism highlights sub-cultural variations (hooks, 1984; Hill Collins, 1989). Hooks (1984) delineates black feminism, as an alternative theoretical orientation to white Western feminism, one that illustrates experiential differences between black and white feminists. She describes black feminism as a theoretical perspective that capitalizes on the unique position of black women at the "margin" rather than at the "center" of the discipline, and she encourages black women to continue to engage in a "feminist struggle," by taking advantage of their "marginality." She goes on to say state that,

> It is essential for continued feminist struggle that black women recognize the special vantage our marginality gives us and make use of this perspective to criticize the dominant racist, classist, sexist hegemony as well as to envision and create a counter-hegemony. I am suggesting that we have a central role to play in the making of feminist theory and a contribution to offer that is unique and valuable (Hooks, 1984, p. 15).

Further, hooks' (1984) description of black feminism as counter-hegemonic acknowledges what Hebdige (1987) termed "the presence of difference" (p. 3), highlighting tensions between domininant (white) and subordinate (black) groups in America. Hill Collins (1989) makes the same point when she describes African American women as belonging to an oppressed group and white women to an oppressive one. Hooks (1984) and Hill Collins (1989) both discuss the exclusion of black feminist perspectives from the main body of feminist theory. As a consequence, they call for revolutionary changes in the discipline, by advocating a "mass-based feminist movement" with a "liberatory ideology" shared by everyone and by promoting a theoretical orientation (Afrocentric feminism) that would give African-American women tools to oppose their own subordination.

While black and Afrocentric feminisms share a strong grounding in black Western experience, the latter draws from an additional set of Afrocentric values that contrast with Eurocentric ones (Asante, 1987). The Afrocentric feminist epistemology outlined by Hill Collins (1989) is based on the concept that black people share a common experience of oppression either in the form of racism, imperialism or colonialism:

> In spite of varying histories, Black societies reflect elements of a core African value system that existed prior to and independently of racial oppression. Moreover, as a result of colonialism, imperialism, slavery, apartheid, and other systems of racial domination, Blacks share a common experience of oppression. These similarities in material conditions have fostered shared Afrocentric values that permeate family struc-

> ture, religious institutions, culture, and community life of Blacks in varying parts of Africa, the Carribbean, South America and North America. This Afrocentric consciousness permeates the shared history of people of African descent through the framework of a distinctive Afrocentric epistemology (Collins, 1989, p. 755).

While Hill Collins states that a "shared history of people of African descent" is what delineates Afrocentric consciousness, she also makes the point that "Black societies" have "varying histories." Her characterization of the role of history in Afrocentric feminist consciousness is confusing. Instead of elucidating a shared history for people of African descent, she promoted the idea of a "common experience of oppression" for all black people, resulting in an a-historical Afrocentric consciousness.

While Afrocentric consciousness seeks to meld black American and African conceptual frameworks, Steady's version (1996) of African feminism (a.k.a. inclusive, humanistic, or diaspora feminism) links African and diaspora values. She states that, "African feminism combines racial, sexual, class, and cultural dimensions of oppression to produce a more inclusive brand of feminism through which women are viewed first and foremost as human, rather than sexual beings." Steady's African feminism incorporates African values, including: 1) a balance between humans, the material and metaphysical realms; 2) respect for cooperation between people rather than the privileging of individualism; 3) acknowledgement of parallel, rather than hierarchical relationships between women and men; 4) consideration of polygamy in patrilineal and matrilineal kin systems; and, 5) the presentation of African women's autonomy, power and self-reliance in relation to their integral and changing roles in societies. By defining African feminism, Steady (1996) illustrates critical differences between African and Western experiences and perspectives.

Feminist perspectives that stress diverse conceptual and experiential frameworks, highlight African cultural values, and examine the social and historical construction of gender identity, will aid in the following analysis of Okonkwo and the women of Umuofia (Amadiume, 1987; Arndt, 2000; Collier & Yanagisako, 1987; Hill Collins 1989; hooks, 1984; Ifeka-Moller, 1975; Lamphere, 2001; Leacock, 1978; Ogunyemi, 1996; Oyewumi, 2000; Sanday, 1978; Silverblatt, 1987; Van Allen, 2001). Perhaps the feminist theoretical orientation that goes the farthest toward establishing a new and vibrant perspective for the discipline is Steady's (1996) inclusive feminism.

An Analysis of *Things Fall Apart*: Okonkwo and the Women of Umuofia

Although Okonkwo (the tragic hero in *Things Fall Apart*) was a proud and accomplished Igbo man, the events in his life ultimately led him to commit suicide by hanging. Having died a dishonorable death, even his best friend was prohibited from providing a funeral for him. Instead, Okonkwo's body was cut down from a tree by "strangers" (British colonial officials) and thrown into the "bad bush" (*Ojo ahia*). Okonkwo's dishonorable death was made all the more tragic by the fact that he lived an exemplary life in so many ways.

Okonkwo was a man who was singularly focused on a quest for personal prestige. Although a high degree of achievement orientation has been noted among the Igbo, Okonkwo's character provides an extreme example. Uchendu (1965) described Igbo achievement beliefs as follows:

> The Igbo achievement orientation has two important social effects. In the first place, it makes the Igbo world a highly competitive one in which the rules of competition may be manipulated by the status seeker in order to attain his goals. Second, it fosters a sociopolitical system which is conciliar and democratic. A forward-moving, and talented young man who can acquire wealth and convert it into the traditionally

> valued status symbols (such as title taking) is allowed to wield political power over his peers and elders. This is a further demonstration of the Igbo saying that "no one knows the womb that bears the chief." It is not surprising that chiefship among the Igbo must not only be achieved, but be constantly validated to be retained (p. 20).

Okonkwo provides a good example of a young Igbo man who wished to achieve the highest level of prestige in his community (Umuofia), by attaining the *Ozo* title. Unfortunately for Okonkwo, his quest was interrupted when he accidentally shot a clansman's son at the father's funeral. He was automatically exiled for seven years for shedding the blood of a kinsman and had no choice but to flee Umuofia and establish residence in his maternal village of Mbanta.

Being the best at everything he did was Okonkwo's cherished ambition, yet it was far too important to Okonkwo that he maintained the respect of his fellow Umuofia residents. He dreaded the thought that people would associate him with his father Unoka, who had been a sensitive, yet ineffectual man, of whom he had very negative memories.

For when Unoka died he had taken no title at all and he was heavily in debt. Any wonder then that his son Okonkwo was ashamed of him? (Achebe, 1994, p. 8).

Okonkwo didn't have much of a childhood. He was jolted into adulthood by the necessity to help support his family. His father was lazy, and consequently the family never had enough food or money. As a result of these early experiences, Okonkwo had no patience for other people's weaknesses, particularly those of unsuccessful men because they reminded him of his father. In fact, Okonkwo had very little patience for men or women who didn't act the way he thought they should, and he was quick to judge weak men as too feminine.

Compared to the actions of the reasonable men of Umuofia and Mbanta, Okonkwo's behavior was not normal. In fact, several men warned him about his behavioral excesses, which included striking his youngest (second) wife (Ojiugo) during the Week of Peace. He was heavy-handed with his wives and his children, striking them when they did not do what he thought they should have done. He was equally rough with females and males. Achebe describes Okonkwo frequently hitting his oldest son Nwoye. However, it was Okonkwo's violence against Ikemefuma (the boy that Umuofia sacrificed in repayment for the murder of a village sister) that ultimately drove Nwoye to leave home and join a Christian Mission. In retrospect, it seems that Okonkwo's actions were not inspired by sexism but by other factors, including an extreme fear of failure and the confusion of sensitivity with failure.

Some scholars have insisted that Okonkwo was sexist by virtue of his heavy-handed dominance of his wives and that Achebe's portrait of Igbo society in his novel symbolizes the omission of women in African cultural discourse (Boyce Davies, 1986; Jeyifo, 1993). Boyce Davies (1986) states that Achebe's portrayal of females in the novel was one where they were entirely under the control of men. Jeyifo (1993) insists that Achebe's description of Okonkwo's mother was sexist because she was not referred to by her name and mentioned only once in conjunction with a story that she told Okonkwo as a child about Mosquito and Ear.

The story was an Igbo parable that explained why mosquitoes buzz around people's ears and taught a lesson about the importance of not judging people by their appearance. Mosquito came to court ear, asking her to marry him. Ear refused Mosquito's romantic advances and dismissed him as bare skeleton. Despite the fact that Mosquito had been summarily dismissed by his love interest he still had the stamina to let her know he survived. In fact, every time he was in the area, he buzzed by Ear.

In contrast to the characterizations by Boyce Davies (1986) and Jeyifo (1993), I argue that Achebe depicts a multitude of powerful female images throughout *Things Fall Apart*. Further, Jeyifo (1993) is mistaken about the number of references made to Okonkwo's mother in the novel, and the importance of the descriptions as well. For example, rather than one, Achebe in fact makes several references to Okonkwo's mother.

Powerful Women

The first description of a powerful woman in *Things Fall Apart* occurs when Achebe described the reason that Umuofia almost went to war with the neighboring village of Mbaino. Umuofia residents were offended when the wife of a titled man (Ogbuefi Udo) was murdered while she visited the market at Mbaino. As safe passage for trade between villages was (and still is) extremely important, it was a significant breech of custom when Ogbuefi Udo's wife was killed. As a result, Umuofia residents considered going to war with their Mbaino neighbors, yet chose instead to have them provide two people in exchange for the life of Ogbuefi Udo's wife. Mbaino gave Umuofia a boy (Ikemefuma) and a female virgin as compensation. It was up to Umuofia residents to decide whether or not the boy and the girl would be sacrificed or allowed to live. From Achebe's description, it seems that the girl may have been immediately sacrificed, as Ikemefuma reported never having seen her. Ikemefuma, on the other hand, lived in Umuofia in Okonkwo's family compound for several years until the Oracle of the Hills and Caves ordered his sacrifice.

In the third chapter, another reference is made to the powerful woman, Anasi, the senior wife (*lolo*) of the wealthy and titled man Nwakibie. As Okonkwo was not able to ask his own father (Unoka) for yams, or a means to start an independent life with a wife (or wives), he sought help from Nwakibie. Oknokwo's own father had become indebted during his lifetime and, as noted earlier, died a dishonorable death. When Okonkwo arrived at Nwakibie's family compound, he was greeted with kola nuts and something to drink, yet before the welcoming ceremony could proceed, Anasi had to be present. In deference to her prestigious status, none of her junior co-wives were allowed to drink before she did. Okonkwo, as a man of lesser fortune than Nwakibie, had to wait for the titled man's wife to arrive before making his request. Achebe (1994) described Nwakibie's wife as,

> .... a middle-aged woman, tall and strongly built. There was authority in her bearing and she looked every inch the ruler of the womenfolk in a large and prosperous family. She wore the anklet of her husband's titles, which the first wife alone could wear (p. 20).

Although Okonkwo was forced to appeal outside his family for help, Nwakibie was impressed by the young man's fortitude and motivation. He awarded Okonkwo 800 yams to start his own *oba ji* (yam barn) and farm. Unfortunately, there was a very bad yam harvest the year Okonkwo started his farm, but with perserverance and determination his luck changed. Subsequently, he had a good harvest, and successively married three wives.

Achebe mentioned several other powerful women in chapter two, when he introduced the senior of Okonkwo's three wives (whom he referred to as Nwoye's mother), and his second wife, Ekwefi, of whom Okonkwo was particularly fond. Igbo custom dictates that the senior or first wife has the highest status of all the wives. Therefore, Okonkwo's first wife's status was higher than that of her other two co-wives. Achebe first mentioned Nwoye's mother when Okonkwo brings Ikemefuma (the boy given to Umuofia by Mbaino in recompense for the murder of Ogbuefi Udo's wife) to his family compound to live. Nwoye's mother takes the boy into her house to care for as one of her own children.

Thus, Ekwefi provides another strong female image in the novel, yet in a different manner than that of Nwoye's mother. Rather than being the esteemed first wife (like Nwoye's mother), Ekwefi was the cherished second wife. Further, Okonkwo's marriage to Ekwefi was not arranged between families as was customary. Instead, Ekwefi chose to be with Okonkwo out of love and admiration for him. She fell in love with him when she saw him beat the formidable athlete, Amalinze, "the Cat", in a wrestling contest. In turn, Okonkwo was very proud of the fact that she was the town's beauty, and consequently was extremely fond of their daughter Ezinma. In essence, Ekwefi can be viewed as a powerful woman because she has Okonkwo's love and admiration and is in a position to influence his actions.

Ezinma (Ekwefi's daughter) is also a powerful young woman. Although Okonkwo does not freely show his emotions, he is secretly very proud and fond of Ezinma. Her importance is highlighted throughout the novel against the backdrop of Ekwefi's (Ezinma's mother) maternal misfortunes. Ekwefi has suffered through the deaths of many children and is constantly in fear of losing Ekwefi, the child that lived. It is clear that Okonkwo respects Ekwefi and admires Ezinma. In fact, Okonkwo wished that Ezinma had been born male so that he could have initiated her into Umuofia male society. Ezinma displays such a combination of intuition and intelligence that Okonkwo regrets that his sons were not more like her.

Powerful women in Achebe's classic novel include women who occupy positions of authority in polygynous households as first wives (Anasi and Nwoye's mother), esteemed and valued junior wives who marry out of a feeling of overwhelming love (Ekwefi), and insightful, sensitive, intelligent daughters such as Ezinma.

Female Religious Symbols, Oracles, Priestesses and Goddesses

While many references are made to powerful women as wives and mothers, there are also multiple descriptions of female religious symbols, oracles, priestesses and goddesses. For example, in the second chapter of *Things Fall Apart* Achebe mentions *agadi nwayi* (old woman), the most powerful principle in Umuofia's "war-medicine." The war-medicine was named after an old woman with one leg. It is important to point out at this juncture that Umuofia was known for its strength in war, and therefore respected by surrounding communities for this reason. In fact, Umuofia had a shrine dedicated to the medicine of the old woman.

> Umuofia was feared by all its neighbors. It was powerful in war and in Magic, and its priests and medicine men were feared in all the Surrounding Country. Its most potent war-medicine was as old as the clan itself. Nobody knew how old. But on one point there was general agreement. The active principle in that medicine had been an old woman with one leg. In fact, the medicine itself was called *agadi-nwayi*, or old woman. It had its shrine in the centre of Umuofia, in a cleared spot. And if anybody was so foolhardy as to pass by the shrine after dusk he was sure to see the old woman hopping about (pp. 11-12).

Another powerful female image employed in Achebe's novel is implicit in the symbolism of the *agbala* (Oracle of the Hills and Caves) which is associated with a priestess who alone had the power to appeal to the Oracle. In essence, the priestess communicates with the Oracle, acting as an intermediary between Umuofia residents and the *agbala.* An important example of the Oracle's function was evident when Umuofia residents were considering going to war. Only the *agbala* or the Oracle of the Hills and Caves could sanctify or forbid war. If Umuofia residents attempted to fight a war without the approval of the Oracle, then the village's strongest war-medicine (*agadi nwayi* or old woman) could not be employed. In order to go to war, Umuofia needed the blessing of the Oracle of the Hills and Caves that could only be received by communication through the priestess. The priestess acted as a powerful intermediary between the Oracle of the Hills and Caves and Umuofia residents.

Chika was the priestess to the Oracle of the Hills and Caves during Okonkwo's childhood; Chika is said to be "full of the power of her god, and she was greatly feared" (p. 17). Further, Chika was the woman who assessed Unoka's (Okonkwo's father) misfortune, concluding that it was not bad luck, but lack of ambition that held him back. She told Unoka that he hadn't offended any of the gods or goddesses, but that he was not wealthy because of his laziness (p. 17).

Chielo was another strong woman in the novel. Like Chika, she was a priestess to the Oracle of the Hills and Caves. It is Chielo who carried away Okonkwo's favorite daughter (Ezinma) in the middle of the night. As a priestess, Chielo had the ability to become "possessed by the spirit of her god" and to prophesy (p. 100).

Later in the novel, when Okonkwo returned from his seven-year exile in his maternal village of Mbanta and takes up residence in Umuofia again, he was confronted with many contradictions raised by colonialism and missionary activities in Nigeria. One prominent contradiction was raised by Mr. Brown, a missionary who had built a Christian Church in Umuofia and begun to evangelize in the town. Mr. Brown preached a Christian doctrine that forbade Umuofia people to worship the earth goddess (*Ani*, a.k.a. *Ala*). He told residents that there was only one God and that it was *Chukwu,* the High [Male] God. He extolled the merits of monotheism and actively discouraged polytheism. When Okonkwo returned from Mbanta, he was deeply disturbed by the changes that he saw. "Okonkwo was deeply grieved. And it was not just personal grief. He mourned for the clan, which he saw breaking up and falling apart..." (p. 183).

At this point it should be mentioned that even with the advent of Christianity in Southeastern Nigeria, the earth goddess played an influential role in village life. Njaka (1974) noted that the earth goddess was the deity who judged whether an event was against Igbo custom (*omenala Igbo*) and should therefore be considered an offense against the land, taboo or *nso Ala* (a.k.a. *nso Ani*). In particular, *Ani* (a.k.a. *Ala*) helped to maintain law and order in Igboland prior to the implementation of formal courts (Njaka, 1974). Achebe describes the widespread observance of the New Yam Festival, which is held annually in honor of the earth goddess. He depicted the New Yam Festival as an opportunity for Umuofia residents to thank the earth goddess, "the source of all fertility" (p. 36). Although *Ala* or *Ani* is the source of all fertility, she is also the ultimate judge of morality and conduct and maintains close communication with deceased clan members whose bodies are then buried in the earth. In fact, *Ala* or *Ani* the earth goddess is one of the most important among the Igbo pantheon (Achebe, 1994; Uchendu, 1965). Therefore, when Okonkwo committed offenses against *Ani*, it was particularly meaningful in the context of the Igbo society of Umuofia.

During the Week of Peace (celebrating the earth goddess) Okonkwo lost his temper with his youngest (second) wife (Ojiugo) who had gone to plait her hair instead of providing dinner for him and their children. When Ojiugo returned, Okonkwo hit her. Although his other two wives ran out and tried to stop him, particularly because he raised his hand to somebody during the Week of Peace, he did not listen and consequently was punished by Ezeani (a.k.a. *Ezeala*), the priest of the earth goddess.

Okonkwo's involvement in the ritual killing of Ikemefuma was also against the laws of the earth goddess. It had come to his attention that the Oracle of the Hills and Caves had requested that Ikemefuma be sacrificed. The Oracle's request was difficult for Okonkwo and his family because, for several years, Ikemefuma had lived in their compound and had come to regard Okonkwo as his father. One of Okonkwo's friends noted this and asked him not to take part in the ritual killing of the boy. Stubbornly, however, Okonkwo disregarded his friend's advice and went ahead with the deed.

As the man who had cleared his throat drew up and raised his machete, Okonkwo looked away. He heard the blow. The pot fell and broke in the sand. He heard Ikemefuma cry, "My father, they have killed me!" as he [Okonkwo] ran towards him [Ikemefuma]. Dazed with fear, Okonkwo drew his machete and cut him [Ikemefuma] down. He [Okonkwo] was afraid of being thought weak (p. 61).

As previously mentioned, Okonkwo committed more than one offense against the earth goddess; it was the most grievous one that got him exiled from his fatherland (Umuofia) for seven years. Okonkwo accidentally shot Ezedu's 16-year-old son at Ezeudu's funeral celebration. As it is *nso Ani* or taboo to kill a clansman, Okonkwo had no choice but to leave Umuofia for his maternal village (Mbanta), until he and his family could return. Tragically, shooting Ezeudu's son was not the last offense that Okonkwo committed against the earth goddess. His final act, his suicide by hanging, was also against the laws of the earth goddess.

Okonkwo's exile from his fatherland (Umuofia) provides the most important and powerful of all female images in *Things Fall Apart*, as it forced him to re-examine the importance of his motherland (Mbanta). It was very hard for Okonkwo to leave his fatherland. He was a proud man who had intended to live all his days in his paternal village, acquiring wealth and taking prestigious titles, yet his plans had been thrown asunder by the accidental death of Ezeudu's son. Okonkwo was depressed by the unfortunate turn of events. In Mbanta, his maternal uncle (Uchendu) noticed his sadness, and arranged for a family meeting in which he addressed everybody and offered some pointed advice to Okonkwo. The meeting was dignified by the presence of the *umuada*, or daughters of the village, who had come to the aid of their relatives for dispute settlement and funeral celebrations (Green, 1964; Okonjo, 1976).

Uchendu began by simply stating that Okonkwo was living in his maternal, rather than paternal village. In a compassionate way, Uchendu gently chided Okonkwo to remember his responsibilities to his family by appreciating the importance of his maternal relatives. By doing this, Uchendu stated, he would honor the memory of his mother and not anger the dead ancestors. He then asked Okonkwo a very important question:

Can you tell me Okonkwo why it is that one of the commonest names we give our children is Nneka, or "Mother is Supreme"? We all know that a man is the head of the family and his wives do his bidding. A child belongs to its father and his family and not to its mother and her family. A man belongs to his fatherland and not to his motherland. And yet we say Nneka-'Mother is Supreme'. Why is that? (Achebe, 1994, p. 133)

When Okonkwo did not know the answer to his uncle's question, Uchendu said,

> You do not know the answer? So you see that you are a child. You have many wives and many children—more children than I have. You are a great man in your clan. But you are still a child, my child. Listen to me and I shall tell you. But there is one more question I shall ask you. Why is it that when a woman dies she is taken home to be buried with her own kinsmen? She is not buried with her husband's kinsmen. Why is that? Your mother was brought home to me and buried with my people. Why was that? (Achebe, 1994, pp. 133-134)

Okonkwo was still unable to answer his uncle's questions, and Uchendu proceeded,

> Then listen to me, he said and cleared his throat. It's true that a child belongs to its father. But when a father beats his child, it seeks sympathy in its mother's hut. A man belongs to his fatherland when things are good and life is sweet. But when there is sorrow and bitterness he finds refuge in his motherland. Your mother is there to protect you. She is buried there. And that is why we say that mother is supreme. Is it right that you, Okonkwo, should bring to your mother a heavy face and refuse to be comforted? Be careful or you may displease the dead. Your duty is to comfort your wives and children and take them back to your fatherland after seven years. But if you allow sorrow to weigh you down and kill you, they will all die in exile.... These are your kinsmen now

(Achebe, 1994, p. 134).

The metaphorical image of Okonkwo's mother welcoming him back to Mbanta is arguably the most important female image in the book, as it illustrates the power, importance and prestige of women as mothers among the Igbo.

Secondary Female Imagery

While primary images of women as mothers, wives, daughters, priestesses and goddesses are described by Achebe (1994), he also includes secondary female images. For example, in the early portion of the book, Ikemefuma (the young man who was ritually sacrificed) made Nwoye (Okonkwo's first son) laugh by telling him where the "corn" came from. Ikemefuma called corn "*Eze Agadi Nwayi*" or old woman's teeth (Achebe, 1994, p. 34). Achebe's reference to *Eze Agadi Nwayi* signified one of the few light-hearted moments in Nwoye's life, one that he thought back on with fondness. The reference was also important because it indicated the close relationship between Nwoye and Ikemefuma, who treated one another as brothers.

In contrast, Nwoye and his father Okonkwo did not have a good relationship. Okonkwo continuously tried to force his eldest son to be less sensitive by telling him stories that were "full of violence and bloodshed" (Achebe 1994, p. 53), actively discouraging Nwoye's preference for "motherlore" or stories and parables that his mother told him. Okonkwo himself suppressed memories of his mother's stories, such as the one about 'Mosquito and Ear' in favor of those that he thought were more masculine. Of course, Okonkwo equally suppressed images of his ineffectual and overly sensitive father as well. Tragically, in the end, Nwoye lost respect for his father because of Okonkwo's involvement in Ikemefuma's ritual killing. Something in Nwoye's psyche snapped when he realized that his father had just killed his "brother." Subsequently, Nwoye joined the Christian church and literally left his father behind; he even adopted Isaac as his new Christian name.

Conclusions Regarding Female Imagery in *Things Fall Apart*, Women's Power and Feminism in the New Millennium

It is clear that relegating *Things Fall Apart* to a metaphorical shelf designated for sexist literature is neither accurate nor fair (Boyce Davies, 1986; Jeyifo, 1993). A multitude of powerful female images appear throughout Achebe's (1994) novel, including descriptions of women as wives, mothers, daughters, priestesses and goddesses. Furthermore, there is a rich subtext of *secondary female imagery* in the book.

Some of the most powerful female images in the novel involve women as wives, mothers, daughters and priestesses. Achebe (1994) depicted strong, insightful and intelligent women with the ability to influence the lives of others including Anasi (Nwakibie's wife), Nwoye's mother, Okonkwo's second wife Ekwefi and their daughter Ezinma. Female priestesses such as Chika of Okonkwo's childhood and Chielo of his adulthood are also powerful women. Chika and Chielo had the ability to communicate with the Oracle of the Hills and Caves and were intimately associated with Umuofia's war medicine (*agadi nwayi* or the old woman that hopped on one leg). Furthermore, priestesses, like Chika and Chielo, had the right to sanction or refuse Umuofia's involvement in war. As Umuofia was famous for its fierceness in war, the power of the priestesses was awesome.

The novel is replete with female religious symbols including discussions of the significance of *Ani* or *Ala* the earth goddess, The Week of Peace and the New Yam Festival honoring her. In addition, Okonkwo's fate was intimately entwined with *Ani* the earth goddess. On more than one occasion he broke her laws or customs (*Omenala Igbo* or Igbo customs) and commits crimes against the land which are considered taboo or *nso Ala* (a.k.a. *nso Ani*). For example, he struck Ojiugo (his youngest wife) during the Week of Peace, took part in the ritual killing of Ikemefuma, accidentally shot a clansman, and ultimately hung himself.

The fact that Okonkwo consistently ignored the laws of the earth goddess may be the most important message in the novel. In fact, Okonkwo's lack of respect for the important female Igbo deity is symbolic of events that took place during colonial era Nigeria (1914-1960). Many Igbo youth turned away from *Ani* the earth goddess in favor of a Christian prophet and the Igbo male High God (*Chukwu*). In essence, one of the powerful sub-plots in *Things Fall Apart* is that Jesus Christ and *Chukwu* (both male) gain ascendance over *Ani* and *Igwe (a male/female pair in the Igbo pantheon).* Crimes against the earth goddess were considered particularly grievous among the Igbo, as Ani was considered the source of all fertility. Since she had the right to give or withhold yams and other food crops, an offense against her may imply starvation, a point that was raised by Ezeani after Okonkwo's behavioral infraction (p. 30).

If Western feminist analysis alone is applied to *Things Fall Apart*, the conclusions would probably be that Okonkwo is sexist, that he ignores his mother and oppresses his wives and daughters. From this perspective, Achebe's (1994) portrayal of Igbo (Umuofia) culture would probably also be viewed as sexist by virtue of the fact that he omitted Okonkwo's mother's name and therefore symbolically excluded women from African post-colonial discourse (Jeyifo, 1993). In contrast, an inclusive or new feminist reading of the novel highlights African values and experiential frameworks in the context of colonial era Nigeria. It should be remembered that Okonkwo was a proud, highly-motivated Igbo man who lived to see Umuofia's religion and social system seriously challenged by Western colonialism. Furthermore, Okonkwo had an extreme fear of failure and a heightened aversion to emotional sensitivity, because of childhood experiences. Therefore, it was his fear of failure and sensitivity that led him to be heavy-handed with his wives, daughters and son.

Examining Okonkwo's wives from a purely Western feminist perspective may be to equate differing Umuofia male/female roles with either equality or inequality in a mutually exclusive manner. In contrast, if the Igbo cultural ideal of complementary duality is considered, a different picture of gender relationships comes to light. Parallel male/female roles and power differentials between women become apparent. For example, Achebe (1994) depicts Anasi's (Nwakibie's first wife) important role in welcoming Okonkwo to Nwakibie's family compound, while describing her senior status in relation to the other women of the household. As noted, Achebe (1994) described Anasi as a strong middle-aged woman who is the ruler of the women in their prestigious family compound. Nwoye's mother (Okonkwo's first wife) holds a similar position in the family compound.

Ekwefi (Okonkwo's second wife) exudes a different kind of power. Although she is not the first or senior among wives, she is particularly treasured by her husband and thus potentially able to influence Okonkwo's decisions. Ekwefi married Okonkwo out of an overwhelming feeling of love for him. As previously noted, their marriage was not arranged. In fact, she stole away from her former husband during the night in order to be with Okonkwo. Ezinma (Ekwefi and Okonkwo's daughter) is a powerful young woman for several reasons, including her stunning beauty and intelligence. As both beauty and intelligence are female attributes that are highly prized among the Igbo, Ezinma provides another example of a strong woman. In addition, Ezinma is intuitive and cares deeply for her father. In turn, Okonkwo respects and admires her.

In conclusion, there are many examples throughout *Things Fall Apart* of powerful female imagery, yet they may be overlooked if the novel is read exclusively from a Western feminist perspective. In contrast, a new or inclusive feminist perspective is needed, one that considers African experiences and conceptual frameworks, Igbo cultural norms, and the historically constructed nature of gender relationships.

References

Abu-Lughod, L. (1990). The romance of resistance: Tracing transformations of power through Bedouin women. *American Ethnologist* 17, (1).

Achebe, C. (1994). *Things fall apart.* New York: Anchor Books.

Afigbo, A. (1972). *The warrant chiefs: Indirect rule in southeastern Nigeria 1981-1929.* New York: Morrow.

Amadiume, I. (1987). *Male daughters/female husbands: Gender and sex in an African society*. London: Zed Books Limited.

Arndt, S. (2000). African gender trouble and African womanism: an interview with Chikwenye Ogunyemi and Wanjira Muthoni. *Signs*, 25, (3), 709-726.

Asante, M. (1987). *The Afrocentric idea*. Philadelphia: Temple University Press.

Barlow, T. (2000). International feminism of the future. *Signs*, 25, (4), 1099-1106.

Boyce, D. C. (1986). Motherhood in the works of male and female Igbo writers: Achebe, Emecheta, Nwapa and Nzekwu. In Boyce, D. C. & Graves, A. A. (Eds.). *Ngambika: Studies of women in African literature*. Trenton, NJ: Africa World Press.

Collier, J. (1974). Women in politics. In Rosaldo, M. & Lamphere, L. (Eds.). W*oman, culture and society*. Stanford: Stanford University Press.

Collier, J. & Yanagisako S. (1987). Introduction. In Collier, J. & Yanagisako, S. (Eds.). *Gender and kinship, essays toward a unified analysis*. Stanford: Stanford University Press.

Foucault, M. (1987). *The history of sexuality. Vol. 1. An introduction*. New York: Random House.

Geertz, C. (1973). *The interpretation of cultures.* New York: Basic Books.

Green, M. M. (1964). *Ibo village affairs.* New York: Frederick A.

Praeger.

Hebdige, D. (1999). *The meaning of style.* London: Routledge.

Hewlett, B. (2001). The Cultural Nexus of Aka Father-Infant Bonding. In Brettell, C. & Sargent, C. (Eds.). *Gender in Cross-Cultural Perspective*. New Jersey: Prentice Hall.

Hill Collins, P. (1989). The social construction of Black feminist thought. *Signs* 14, (4), 745-773.

Hooks, b. (1984). *Feminist theory from margin to center.* Boston: South End Press.

Ibechem, C. (2000). *When women leave the village: An evaluation of women's power and their protest actions in Ofodim, Umuneke, Imo State, Nigeria.* Ann Arbor: UMI Dissertation Services.

Ifeka-Moller, C. (1975). Female militancy and colonial revolt: The women's war of 1929, Eastern Nigeria. In S. Ardener (Ed.) *Perceiving women*. New York: John Wiley & Sons.

Jeyifo, B. (1993). Okonkwo and his mother: Things fall apart and issues of gender in the constitution of African postcolonial discourse. *Callaloo* 16, (4), 847-858.

Lamphere, L. (2001). The domestic sphere of women and the public world of men: The strengths and limitations of an anthropological dichotomy. In Brettell, C. & Sargent, C. (Eds.) *Gender in cross-cultural perspective*. New Jersey: Prentice Hall.

Landsman, G. & Krasniewicz, L. (1992). A native man is still a man: A case study of intercultural participation in social movements. *Anthropology and Humanism Quarterly* 15, (1), 11-19.

Leacock, E. (1978). Women's status in egalitarian society: Implications for social evolution. *Current Anthropology* 19, (2), 247-275.

McCall, J. (2000). *Dancing histories: Heuristic ethnography with the Ohafia Igbo*. Ann Arbor: University of Michigan Press.

______. (1996). Portrait of a brave woman. *American Anthropologist*

98, (1), 127-136.

Mead, M. (1960). *Coming of age in Samoa*. New York: Morrow.

Njaka, M. (1974). *Igbo political culture*. Evanston: Northwestern University Press.

Ogunyemi, C. (1996). *Africa wo/man palava: The Nigerian novel by women.* Chicago: University of Chicago Press.

Okonjo, K. (1976). The dual-sex political system in operation: Igbo women and community politics in midwestern Nigeria. In Hafkin, N. & Bay, E. (Eds.) *Women in Africa: Studies in social and economic change*. Stanford: Stanford University Press.

Ortner, S. (1974). Is female to male as nature is to culture? In Rosaldo, M. & Lamphere, L. (Eds.). *Woman, culture and society*. Stanford: Stanford University Press.

_______. (1979). On key symbols. In Lessa, W. & Vogt, E. (Eds.). *Reader in comparative religion: An anthropological approach.* Harper Collins.

Oyewumi, O. (2000). Family bonds/conceptual binds: African notes on feminist epistemologies. *Signs* 25, (4), 1093-1098.

Rapp, R. (2001). Thinking about women and the origin of the state. In Brettell, C. & Sargent, C. (Eds.). *Gender in cross-cultural perspective*. New Jersey: Prentice Hall.

Rosaldo, M. & Lamphere L. (1974). Introduction. In Rosaldo, M. & Lamphere, L. (Eds.) *Woman, culture and society.* Stanford: Stanford University Press.

Sanday, P. (1974). Female status in the public domain. In Rosaldo, M. & Lamphere, L. (Eds.). *Woman, culture and society*. Stanford: Stanford University Press.

_______. (1978). *Female power and male dominance: On the origins of sexual inequality*. London: Cambridge University Press.

Silverblatt, I. (1987). *Moon, sun and witches: Gender ideologies and class in Inca and colonial Peru*. Princeton: Princeton University Press.

Steady, F. (1996). African feminism: A worldwide perspective. In Terborg-Penn, R. & Rushing, B. (Eds.). *Women in Africa and the African diaspora*. Washington DC: Howard University Press.

Strobel, M. (1992). Introduction. In Johnson-Odim, C. & Strobel, M. (Eds.). *Expanding the boundaries of women's history: Essays on women in the third world.* Bloomington: Indiana University Press.

Uchendu, V. (1965). *The Igbo of Southeast Nigeria*. Fort Worth: Holt, Rinehart, and Winston Inc.

Van Allen, J. (2001). "Aba riots" or "Igbo women's war"? Ideology, stratification, and the invisibility of women. In Brettell, C. & Sargent, C. (Eds.). *Gender in cross-cultural perspective*. New Jersey: Prentice Hall.

White, E. (1992). Africa on my mind: Gender, counter discourse, and African-American nationalism. In Johnson-Odim, C. & Stroebel, M. (Eds.). *Expanding the boundaries of women's history: Essays on women in the third world.* Bloomington: Indiana University Press.

CHAPTER 12

AFRICAN AESTHETICS AND AFRICAN LITERATURE:

DEVELOPING AN AFRICAN CENTERED LITERARY THEORY FROM EXISTING PHILOSOPHICAL CONCEPTS

Nzingha V. Gaffin
Doctoral Candidate
Temple University

Introduction

Although most African countries have been independent since the 1960's, criticism of each country's art and culture continues to be influenced by constructs from European literary models. In other words, the evaluative criterion used to analyze the literature is heavily drawn from European *utamawazian* concepts. As such, critical interpretation falls short of the intended message of the respective authors and in many respects contradicts the worldview and ethos of the people whose very culture informs the various works.

African literature, especially the novel, is then judged to possess little literary worth, often dismissed as mere journal entries. Structurally, too, the novels are said to suffer from inadequate characterization, motivation, and psychological depth. They are also said to possess unrealistic and awkward dialogue with problems regarding the conceptualization of time and space. The themes of the works are denounced as being merely situational, lacking complex or interesting plots. Some Eurocentric critics also malign the African novel as being either too biographical, or obsessed with the past with an inordinate stress on cultural conflict. The misrepresentation of these novels goes beyond mere structural issues; the novels are also denigrated on ideological grounds. While some critics view them as being too didactic, others say they lack the right type of moral attitude and are merely exercises in the art of 'protest literature.'

My main objective here is to offer an alternative model of literary analysis based on principles derived from an African worldview and cultural traditions with specific reference to language and aesthetics, as suggested in Marimba Ani's *Yurugu (1994).* The analytical thrust will be on the special branch of Eurocentric, post-colonial critics. Even though we are aware of the constraints the colonial situation puts on the African novel, these critics insist on analyzing African literature from the perspective of European culture and traditions. They often view the African as, what Marimba Ani and others have referred to, 'the cultural other', "an apprentice European whose literary productions has no other canon to adhere to but Western tradition" (Ngugi, 1986). Critics, both African and non-African, within the postcolonial school of thought, do not concede the autonomy of African literature. These critics play down the significance of African literature because, in many cases, it does not enhance or promote European hegemony. In light of this line of thinking, we should not use European ideology in analyzing Africana literature, less we reach the same negative conclusions about our own works.

I will proceed with a discussion of postcolonial, anti-postcolonial, and Afrocentric theorists. This analysis will begin with postcolonial theorists to lay the groundwork for an *asilian* discussion. The implications and assumptions of the "Postcolonial Triad" Edward Said, Homi Bhabha, and Gayatri Spivak—are critical to understanding the effect of western hegemony and pedagogy, which their critiquing ideology brings to the discussion.

Postcolonial theory is an umbrella term levied upon all literary criticism applied to works produced from postcolonial countries. This school of thought has yet to define or agree on when, where, who, or what actually falls under this term. However, the literature is heavily laden with terminologies such as 'minority literature,' 'standard literary criticism,' 'colonial theorist,' and 'phases of imperialism'–terms which should assault Afrocentric sensibilities. The analysis of works from Africa, Asia, India, Australia and the Caribbean are all included in this cultural melting pot.

I will then move on to the anti-postcolonial theorists, where I include Marimba Ani, Chinweizu, Frantz Fanon and Ngugi Wa Thiong'o. These theorists declare that African literature has its own traditions and models to build upon and they argue against using alien western standards. Their works are infused with a *kugusa mtimaic* spirit, an important logical progression and important to the development of an African centered literary framework.

The research model will conclude by investigating Afrocentric theorists, such as Molefi Asante, Cheikh Anta Diop and Kariamu Welsh-Asante. Their contributions liberates African consciousness and provides the community with the necessary analytical tools and the scientific method to view phenomena located in an African perspective. The *kuntuic* approach arms African people with an intellectual orientation of determination that is a powerful force steeped in African culture.

Understanding the Cultural Matrix: Postcolonial Literary Theorists

In *Orientalism*, Edward Said (1979) makes the following observation:

> The Orient is not only adjacent to Europe: it is also the place of Europe's greatest and richest and oldest colonies, the source of its civilizations and *languages, its cultural contestant, and one of its deepest and* most recurring images of the Other (p. 1).

He goes on to say that,

> Anyone who teaches, writes about, or researches about the Orient–and this applies whether the person is an anthropologist, sociologist or historian–either in its specific or in general aspects, is an Orientalist, and.... What he or she does is Orientalism.... Orientalism lives on academically through its doctrine and theses about the Orient and the Oriental.

Postcolonial theory is based in the cultural *asili* of "Orientalism;" African literature is analyzed from this political location. Said is entangled within the very Eurocentric colonized discourse he seeks to expose. Postcolonial theory has defined the boundaries for the discussion, but Africa was not included in setting those boundaries.

The West is the standard bearer throughout Edward Said's work. With the addition of other texts including *Beginnings, Literature and Society,* and *Culture and Imperialism*, Said's philosophy has accomplished for postcolonial theory much the same as the Hegelian worldview did for the study of Africa in general. Understanding this concept is critical to understanding the need for this area of research.

In *Location of Culture*, Homi Bhabha sets out what he feels is the conceptual imperative and political consistency of the postcolonial intellectual project. He explains why the culture of the west must be relocated away from postcolonial perspectives:

> Postcolonial criticism bears witness to the unequal and uneven forces of cultural representation involved in the contest for political and social authority within the modern world order. Postcolonial perspectives emerge from the colonial testimony countries and the discourses of 'minorities' within geopolitical divisions of East and West, North and South. They intervene in those ideological discourses of modernity that attempt to give a hegemonic 'normality' to the uneven development and the differential, often disadvantaged, histories, nations, races, communities and people (Bhabha, 1990, p. 171).

This excerpt from *Postcolonial and Postmodern: The Question of Agency*, has not given agency to the very colonized masses it purports to speak for. Bhabha's use of terms like 'minorities' locates him squarely within the European *asili*. His analysis is based in the Marxist tradition where globalization and materialistic dialectic is prized. The methodology inherent within the Marxist does not have the cultural consciousness of African people at its core. Bhabha does critic western inconsistencies, but his language and philosophy remain within European hegemony. Despite appearances, rules of the dominating discourse articulate signs of the colonial power. The oppressors' methods can not be applied to African production with the expectation of a positive result!

It is well known that the notion of the feminine (rather than the subaltern of imperialism) has been used in a similar way within deconstructive criticism and within certain varieties of feminist criticism. In the former case, a figure of 'woman' is an issue, one whose minimal predication as indeterminate is already available to the phallocentric tradition. Both as object of colonist historiography and as subject of insurgency, the ideological construction of gender keeps the male dominant. If in the context of production, the subaltern has no history and cannot speak, the subaltern as female is even more deeply in shadow (Ashcroft, et al., 1995, p. 28).

In this description of Gayatri Spivak's philosophical contribution to postcolonial theory is a terminology that again should flag Afrocentric sensibilities. First, the Afrocentric paradigm affirms male-female relationships as inspirational and intellectual. The feminist perspective works against African cultural unity. Many feminist critics have analyzed African novels from this location and missed the crux of the production. Observation of any African character affects the African community at large.

Secondly, African people must rely on their own history and take agency to speak for themselves. The subaltern's history is not African history; African truth resides in African experiences and African history must be told from an African perspective. Neither feminist nor Marxist ideologies define the African experience, yet both of these philosophies are applied to African literature as analytical tools.

African postcolonial literature expresses the tension between European and African *asilis*. Postcolonial studies are based in the historical experiences of European colonialism and the diverse effects this phenomenon created. The subject is Europe, the perspective is European and the analytical tools are European. The Afrocentric worldview rejects this hegemonic approach to scholarship and that perspective motivates this research model.

The Process of Cultural Awareness: The Anti-Postcolonial Theorist

> Europe's political domination of Africa and much of the 'non-European' world has been accompanied by relentless cultural and psychological rape and by devastating economic exploitation. . . beneath this deadly onslaught lies a stultifying intellectual mystification that prevents

> Europe's political victims from thinking in a manner that would lead to authentic self-determination. Intellectual decolonization is a prerequisite for the creation of successful political decolonization and cultural reconstruction strategies. Europe's political imperialistic success can be accredited not so much to superior military might, as to the weapon of culture . . . Culture carries rules for thinking, and that if you could impose your culture on your victims you could limit the creativity of their vision (Ani, 1994, p. 1).

Marimba Ani's *Yurugu* lays out in systematic detail, European consciousness and she explains global domination from an African centered perspective. The core structure and key components of her framework offer us the tools for grappling with European hegemony. Ani applies African names to African sensibilities and leads the reader into an African intellectual space that is fruitful for investigation. She relies on African philosophy as the foundation for inquiry and builds from that worldview. *Yurugu* is ***kugusa mtimaic*** in that it transforms the reader's consciousness. She methodically explores and exposes the affects of Christianity and colonialism and the West's purposeful creation and follow-up treatment of the 'cultural other'. Marimba Ani's scholarship is critical to this project.

> How can our critics support and aid our writers in their efforts to decolonize and Africanize their techniques? In posing this question in this manner, we wish to emphasize that the role of the critic is secondary. Their proper role is that of helper, not legislator, to writers and audience. Their authority exists only insofar as they remain representatives of the society for which the writers produce. . . In the ideal state of things where everybody in the society is sufficiently educated to serve as his or her own critic, the role of critic ought to disappear (Chinweizu, et al., 1983, p. 285).

Chinweizu and Madubuike's *Toward the Decolonization of African Literature* (1983) offer the reader the ideology of African agency in the role of the critic. At the anti-postcolonial level, we witness an elevation of African consciousness beyond postcolonial theory. Chinweizu and Madubuike references their culture and the conflict between European and African *asili*. In his *The West and the Rest of Us: White Predators, Black Slaves and the African Elite*, Chinweizu points out that,

> One of the most devastating legacies of our satellization to the West is that our culture has become eccentric. Instead of being Afrocentric in our thought and actions, we are Eurocentric. What Europe does we automatically assume as the standard we must imitate in order to appear civilized. As a result, we have lost our ability to define ourselves... Without a strong sense of ourselves we accept what the West wants us to believe is our past. We refuse to define our cultural and political constituency for what it is—Africa, black Africa. That is our pan-African constituency, a constituency defined by our separate history, our separate historical situation (Chinweizu, 1975, p. 493).

An Afrocentric literary theory requires both historical reliance and agency. This is accomplished at the *kugusa mtimaic* level where cultural maturation expands African consciousness.

> As long as the black man is among his own, he will have no occasion, except in minor internal conflicts, to experience his being through others. There is of course the moment of 'being for others' of which Hegel speaks, but every ontology is made unattainable to a colonized and civilized society. It would seem that this fact has not been given sufficient attention by those who have discussed the question...The black man among his own in the twentieth century does not know at what moment his inferiority comes into being through the other. In America, Negroes are segregated. In South America, Negroes are whipped in the streets, and Negro strikes are cut down by machine-guns (Fanon, 1976, pp. 109– 110).

Frantz Fanon mentions at least three issues critical to understanding the *kugusa mtimaic* analysis: white supremacy is throughout the non-European world, sovereignty in the African world is not yet realized and yet African cultural reliance is vital to the African psyche. In the *Wretched of the Earth: The Handbook for the Black Revolution That is Changing The Shape of the World,* he guides the reader to an understanding of European *asili.* Without political activism and scholarly intervention, white supremacy will render Africans as mere European objects.

The aim of colonialism was to control the people's wealth: what they produced, how they produced it, and how it was distributed; to control,

> other words, the entire realm of the language of real life. . . For colonialism this involved two aspects of the same thing: the world has been accompanied by destruction or deliberate undervaluing of a people's culture, their art, dances, religions, history, geography, education, orature, and literature, and the conscious elevation of the language of the colonizer...Since culture is a product of the history of a people which in it turn reflects, the child was now being exposed exclusively to a culture that was a product of a world external to himself (Wa Thiong, 1986, p. 16).

Through *Writers in Politics, Decolonising the Mind and Moving the Centre*, Ngugi Wa Thiong provides a perspective that uniquely highlights the pitfalls in the colonizer's worldview. Today, we recognize that the anti-postcolonial theorists rely on European literary constructs. Neither the feminist nor Marxist paradigm was designed to have a sufficient grasp on African consciousness. From the feminist and Marxist centers, African realities are invisible. The development from postcolonial theorist to anti-postcolonial theorist is the vital understanding and centeredness in one's own culture as a point of departure. And yet, cultural awareness alone will not lead a text or community to victorious action.

The *Kuntuic* Power of Change: The Afrocentric Theorists

Although the Afrocentric project builds on the research of previous African and diasporian African scholars like Marcus Garvey, W.E.B. DuBois, Malcolm X, Cheikh Anta Diop, Yosef ben-Jochannan, Walter Rodney and many others, it was the Temple University School of Thought, lead by Molefi Asante, that had the vision to formulate the Afrocentric paradigm, pinpointing Africa as the starting point of our discourse:

> Afrocentricity is the most complete philosophical totalization of the African being-in-the-center of his or her existence. It is not merely an artistic or literary movement. Nor only is it an individual or collective quest for authenticity, but it is above all the total use of method to effect psychological, political, social, cultural and economic change. The Afrocentric idea is beyond decolonization of the mind (Asante, 1987, p. 125).

Herein lies the crux of this project, the very basis and essence of the Afrocentric paradigm. Molefi Asante's vision and scholarship have provided African people a place to stand and the lens through which to view African phenomenon. In *Afrocentric Idea*, he places our African culture center stage and we are handed the analytical tools to start a shift from Africans-as-objects to Africans-as-subjects of discourse. Asante underlines and underscores the value of establishing an African worldview, located in and on African ground, to observe the world and Africans' relationship to it. Several of his texts, including *Afrocentricity (1988)*, and *Kemet, Afrocentricity and Knowledge (1990)*, continue to focus the Afrocentric lens. The most meaningful contribution to this project is African agency, centering one's intellectual investigation in African culture as the starting location.

Cheikh Anta Diop's main interdisciplinary thesis, that historical, archeological, linguistic and anthropological evidences support the theory that the civilization of ancient Egypt was Black, profoundly influenced the thinking about Africa around the world. Diop's 'Two Cradle' theory and his declaration that ancient Egypt is to Africa what ancient Greece is to the West, form the basis for the Afrocentric idea. Diop reconstructs, reinserts and reclaims thousands of years of African and therefore a world history that had been suppressed by western scholars. Diop's illustration of an African agency in noteworthy:

Cheikh Anta Diop's Two Cradle Theory (at a glance)

African Utamawazo (Matriarchy)	**European Utamawazo (Patriarchy)**
Bride Wealth	Dowry
Sedentary/Agricultural	Nomadic
Social Collective	Individualism
Central Power	Survival of the Fittest
Hospitality	Xenophobic
City/State	Territorial
King/God	Fire Worship
Cosmic Triad	Family DiVinity
Burial	Cremation

(Diop,1955)

From *The African Origin of Civilization: Myth or Reality* in to *The Cultural Unity of Black Africa: The Domains of Matriarchy & Patriarchy in Classical Antiquity,* published posthumously in 1989, Cheikh Anta Diop's legacy acts as a transforming agent which centers and redirects vigilant scholars to victorious Afrocentric endeavors.

Kariamu Welsh-Asante's edited texts, *African Culture: The Rhythms of Unity (1990*) and *The African Aesthetic: Keeper of the Traditions (1993),* examine the link between African and African American aesthetic. I depend on her collection for the introduction and interpretation of existing African philosophical concepts–*kugusa mtima and kuntu*–which I in turn juxtapose with existing postcolonial literary terminology to establish the basic framework for an Afrocentric literary terminology.

> It is a diasporian African's privilege and position that allows her to see Africa as a concept as well as a diverse and multicultural continent. This conscious vision and perspective of the Africa in America, has guided, informed and inspired the African to reclaim Africa politically as well as historically and aesthetically. An understanding of the African aesthetic(s) facilitates any paradigm or blueprint for the artistic, literary and philosophical criticism and scholarship (Welsh-Asante, 1993, p. 1).

Yemoja/Olukun: Completing the Circle of Cultural Fidelity

This idea enables the reader to understand post-colonial theorists' works at the *asilian* level. Within the Afrocentric literary framework, the *asilian* level is the starting point for analysis. At this level, as shown through the works of the 'post-colonial triad,' critics rely on foreign *utamawazian* pedagogy and ideology to critic works outside of their cultural grasp. All so-called post-colonial countries' artistic productions are lumped together and then devalued using evaluative measures unrelated to the cultural material. From the Afrocentric perspective, an *asilian* assessment serves the purpose of drawing attention to itself.

One level deeper into our Afrocentric literary framework is the point where one's own cultural consciousness enables the theorist to analyze our productions steeped in our own cultural center–the center that produced the work. Here, instead of grappling with European hegemony, we rely on African sensibilities that lead the scholar into an

African intellectual space. At the level of ***kugusa mtimaic*** investigation, the analysis relies on African philosophy as the foundation for inquiry and builds from that worldview. Anti-postcolonial theorists who rely on feminist or Marxist traditions certainly contribute to the cause;

however, their entrapment within European hegemony limits their ability to stand on firm African grounding. Awareness of cultural differences alone will not lead a text or community to victorious action.

Finally, theoretical concepts must evolve to the third and deepest level of analysis. If the work has developed through mere cultural conflict and progressed beyond cultural identification, the work may reach the ***kuntuic*** level. Here, the production carries a purposely developed conscious awareness of African affirmation and orientation. The text is now an eliminator of chaos, a transformative circuit, and has most importantly become a victorious 'agent for change'–***kuntuic***. The ***kuntuic*** character/text/author can be identified through victorious thought, word and deed and will function in the literature ***kuntuicly***. Examining our work from a location of ***kuntuic*** spirit, distinctly rooted in African sensibilities, will promote evaluative criteria with cultural integrity. This is not only an additional step toward African autonomy and cultural repair; it is also laying the foundation for our own functional literary theory.

Glossary of Terms

Asili: The logos of a culture within which its various aspects cohere. It is the developmental germ/seed of a culture. It is the cultural essence, the ideological core, the matrix of a cultural entity which must be identified in order to make sense of the collective creations of its members (Ani, 1994, p. xxv).

Cultural Other: A conceptual/existential construct, which allows Europeans to act out their most extreme aggression and destructiveness, while simultaneously limiting their collective self-destruction on a conscious level (Ani, 1994, p. xxv).

Kugusa Mtima: The African experience of being touched, moved or affected by a self-consciously created form/phenomenon. The concept of ***kugusa mtima*** takes aesthetic beauty and pleasure, expands it and places it into the context of the profound African experience of understanding the universe. A progression through stages of cultural maturation, requiring the development of the whole person, physically, mentally, intellectually, spiritually and ideologically. This process is facilitated by the contemplation and use of symbols which intensify in complexity requiring progressively more astute powers of comprehension and wisdom. ***Kugusa Mtima*** is the process of expanding African consciousness (Welsh-Asante, 1993, p. 69).

Kuntu: A category of African philosophy, a modality of expression. It is that expression of truth, uniquely suited to African sensibilities. It is not power-over-the-other, but power to move, to do, to effect, to feel—the African conception of power as energy and force. The power to make things happen, an agent for change (Welsh-Asante, 1993, p. 68).

Utamawazo: Culturally structured thought. It is the way in which cognition is determined by a cultural ***asili.*** It is the way in which the thought of members of a culture must be patterned if the asili is to be fulfilled (Ani, 1994, p. 13).

Yemoja/Olukun: From the Yoruba tradition, used metaphorically to indicate bottom and /or top, light and/or dark, male and/or female, chaos/ clarity, beginning and end—a summation.

References

Ani, M. (1994). *Yurugu: An African-centered critique of European thought and behavior.* Trenton, NJ: Africa World Press, Asante, Molefi K. *The Afrocentric idea*. Philadelphia: Temple University Press. 1987.

_______. *Afrocentricity*. Trenton, NJ: Africa World Press, 1988.

_______. *Kemet, Afrocentricity and knowledge*. Trenton, NJ: African World Press, 1990.

Asante, M. K. & Abarry, A. S. (1996). *African intellectual heritage. A book of sources.* Philadelphia: Temple University Press.

Asante, M. K. & Welsh, K. (1990). *Asante African culture: The rhythms of unity*. Trenton: Africa World Press.

Ashcroft, B., Griffiths, G. & Tiffin, H. (1995). (Eds.). *The post colonial studies reader*. London: Routledge Press.

Bhabha, H. K. (1990). *Nation and narration*. London and New York: Routledge Press.

_______. (1994). *The location of culture*. London and New York: Routledge

Childs, P. & Williams, P. (1997). *An introduction to post-colonial theory*. London: Prentice Hall.

Chinweizu. J. O. (1975). *The west and the rest of us: White predators black slavers and the African elite*. New York: Vintage Books.

Chinweizu, J. O. & Madubuike, L. (1983). *Towards decolonization of African literature*. Washington: Howard University Press.

Diop, C. A. (1984). *The African origin of civilization: Myth or reality*. Westport: Lawrence Hill & Co.

_____, (1987). *Precolonial Black Africa*. Westport: Lawrence Hill & Co.

_____, (1989). *The cultural unity of Black Africa: The domains of matriarchy and of patriarchy in classical antiquity*. London: Karnak House.

_____. (1991). *Civilization or barbarism: An authentic anthropology*. Westport Lawrence Hill & Co.
_____. (1996). *Towards the African renaissance: Essays in culture & development*. London: Karnak House.
Fanon, F. (1963). *The wretched of the earth: The handbook of the Black revolution that is changing the shape of the world.* New York: Grove Weidenfeld Press.
_____. (1967). *Black skin, White masks.* New York: Grove Weidenfeld Press.
Gikandi, S. (1987). *Reading the African novel*. London: Heinemann.
_____. (1997). *Tradition and modernity: Philosophical reflections on the African experience*. New York: Oxford University Press.
Keto, C. T. (1989). *The Africa centered perspective of history.* Blackwood: K. A. Publications.
Mbiti, J. S. (1992). *Introduction to African religion.* Oxford: Heinemann.
Ngugi, W. T. (1981). *Writers in politics: A re-engagement with issues of literature & society*. Oxford: James Currey LTD.
_____. *Decolonising the mind: The politics of language in African literature.* Oxford: James Currey LTD. 1986.
_____. *Moving the centre: The struggle for cultural freedoms.* Oxford: James Currey LTD, 1993.
Said, E. W. *Beginnings: Intention and method.* New York: Basic Books, Inc, 1975.
_____. *Orientalism*. New York: Vintage Books, 1979.
_____. (ed) *Literature and society.* Baltimore: The Johns Hopkins University Press, 1980.
_____. *Culture and imperialism*. New York: Alferd A. Knopf, 1993.
Spivak, G. C. *Outside the teaching machine*. New York: Routledge, 1993.
Spivak, G. C. *A critique of postcolonial reason: Toward a history of the vanishing present*. Cambridge: Harvard University Press, 1999.

Welsh-Asante, Kariamu. (Ed.). *The African aesthetic: Keeper of the traditions*. Westport: Praeger, 1993.

________. (1996). *African dance: An artistic, historical, and philosophical inquiry.* Trenton: Africa World Press, 1996.

Williams, P. & Chrisman, L. (Ed.). *Colonial discourse and post-colonial theory*. New York: Columbia University Press, 1994.

CHAPTER 13

THE REJECTION OF BLACKNESS IN AFRICAN AMERICAN LITERATURE

John K. Marah
Associate Professor and Chair
African and Afro American Studies Department
State University of New York at Brockport

The rejection of African people's blackness has been well documented by various writers, practical thinkers, philosophers, and countless others around the globe (Wagatsuma, 1967; Beteille, 1967; Brown, 1967; Lewis, 1970; Cose, 1995; Herskovits, 1968). Thus, everywhere we look, African people's black skin, prognathism, and culture are denounced and depicted as ugly and repulsive. W.E.B. DuBois' famous assertion that the problem of the twentieth century is the problem of the color line still holds true in the twenty-first century.

African people's blackness still evokes negative reactions from Europeans and other non-African people. Even though there has been a long contact between blacks, whites, and others, black people remain the least accepted on account of their looks, their prognathism, and black skin.

Wagatsuma (1967), in his seminal essay "The Social Perception of Skin Color in Japan" tells us that "long before any sustained contact with either Caucasoid Europeans or dark skinned Africans or Indians, the Japanese valued 'white' skin as beautiful and depreciated 'black' skin as ugly" (p. 407). In 1860, when the then Japanese government sent an envoy to the United States, some members of the visiting party recorded some of their impressions about white American women; "American women are better because their skin is whiter than that of Japanese women; the girls didn't need the help of powder or rouge" (pp. 414-415).

When these Japanese stopped at an African coast, on their way back to their homeland, they were 'repulsed' by black African features; the curly hair of blacks reminded them of animals, like "that of a monkey" (p. 415). The black skin of Africans "…is associated in the Japanese mind with many undesirable traits: death, vice, despair… something unclean… not the natural state of things" (p. 431). This Japanese writer (Wagatsuma) goes on to say that "The type of Negro the Japanese think attractive or handsome, or the least objectionable, is a light-skinned individual with Caucasian features; and that the Japanese are not ready to appreciate a very Negroid Negro as attractive…" (p. 432).

Bernard Lewis (1970), a Jewish writer, on the other hand, tells us that, though "the Quran expresses no racial or color prejudice" (p. 20), white Arabs are not without their 'hatred' for Black Africans. Blacks could be Muslims, pious, intelligent, but they are often perceived as lower than white Arabs; "blackness (is) viewed (as) an affliction" (p. 21). Professor Lewis goes on to cite even some Islamic black poets that penned their distaste for their own very African color (pp. 21-23). Even the prophet Mohammed ".... is quoted as saying of the Ethiopian: 'When he is hungry, he steals, when he is sated he fornicates' and that the Arabs or Muslims should "obey whoever is put in authority... even if he be a crop-nosed Ethiopian slave" (p. 24).

To Europeans and Arabs, Black people's "frizzy hair, thin eyebrows, broad nostril, thick lips, pointed teeth, smelly skin...," set them apart from other human beings; "they are people distant from the standards of humanity" (p. 27). Arabs also believe that Blacks are natural slaves, because the almighty God had so decreed; we are told that "A common explanation of this status, is that the ancestor of dark skinned people was Ham the son of Noah who was... damned black for his sin, and that this... curse of blackness... passed to all the black people who are his descendents" (p. 29). Thus a pure Arab of less intelligence could be socially elevated above the accomplished Arabized African. "The Negro's physical appearance," which sets him apart from Europeans and Arabs, "is described as ugly, distorted, or monstrous" (p. 32).

These alien standards of beauty have so inundated black people's psychic that intra-racism (racism within the race based on the degree of skin color) has distorted black male-female relationships, mate selections, and even notions of black female beauty. "Professor Paula Giddings of Duke University reports that as a student at Howard University in the 1960s, the homecoming queen was always light skinned. In 1967, when a dark-skinned black woman won the title for the first time, Giddings said, we knew that Howard, the nation, and the world were changing" (p. 119). Though Howard, the nation and the world have changed since the 1960s, it still appears to be the case that no black woman with classically African features will be chosen as a homecoming queen, Miss America, or Miss Universe, as long as the West dominates in these matters.

Marion Berghahn (1977) writes that "no feature of African reality was seen by the Elizabethans to be more foreign and shocking than the blackness of the skin which they encountered in African peoples;" the English "found the contrast of skins all the more fascinating since the polarity of black and white had a firmly established place in the Western system of symbols" (p. 5).

It was the Belgium "Euroman" (Niehoff, 1996), that "divided Rwanda, issuing identity cards that marked Hutu or Tutsi according to the colonists' own ideas about race. They favored the Tutsi, seen as tall, fine-featured cattle-drivers, over the Hutu, seen as short, rough (and ugly) cultivators" (Fisher, 1999, p. A3). The Black American journalist, Keith Richburg (1997), observed in Rwanda in the early 1990s that, "with their straight noses and sharp features, the Tutsi were considered the more physically attractive tribe... Even with growing wealth and power, what the Hutu really aspired to become was Tutsi" (p. 102), or to be like Mary Jane, or to be Mary Jane, as in Toni Morrison's *The Bluest Eye* (1970). Mr. Richburg himself was to later confess that he was "terrified of Africa" and "would not want to be from (that) place"; he was glad his ancestors made it out of Africa (p. 233). In the Dominican Republic, we are told, "no matter how dark-skinned, most Dominicans describe themselves as dark or light Indian–'indio clara or indio oscura—not black or African" (Wing, 2001, p. 25); we observe a similar phenomenon in Brazil (Robinson, 1999, pp. 105-122); in Mexico, "there is open prejudice...against those whose features come from the darker side of the national gene pool. 'It's one thing to be brown. The black race is something different...'" (Thompson, 2001, p. A10); in Somalia, we are told that:

> the Somali Bantu, also known as the Mushunguli, recount a host of abuses by their Somali compatriots. There were the slurs hurled against them by Somalis with more Arab lineage over their darker skin and African features. Their land and produce were frequently seized; the women and girls among them were often raped by militiamen. Condi-

> tions grew even worse after 1991, when Somalia was divided up into a checkerboard of rival turfs upon the fall of its dictator, Muhammad Siad Barre. Many Somali Bantu, with no warlord to protect them, were caught up in the fighting (Lacy, 2001, p. A6).

In this chapter, I further substantiate that African-Americans have 'abundantly' depicted their rejections of the 'classically' African features in their literature, and have embraced the classically European features as the epitome of beauty, as a result of their colonization, and exposure to westernization and their "dis-Africanization" (Mazuri, 1985, pp. 72-79).

A classical rejection of African blood, and all that that entails is depicted in James Weldon Johnson's Harlem Renaissance novel, *The Autobiography of an Ex-Colored Man*. Mr. Ex-Colored Man, the nameless protagonist in this novel, was initially 'color-blind' while attending an 'all-white' school in the northeast of the United States. A child of a mulatto mother and a white father, Mr. Ex-Colored Man grew up in a genteel household, with books, piano, and he dressed "like a little aristocrat" (p. 7) and "the best blood of the south was in..." him (p. 18).

However, there was also that African blood that he could not get rid–off. That he had African blood in him was one day brought to him in school by his teacher in an educational setting, in front of his peers, and at a tender age, when children are easily impressed or affected by contradictions. To him, the other black boys in his class were "them" (p. 14); he had not seen himself as one of 'them' until he was assured by the principle that he, too, was a Nigger (p. 16). From this instance he became a man of two 'identities' (two souls, two strivings or two personalities), in the words of W.E.B. DuBois (1989, p. 5).

One of the strategies Mr. Ex-Colored Man utilized was flight; he ran away from situations that threatened to identify him for what he was. In all, Mr. Ex-Colored Man engaged in eleven major flights:

(1) from Georgia to
(2) Connecticut
(3) Atlanta
(4) Jacksonville
(5) to Harlem, New York in the 1920s
(6) Europe
(7) Deep South
(8) North
(9) Flight from a theater, where his father, his wife and their daughter were seated;
(10) Flight from the club in Harlem where a white woman had been killed, and
(11) Flight from his mother's people for a mess of pottage.

Even though Mr. Ex-Colored Man was 'visually,' culturally, and experientially a European-American, as his millionaire white friend had reminded him (p. 144), he aspired to be composer of Negro music. To accomplish this, he had to travel to the deep south, to be among Blacks whose intelligence had not yet been quickened by westernization. "These dull, simple people" (pp. 169-170), will provide him with 'authentic' black cultural materials, out of which he'll make classics; these "dialect-speaking 'darkies,' and "happy-go-lucky, laughing, shuffling, banjo-picking" (pp. 167-168) African people, will provide him with the right sorts of materials that he'll elevate into classics; he'll become the 'Negro' composer that would help elevate his race, if not himself. Indeed, his dreams and ambitions were to help his 'mother's people' to obtain respect in American society; but before he could get down to do his work, southern whites 'brought' up a black man, to be burned at the stake.

Mr. Ex-Colored Man's 'cowardice' drove him to flee once again, this time into the hands of the very 'white' race that practiced such inhumanity to a son of Africa, one of his mother's people. After this scene of lynching, Mr. Ex-Colored Man goes back to the north and confesses to his white fiancée that he has a drop of African blood in him, a blood that 'denoted' inferiority, ugliness, stupidity, paganism, barbarism, and blackness, as earlier depicted in Phyllis Wheatley's famous poem, "On Being Brought from Africa to America" and as lately depicted in Richburg's *Out of America* (1997), and Mary Lefkowitz's *Not Out of Africa* (1996). Hyperbolically, Mr. Ex-Colored man felt himself transformed or metamorphosized into a 'classical' Negro under the gaze of his white fiancée:

> ...and bending over her... I said: 'Yes, I love you; but there is something more, too, that I must tell you.' Then I told her, in what words I do not know, the truth. I felt her hand grow cold, and when I looked up, she was gazing at me with a wild, fixed stare as though I was some *object* she had never seen. Under the strange light in her eyes I felt that I was growing *black and thick-featured and crimp-haired.... This was the only time in my life that I ever felt absolute regret at being colored, that I cursed the drops of African blood in my veins and wished that I were really white* (pp. 204-205).

Mr. Ex-Colored Man, a quadroon, felt that the drop of African blood in his veins was perturbingly inconvenient, a badge of inferiority, and symbolized depravity. He gave up his great ambition of being a world renown black composer to become an ordinary white man. In the end, he gave up his mother's people to pass into the world of his father's white race, to obtain, thereby, all the conveniences and privileges that that move provided. Mr. Ex-Colored Man did not want to be associated with the defeated black race, members of which could be despised and lynched with impurity; he would rather have material things than to have to 'permanently' struggle to uplift his mother's unfortunate black race.

Mr. Ex-Colored Man's rejection of that drop of African blood in him appears inevitable in a society that 'worships' whiteness in magazines, movies, and posters; he would rather live with the guilt of abandoning his mother's people than be enough of a man and fight against man's inhumanity to man; he became an individualist and lived with the fear that he could one day be discovered as a colored man.

Mr. Ex-Colored Man's 'passing' illustrates the tremendous pressures on African-Americans to disassociate themselves from Africa; they have to be 'disafricanized' in language, religion, education, tastes, coloration and physical features; since Mr. Ex-Colored Man was practically a white man, why not go for the gusto, go with the ruling race and be assimilated? In this way, his children will at least be 'good looking' and be saved from the numerous slights that even accomplished blacks in the United States are daily confronted with (Cose, 1993; Zaslow, 1998:26; Dumas III, 2001, p. 13A).

But if Mr. Ex-Colored Man could pass for white, there are 'numerous' African-American protagonists, being too black, who are not afforded the 'luxury' of choice. What is the fate of those blacks that can not pass and do not wish to submit to Western standards of beauty, but accept their God-given classical African features? How about, if they're too black, poor, not highly educated, and female? To a large extent, to be female, black, poor, and not be highly educated illustrate Pecola's predicament in Toni Morrison's *The Bluest Eye* (1970). In this novel, we are confronted with a protagonist afflicted with a number of 'impossible' disabilities, in a capitalist, sexist, and a racist society infatuated with classism and European standards of beauty.

Pecola's family, Mr. and Mrs. Breedlove and their son Sammy, are poor, 'uneducated', and had been psychically 'damaged' in internalizing white standards of beauty, depicted in movies, on billboards, by Mrs. Breedlove's employers and their children, white models, infinitum. The Breedloves are so inundated with European paradigms of beauty that they feel they are the epitome of ugliness; they are afflicted with "ugliness by conviction" (p. 34); they had come to believe that they were ugly because the master had told them so, in so many ways. Like Celie in *The Color Purple*, who had been indoctrinated by Mr.

Albert that she was a "black... poor... ugly... woman" (Walker, 1982, p. 182), the Breedloves were also convinced of their stupendous unattractiveness in a white dominated society.

The name "Breedlove" is indeed a misnomer in that no love permeated this Breedlove home on 35th street, in Lorain, Ohio. This was not only a loveless home, but also one in which Mr. Breedlove was an alcoholic, where Pecola's brother, Sammy, used his ugliness to hurt others, and Pecola dreamt about obtaining blue eyes. To be black, ugly, poor, and female spelled disaster for this young girl, who was already experiencing menstruation, which denoted her womanhood, a womanhood that would have to be substantiated by a man's love; but which man was going to love a poor, black, ugly Pecola?

When she goes to Mr. Yacobowaski's grocery store, to buy Mary Jane candies, the 'old' man simply did not recognize Pecola; he didn't glance at her or recognize her as adults normally 'pretend' to be curious about youngsters. As if Mr. Yacobowaski was disgusted by Pecola's 'classically African features', he scoots the three Mary Jane candies towards Pecola; he did not even 'give' them to her. Pecola's sensibilities were insulted; she was humiliated for not being recognized as a valuable human being, for not being like Mary Jane, for not even eliciting, at least, an iota of liking from the 'old' man.

The only persons that seemed to care about Pecola's black-ugly-self were the three prostitutes–China, Poland and Marie; these 'ladies of the night' were not pretentious; they were 'real people' and could therefore perhaps identify with Pecola's predicament in a society that upheld European-American middle class morality, expectations, standards of behavior and, of course, beauty.

In contrast to Pecola, Maureen Peal (Pearl) is described as the epitome of beauty; she likes ice cream and white milk, has springtime eyes, is high-yellow, wears fur coats, is popular among her peers, and has white teeth. Despite her six fingers on each hand (a deformity?), she stands in sharp contrast to the likes of Pecola (p. 53). When Ms.

Maureen Peal, 'velvet back' (p. 53), refers to Pecola, Frieda, and Claudia as "black and ugly" (p. 61), Pecola zeros-in on her own blackness and ugliness, which denoted inferiority and unworthiness. Like Mr. Ex-colored Man, Maureen Peal over-emphasized the European blood in her veins, which goes with wealth and refinement. In the society in which these girls found themselves, they knew that it did not pay to be black, ugly, female and poor; one was forever ridiculed by the media, peers and the Mr. Yocobawaskis. Even when blacks are not poor, they still have to lose their "funkiness," their 'naturalness', and must be constantly vigilant about not slipping back into having kinky hair or ashy skin. All those characteristics that reminded one of Africa must be covered-up, restrained, and de-emphasized, lest one be closely associated with the lower class blacks and the cultural throwbacks.

In Toni Morrison's *The Bluest Eye* a distinction is made between Niggers and Coloreds. Geraldine, a highly educated black woman, has already bought into western standards of beauty. Not as light skinned as Mr. Ex-colored Man, Geraldine makes sure that she is not 'seen' as a typical black woman with affronting African features. She tells her son (Junior) "not to play with Niggers" (p. 71).

> ... In winter his mother put Jergens Lotion on his face to keep the skin from becoming ashen. Even though he was light-skinned, it was possible to ash. The line between colored and nigger was not always clear; subtle and telltale signs threatened to erode it, and the watch had to be constant.

Junior used to long to play with the black boys. More than anything in the world he wanted to play King of the Mountain and have them push him down to the mound of dirt and roll over him. He wanted to feel their hardness pressing on him, smell their wild blackness, and say "Fuck you" with that lovely casualness (p. 71).

Geraldine has so rejected how naturalness, blackness, and her black ancestors that she now derives sexual pleasures from a cat; her western education must have so indoctrinated her that, short and coarse hair, dark and dry skin were too African, and must be minimized at all costs; if she could not deal with the Pecolas of America, it appears obvious that she'll not be able to entertain 'native' Africans, with their classically African features; she had been dis-Africanized and educated to be Eurocentric in her ways of looking at beauty and femininity, and to avoid as far "as possible… any suggestion of wool" (p. 71), or woolen braids, like those of Africans in the 'bush'; like Jadine in Morrison's other novel, *Tar Baby* (1981), Geraldine didn't want to appear to be a cultural-throwback into African funkiness, or wear her hair natural, which will all definitely suggest her Africanity. In rejecting those aspects of herself, she becomes fastidiously concerned about the slightest suggestion that she indeed is a black woman; but the more she tries to be refined and sophisticated, the more she becomes useless to her people, especially those of Pecola's class and shade of color.

If Geraldine rejected the coarse hair, dark and dry skin of black people, Mr. Soaphead Church, also in *The Bluest Eye*, goes further in his rejection of anything associated with Africa. A 'misanthrope' (p. 130), Soaphead Church's ancestors had progressively rejected the African blood in their veins to embrace Anglo-Saxon features, skin-color, culture, mannerisms, and tastes.

Mr. Soaphead Church, the Anglophiliac, received a western education that progressively made him useless; rather than use his education to help people, he became a false prophet, a charlatan, a spiritualist, and a misanthrope. "When he was advised that he had no avocation, he left the island, came to America to study the then budding field of psychiatry" (pp. 134-135).

> But the subject required too much truth, too many confrontations, and offered too little support to a failing ego. He drifted into sociology, then physical therapy. This diverse education continued for six years, when his father refused to support him any longer, until he "found" himself. Elihue, not knowing where to look, was thrown back on his own de-

> vices, and "found" himself quite unable to earn money. He began to sink into a rapidly fraying gentility, punctuated with a few of the white-collar occupations available to black people, regardless of their noble bloodlines, in America; desk clerk at a colored hotel in Chicago, insurance agent, traveling salesman for a cosmetics firm catering to blacks. He finally settled in Lorain, Ohio, in 1931, palming himself off as a minister, and inspiring awe with the way he spoke English. The women of the town early discovered his celibacy, and not being able to comprehend his rejection of them, decided he was supernatural rather than natural (p. 135).

It was to this charlatan spiritualist that the desperate Pecola turns, to obtain the bluest eyes, European characteristics she 'believed' would make her beautiful, and thereby revamp her ugly status. Pecola's aspirations for the impossible illustrate the pressures on African people in western societies to denounce and be ashamed of their God-given African physical characteristics; to even be partially accepted, they must 'shed' their dark skins, African features, behaviors, and cultures. They are made to be daily concerned with whether their noses are "too big," their "hips are too thick," or whether the

> ...hair is too short or too coarse
> ...skin is too dark, blemished, oily or dry
> ...breast are too small or too big
> ...butt is too big
> ...thighs are too thick
> ...legs are shaped funny
> ...feet are too wide (Mcfaddin, 1997, p. 21).

African people, in fiction and in reality, who appear to be at the opposite spectrum of whiteness, go through 'impossible' and elaborate gymnastics to even be partially accepted by the macro-U.S. society. Even within the micro African-American society, 'black' persons with dark skins provide a field day for mulattos, quadroons, octoroons, and others who see themselves as slightly blessed with some European physical attributes. Pecola's infatuation with blue eyes drove her into thinking that to be 'black and beautiful' are incompatible and cannot coexist; rather than worry about her family's socio-economic class, which could be changed with effort, talent, luck and determination, she determined to aspire for the impossible. Even if, by some miracle, she were to obtain blue eyes (not the bluest eyes), these would not have eliminated her dark-skinned-black-self, a source of problems for African people globally, within and without the race.

Intra-racism, or racism within the race, also illustrates the rejection of blackness in African-American Literature. In Zora Neale Hurston's *Their Eyes Were Watching God*, for example, "Mrs. Turner was a milky sort of woman that belonged to child-bed" (p. 133). In Hurstonian terms, "her shoulders rounded a little, and she must have been conscious of her pelvis because she kept it stuck out in front of her so she could always see it" (p. 133). This European 'black' woman came to dislike Tea Cake Woods, Janie Crawford's third husband, for being too black. Mrs. Turner is high-yellow and is not used to associating with dark skinned blacks because, hyperbolically, "they draws hightnin" (p. 134). She doesn't like poor, "black niggers" either, because they are always laughing, singing, joking and making a fool out of themselves in front of whites (pp. 135-136). But, perhaps, on a more serious note,

> ...Tain't de poorness, its de color and de features. Who want any lil ole black baby layin' up in de baby buggy lookin' lak uh fly in buttermilk? Who want to be mixed up wid a rusty black man, and uh black woman goin' down de street in all dem loud colors, and whoppin' and hollerin' and laughin' over nothin'? Ah don't know. Don't bring me no nigger doctor tuh hang over mah sick-bed. Ah done had six chilun- wuzn't lucky enough tuh raise but dat one- and sin't never had uh nigger tuh even feel mah pulse. White doctors always gits may money. Ah don't go in no nigger store tuh buy nothn' neither. Colored folks don't know nothin' 'bout no business. Deliver me!
> Look at me! Ah ain't got no flat nose and liver lips. Ah'm uh featured

> woman. Ah got white folks' features in mah face. Still and all Ah got tuh be lumped in wid all de rest. It ain't fair. Even if dey don't take us wid de whites, de oughta make us uh class tuh ourselves (pp. 135-136). Mrs. Turner's European features- "thin-lips, slightly pointed nose... (and) her buttock in the bos-relief were a source of pride" (p. 134).

With these, she was armed with weapons to insult the sons and daughters of Africa, especially those with classically African features. In her view, light skinned African-Americans should be classed-off as an intermediate group between whites and blacks (p. 134). Because dark-skinned black people 'draws hightenin' and are not 'civilized' or respectable, they tend to 'infect' or bring down the whole black race in the eyes of whites and respectable coloreds like Mrs. Turner, and Geraldine in Toni Morrison's *The Bluest Eye*. Thus, light-skinned, middle, and upper class African-Americans look down and reject those African people with classically African features: "It's de color and de features" of African people that negatively 'stand out' for both Europeans and light-skinned African-Americans (p. 134).

When the macro-society perpetuates blackness as a curse, a liability, and as ugly, dark-skinned African people tend to internalize self-hatred and project a devalued self-worth. Nathan McCall (1995, pp. 13-14) tells us that he was 'indoctrinated' to admire whiteness as a young boy; his grandma Bambosse, who worked for whites, often admonished him for behaving like a nigger (pp. 13-14); furthermore, Sharon, one of the girls McCall and his gang members sexually exploited, was "as dark as night"; she was afflicted with low self-esteem because of her dark skin (p. 143).

Black mothers also often contribute to the low self-esteem of their dark-skinned children by making 'negative' comments about their nappy or bad hair, and make positive comments about those with European features with 'good' hair. When the macro-society and the black community propagate these standards, African people with classically African features are in multiple jeopardy.

The case of Emma Lou in Wallace Thurman's *The Blacker the Berry*, 'epitomizes' the rejection of African people's dark skin in American society, and within the black race itself. It depicts the ways in which one actually sees or defines him or herself in a given society, as one responds to the ways that the larger society sees him/her. Colorism, the preoccupation with color or color consciousness, has been with black people as long as they've been in contact with non-black people, and it appears to be the case that the color black has always taken the lowest rank, within as well as without the black race (Eugene Robinson, 1999). Emma Lou could be described as the overwhelming preoccupation with what we think is wrong with us, which depicts Emma Lou's predicament in *The Blacker the Berry*, as the preoccupation with finding out about one's ancestry, was the focus in Haizlip's *The Sweeter the Juice* (1995); but while Haizlip accepts her mixed, light-skinned ancestry, Emma Lou is greatly perturbed because of her 'unfortunate' dark complexion. This preoccupation with her dark complexion-as-a-liability (a curse), is juxtaposed with the other variables of classism, sexism, and feminism. How does an educated dark-skinned female, from a well-to-do family of a blue-vein community, view herself in a color conscious society? How do other blacks view her in educational institutions, work places, (in the English dictionary), and even in the biblical story of Noah and his sons, one of whom was damned black, to be servants to his brethren, including the generations after him?

Therefore, Emma Lou has a historical as well as a contemporary problem that she must confront. Emma Lou wonders why her mother had married a dark skinned man and why *she* had come out so unfortunately (too) dark. In her blue-vein 'black' community in Boise, Idaho, to be a dark-skinned black man is not as terrible as being a dark-skinned female. What will her diploma do for her, when it comes to romance? Educated black men often marry lighter skinned educated black women. Emma Lou had 'good' hair, but this could not compensate for the dark-skinned color, that made her glaringly conspicuous in an 'all' white school and within her blue-veined 'black' society. Why was it that people stared at her askance, as though there were questions about her humanity?

Emma Lou's immediate community looked down on blackness, a process that had started in the plantation tradition, in which connections to the "Big House" connoted mixed blood, where the mixed blooded 'Africans' denoted superiority; freedom for her family members before the emancipation proclamation gave them an upper hand, and their migration to the West, to Boise, Idaho, took them away from the deep South, away from the down-trodden black masses, progressively negating them from their slave and African roots; and "having some of Massa George's blood in their veins set them apart from (the) ordinary Negroes at birth" (p. 28).

Like Mr. Soaphead Church in *The Bluest Eye*, these light-skinned blacks needed to get lighter and lighter until they could melt (pass) into white society as Mr. Ex-Colored Man did. But Emma Lou's father had been a dark-skinned man, the type that Mr. Ex-Colored Man did not want to look like, or John Howard Griffin, in his *Black Like Me* (1976). Emma Lou came out looking as black as her father, not like her fair skinned mother; she had her father's hair and facial features, like those unmixed Africans with "pork chop lips" and who wore size "ten shoes" (Thurman, 1929, p. 80).

Indeed, it was the African features that disturbed her the greatest. Not to make another abominable mistake like Emma Lou, Emma Lou's mother remarried a red-haired Irish Negro; Irish and Indian features were acceptable, but to have African features was decidedly a curse; because of her deep, dark black self, Emma Lou became an outcast, the black sheep of the family, the marked one, the odd one out, the unwelcomed, and the cursed one. Hated by her mother, grandmother, stepfather, and the blue-veined society at large, what was to become of the Emma Lou of the world? Which educated black man, in his right mind, would love and marry Emma Lou?

Emma Lou's fastidiousness about "hanging out" with the right sorts of persons – the refined, educated, and the European featured 'blacks'–also narrowed the types of persons in each community in which she found herself. When she 'migrated' to the University of Southern California after her high school graduation, she expected to be accepted by the supposedly open-minded university students. Among those cosmopolitan students she hoped to make friends and even obtain a husband.

Where she not too fastidious about befriending the right sorts of persons, Hazel Mason, a fictionalized Zora Neale Hurston, could have been an 'authentic' friend, but Mason's language was too rustic and she had lived mostly among Negroes in the South. Despite Mason's wealth, she was not the right sort of person for Emma Lou; Hazel Mason was not only rustic in her language, but she also appeared uncivilized, barbaric, mentally slow, and God-forbiddingly ugly (p. 43).

Like Zora Neale Hurston, Hazel Mason was too minstrel-like for the 'refined' Emma Lou; Mason's Ebonics and free spiritedness appalled the middle-class Emma Lou who desired to be accepted by 'civilized' blacks who did not dress in all colors and ornaments and come out circus-like looking (p. 55).

As Emma Lou rejected Mason's circus-likeness and 'Africanness,' so did the other black students at the University of Southern California reject Emma Lou's black-Africanness; they referred to her as a Hottentot (p. 48), a South African tribe associated in the European mind as the grotesque product of the connection between apes and African women (Lyons, 1975, p. 13). She was not brown or light skinned enough to join the sorority on campus; she definitely was not brown enough to pass the brown bag test. In the African-American folklore that states,

> If you're light, you're all right.
> If you're yellow, you're mellow.
> If you're brown, stick around.

But if you're black, get back…

Emma Lou was expected to get lost. On the other hand, she was 'repulsed' by illiterate, non-collegiate blacks she considered beneath her dignity. Furthermore, the 'promising' young men on campus were not about to lower their standards by dating her, a step that could lead to a marriage to a dark skinned, educated black woman; "a wife of dark complexion was considered a handicap unless she was particularly charming, wealthy, or beautiful. An ordinary looking dark woman was no suitable mate for a Negro man of (promising) prominence" (p. 60). Even though Emma Lou had her first sexual relationship with Weldon Taylor, a promising, dark-brown medical student, Mr. Taylor did not feel towards Emma Lou the way she felt for him; she was disappointed by the man that had deflowered her at the age of twenty. To Mr. Taylor, having sex with Emma Lou did not necessarily mean love that should culminate into marriage. After all, this was simply a summer affair, and as a dark brown medical student, there could be lighter skinned black women who would want a promising black medical doctor.

After three years at the University of Southern California, Emma Lou migrated to Harlem, New York during the Renaissance period. In Harlem, she involved herself with 'dubious' men that exploited her insecurities about her looks. Here, also, she saw color in everything–in plays, employment agencies, among colleagues, and writers of the Harlem Renaissance period, who were also color-struck. When she searched for a job as a stenographer at a black real estate agency, she was turned down for being too dark skinned or 'coal black' (p. 98).

By the time Emma Lou attained self-actualization, a pyrrhic victory, she had already lost her virginity, family, time, authentic friends, and several opportunities for genuine relationship. Before she could accept her blackness, after several trials and tribulations, she had lost her self-esteem and a number of years that could have been spent on other important things.

> After all, she wasn't the only black girl alive. There were thousands on thousands who, like her, were plain, untalented, ordinary, and who, unlike herself, seemed to live in some degree of comfort. Was she alone to blame for her unhappiness? Although this had been suggested to her by others, she had been too obtuse to accept it. She had even been eager to shift the entire blame on others when no doubt she herself was the major criminal.
>
> What she needed to do now was to accept her black skin as being real and unchangeable, to realize that certain things were, had been and would be and with this in mind begin life anew, always fighting, not so much for acceptance by other people, but for acceptance of herself by herself. In the future she would be eminently selfish. If people came into her life–well and good. If they didn't–she would live anyway, seeking to find herself and achieving, meanwhile, economic and mental independence (pp. 216-217).

In general, Emma Louism is a universal story in that we tend to internalize particular societal values, even those that denounce our individual idiosyncrasies. In the United States, and globally, as we've tried to show, blackness is universally rejected and disrespected. 'All' societies are color-conscious and they tend to put at the bottom rank the classically African features that most black people are born with. Black people appear to have 'accepted' this depreciation of their physical characteristics and have depicted this in their literary works. The examples of Mr. Ex-Colored Man, Mr. Soaphead Church, Mrs. Turner, Emma Lou and others, suggest that blackness in American society is an inconvenience, a liability, and a badge of inferiority. It is one that is closely linked with ugliness, Africa, boorishness, barbarity, and vulgarity. To be dark skinned and have pork chop lips, wear size ten shoes, have nappy hair and large nostrils, etc. is to be devalued in American society at large and within the black community in particular. To be all these and still be generally 'illiterate' as the case of Pecola, is to indeed be at the bottom of the bottom in American society.

Nonetheless, despite Emma Lou's trials and tribulations, she offers us an array of hope. She, unlike Pecola, Mrs. Turner, Soaphead Church, and even Geraldine, finally accepted her blackness. After several failed affairs, she finally grasped the fact that she too had participated in her own self-hatred and oppression. With her education and economic security, she no longer needed the racist and intra-racist of the world to validate her existence. Like Janie Crawford in Zora Neale Hurston's *Their Eyes Were Watching God,* Emma Lou matured emotionally, intellectually and psychologically. "It (was) now clear to her ...that she had exercised the same discrimination against her men and the people she wished for friends that they had exercised against her– and with less reason" (p. 218); she was now aware that she was aware and will never again let herself be exploited by light-skinned men; "just because she was black was no reason why she was going to let some yellow nigger use her" (p. 213).

As it has been made abundantly clear, the African blood in Mr. Ex-colored Man, Pecola, Geraldine, Soaphead Church, Emma Lou and others is the major cause of most of the problems these characters encountered within themselves and in their relationships with others. Of these characters, Emma Lou finally accepted her blackness as blacks should and must accept themselves in fiction as well as in nonfiction. It appears that Blacks must continue to Afrocentrically educate themselves beyond Eurocentrism, so that the psychological scars of self-hatred and self-rejection are radically abated. African people must be taught that they too are human beings, endowed by the creator to be proud of their dark skins as Europeans and others are proud to be who they are. It is further reasonable to opine that ugliness is not monopolized by only the black race and blacks must not accept colonialists' definitions of themselves; they must attain such a self-knowledge so that they appreciate their blackness and all the different shades of color within the black race.

References

Berghahn, M. (1979). *Images of Africa in Black American literature*. Totowa, NJ: Rowmand and Littlefield.

Cose, E. (1993). *The rage of a privileged class*. New York, NY: Harper Collins Publishers, Inc.

DuBois, W.E.B. (1989). *The souls of Black folk*. New York, NY: Penguin Books.

Dumas III, O. (2001). Man is angered, saddened by the racial stereotyping in community. *Democrat and Chronicle*. (Rochester, NY), 11/21/01, 13A.

Fisher, I. (1999). Hutu and Tutsi ask: Is a unified Rwanda possible? *New York Times* 4, (6), A2.

Griffin, J. H. (1960). *Black like me*. New York, NY: Penguin Books.

Haizlip, S. T. (1994). *The sweeter the juice: A family memoir in Black and White*. New York, NY: Simon and Schuster.

Hurston, Z. N. (1990). *Their eyes were watching god*. New York, NY: Harper and Row.

Johnson, J. W. (1990). *The autobiography of an ex-colored man*. New York, NY: Penguin Books.

Lacy, M. (2001). Somali Bantu in search of a country. *New York Times*, 12/9/01, A6.

Lefkowitz, M. (1996). *Not out of Africa: How Afrocentrism became an excuse to teach myth as history*. New York. NY: Hill and Wang.

Lewis, B. (1970). Race and color in Islam. *Encounter*. Vol. XXXV, (2) , 18-36.

Lyons, C. H. (1975). *To wash an Aethiop White: British ideas about Black African educability*. New York, NY: Teachers College Press.

McCall, N. (1994). *Makes we wanna holler: A Black man in America*. New York, NY: Vintage Books.

McFaddin, T. (1997). *God made me beauty-full*. Marina del Rey, CA:

Quiet Time Publishing.

Morrison, T. (1970). *The bluest eye.* New York, NY: Pocket Books.

_______. (1981). *Tar baby*. New York, NY: New American Library.

Niehoff, A. (1996). *Take over: How Euroman changed the world.* Bonsall, CA: The Hominid Press.

Richburg, B. K. (1997). *Out of America: A Black man confronts Africa.* New York, NY: Basic Books.

Robinson, E. (1999). *Coal to cream: A Black man's journey beyond color to an affirmation of race*. New York, NY: the Free Press.

The Editors. (1999). For Black college students in the 1930s, respectability depended on passing the brown bag test. *The Journal of Blacks in Higher Education*. 25, 119.

Thompson, G. (2001). *New York Times.* 11, /11, A10.

Thurman, W. (1996). *The blacker the berry*. New York, NY: Simon and Schuster.

Wagatsuma, Hiroshi. (1967, Spring). The social perception of skin color in Japan. *Daedalus: Journal of the American Academy of Arts and Sciences*. 96, (2), 407-443.

Walker, A. (1982). *The Color purple.* New York, NY: Washington Square Press.

Wheatley, P. (1971). On being brought from Africa to America, p. 34, in Miller, R. (Ed.). *Black American literature*. Encino, CA: Glencoe Publishing Co., Inc.

Wing, B. (2001, Summer). Indio Claro O Oscuno. *Color Lines*. 24-25.

Zaslow, J. (1998, March). Straight talk: John Hope Franklin, *USA Weekend*. 20-22, 26.

INDEX

J

K

L

M

N

O

P

R

S

T

U

W

X

Y

Z

ABOUT THE CONTRIBUTORS

Ranahnah A. Afriye is currently obtaining her Master's degree at Cornell University's Africana Studies and Research Center. Born in New York City, she struggled through school systems that neither affirmed nor acknowledged her identity as an African woman. She now explores more viable educational models that will foster the positive self-transformation of African youth. For several years, she has worked in youth development and educational programming both in the U.S. and Tanzania. She has also co-authored a book: *Preventing Teen Pregnancy: Youth Development and After-School Programs.*

Seth N. Asumah is an Associate Professor in the Political Science Department and Coordinator of the African American Studies Program at the State University of New York – College at Cortland, New York. He is the co-author two editions of *Issues on Multiculturalism: Cross National Perspectives* (Whittier Publications, Inc., 1995 and 1999) and *Educating the Black Child in the Black Independent School*

(Global Publications, 2001). Also, he co-edited *Issues in Africa and the African Diaspora in the 21st Century* (Global Publications, 2001). He has published several articles in many professional journals including the *Journal of Black Studies*, The *Western Journal of Black Studies* and *The 21st Century Afro Review*. Professor Asumah was a 2002 winner of Teaching Excellence Award of Infusing Diversity in Teaching and the1999 winner of the Rozanne Brooks Teaching Excellence and Dedication Award, SUNY Cortland. He was Vice President and President of the New York African Studies Association (NYASA), (1998-1999, 1999-2000) and currently serves on NYASA's Executive Board. His research interests are in the areas of multicultural and racial dynamics in the United States, African politics, politics of the developing world, and international relations.

Nzingha V. Gaffin is a Ph.D. candidate in the Department of African American Studies at Temple University in Philadelphia, PA. Her research area is African and African American literature focusing on aesthetics and literary theory. She has presented papers at the University of Michigan, Medgar Evers College in Brooklyn, University of Maryland Eastern Shore, Asante Tours in Aswan Egypt, and the Cheikh Anta Diop Conference in Philadelphia, PA. Her articles include "Mission Literature in Africa: Problems and Prospects, Discord in the Discourse: An Afrocentric Analysis of Postcolonial Theory, and Diopian Concepts and Kuntuic Spirit: Other Ways of Knowing African Literature." Nzingha Gaffin has traveled extensively in Egypt, Ghana and Kenya.

Paulin J. Hountondji is Professor of Philosophy at the National University of Benin, Cotonou. He is editor of and contributor to *Philosophical Research in Africa: A Bibliographic Survey* and *Endogenous Knowledge: Research Trails.* Hountondji is former Minister of Culture and Communication and Special Advisor to the Head of State of Benin Republic.

Cindy Ibechem was an Assistant Professor of Anthropology at Hartwick College (2000-2001). Prior to teaching at Hartwick College, she was an adjunct faculty member at several Pennsylvania colleges. Presently, she is rewriting her dissertation for publication. Her research interests include gender and feminist issues in African Studies through the discipline of Anthropology.

Ibipo Johnston-Anumonwo is Associate Professor of Geography at the State University of New York at Cortland. She is a Past President of NYASA, coauthor of *Issues in Africa and the African Diaspora in the 21st Century* (Global Publications, 2001), and co-author of two editions of *Issues in Multiculturalism: Cross National Perspectives* (Whittier Publications Inc., 1995 and 1999). Her research on differential access to employment, and gender and development in Africa are published in several refereed journals and book chapters.

Lori Lee is an Anthropology Ph.D. candidate at Syracuse University. Her current research focuses on identity construction, labor relations, and consumption through their articulation in the material culture of the African Diaspora in the Caribbean and southeast United States.

John K. Marah is an Associate Professor and Chair of the African and Afro American Studies Department at the State University of New York at Brockport. He is the author of a number of books including *African People in the Global Village: An Introduction to Pan-African Studies* (University Press of America, 1998). Dr. Marah is a member of the NYASA Executive Board.

Thomas O. Mwanika is Professor of Communication Studies at the State University of New York at Cortland, New York. He is the Director, SKEP Project: State University of New York-Kenya Educational

Partnership Project funded by USAID/ALO. He is the founding Chair, Department of Communication Studies at SUNY Cortland, which he chaired for seven years, as well as the founding Director, Center for International Education at SUNY Cortland (1997-1999). His teaching and research interests include intercultural communication, interpersonal communication, development communication, communication in Africa, language and language behavior, public speaking, critical thinking, general semantics, African education, instructional and communication technologies, multiculturalism, statistics and statistics anxiety, context in human affairs, and semiotics and structuralism. He has published articles, presented several papers at local, regional, and international professional conferences, and received several grants in many of those teaching and research areas.

Darryl C. Thomas is an Associate Professor of the Africana Studies, Political Science and Philosophy, Interpretation, and Culture Graduate Program at Binghamton University. He is chair of the Africana Studies Department at the same University. His research and publications have focused on International Relations of the Third World, Comparative Political Economy, Comparative Politics, and African and Africana Studies. His most recent publication includes *The Theory and Practice of Third World Solidarity,* Praeger Publishers, 2001.

Davidson C. Umeh is an Associate Professor in the Department of Physical Education and Athletics at John Jay College of Criminal Justice, City University of New York. He has published several articles in professional journals and presented papers on health issues in Africa. He is the editor of *Confronting the AIDS Epidemic: Cross-Cultural Perspectives on HIV/AIDS Education* by Africa World Press and *Protect Your Health: A Health Handbook for Law Enforcement Professionals* by Looseleaf Law Publications, 1999.

Kenneth Vincent has a Bachelor of Arts degree in Foreign Affairs from the University of Virginia, Charlottesville. His research has concentrated on international monetary policy in Africa and the political economy of oil development in Africa. He plans to dedicate his career to the study of the continent.

Judi Wangalwa Wakhungu is an Associate Professor of Science, Technology, & Society at Penn State. She is also the Director of Penn State's Women in the Sciences & Engineering (WISE) Institute. Dr. Wakhungu's research interests include: Energy Resources Management; Energy Policy & Development; Science, Technology & Development; and Gender Issues in Science & Technology Policy. She has served as Principal Investigator (PI) on several research projects in these fields. Her publications include "Renewable Energy Technologies in Africa: Retrospect & Prospects" in the *Bulletin of Science, Technology, & Society;* and "A Crisis in Power: Energy Planning for Development", in *Missing Links: Gender Equity in Science & Technology for Development.*

Dr. Wakhungu received a BS in Geology from St. Lawrence University in New York, a MS degree in Petroleum Geology from Acadia University in Nova Scotia, Canada, and her Ph.D. in Energy Resources Management from Penn State. She has held a number of energy sector positions in the civil service, industry, and higher education in her native country of Kenya, where she has a long list of "firsts". She was the first woman geologist in the Ministry of Energy & Regional Development, where her duties entailed exploring for geothermal energy in Kenya's Rift Valley. Dr. Wakhungu was also the first woman petroleum geologist in the National Oil Corporation of Kenya. She was also the first female faculty member in the Department of Geology at the University of Nairobi.

Dr. Wakhungu has served on many boards and committees, both nationally and internationally. She was the Research Director of the Global Energy Policy & Planning Program of the International Federation of Institutes for Advanced Study (IFIAS) which is based in Toronto, Canada. She has served as the Project Leader of the Renewable Energy Technology Dissemination Project of the Stockholm Environment Institute (SEI). Dr Wakhungu also has the distinction of being the "designated energy expert" for the United Nations Commission of Science and Technology for Development (Gender Working Group). Most recently, she served as the Executive Director of the African Technology Policy Studies (ATPS) Network.